The
Economist

=== **POCKET** ===
EUROPE
IN FIGURES

THE ECONOMIST IN ASSOCIATION WITH
PROFILE BOOKS LTD

This fifth edition published in 2001 by Profile Books Ltd,
58A Hatton Garden, London EC1N 8LX

Material researched and compiled by
Andrea Burgess, Marianne Comparet, Mark Doyle, Lisa Foote,
Robert Eves, Andrew Gilbert, Conrad Heine, Carol Howard,
Stella Jones, David McKelvey, Simon Wright

Typeset in Univers by MacGuru
info@macguru.org.uk

Printed by
LEGO S.p.a. – Vicenza – Italy

A CIP catalogue record for this book is available
from the British Library

ISBN 1 86197 381 0

Contents

CONTENTS

Highest mountains
Metres

1	Elbrus	Russia	5,642
2	Mount Shkhara	Georgia	5,203
3	Rustiveli	Russia	5,201
4	Dykh-Tau	Russia	5,198
5	Mount Ararat	Turkey	5,165
6	Kazbek	Russia	5,047
7	Mont Blanc	France/Italy	4,807
8	Klyuchevskaya	Russia	4,750
9	Ushba	Russia	4,710
10	Dufourspitze	Switzerland	4,634
11	Dom	Switzerland/Italy	4,545
12	Bazar-Dyuzi	Azerbaijan	4,480
13	Matterhorn	Italy/Switzerland	4,478
14	Dente Blanche	Switzerland/Italy	4,357
15	Nadelhorn	Switzerland/Italy	4,327

Longest rivers
Km

		Outflow	
1	Volga	Russia	3,530
2	Danube	Romania	2,860
3	Dnieper	Ukraine	2,200
4	Don	Russia	1,870
5	Northern Dvina	Russia	1,860
6	Pechora	Russia	1,810
7	Kama	Russia	1,800
8	Oka	Russia	1,500
9	Belaya	Russia	1,430
10	Kura	Azerbaijan	1,360
11	Dniester	Moldova	1,350
12	Rhine	Netherlands	1,320
13	Vyatka	Russia	1,310
14	Vistula	Poland	1,200
15	Elbe	Germany	1,160

Longest coastlines
Km

1	Russia	37,653	14	Germany	2,389
2	Norway	21,925	15	Portugal	1,793
3	Greece	13,676	16	Ireland	1,448
4	United Kingdom	12,429	17	Estonia	1,393
5	Turkey	7,200	18	Finland	1,126
6	Croatia	5,790	19	Cyprus	648
7	Italy	4,996	20	Latvia	531
8	Iceland	4,988	21	Poland	491
9	Spain	4,964	22	Netherlands	451
10	France	3,427	23	Albania	362
11	Denmark	3,379	24	Bulgaria	354
12	Sweden	3,218	25	Georgia	310
13	Ukraine	2,782	26	Romania	225

Saving nature

Protected areas
Number, latest

#	Country	Value	#	Country	Value
1	Czech Republic	1,789	19	Norway	180
2	Germany	1,398	20	Latvia	158
3	France	1,341	21	Romania	157
4	Slovakia	1,039	22	Bulgaria	127
5	Belarus	903	23	Serbia & Montenegro	104
6	Austria	695	24	Greece	88
7	Poland	522	25	Netherlands	82
8	United Kingdom	515	26	Iceland	79
9	Italy	422		Lithuania	79
10	Sweden	348	28	Belgium	72
11	Spain	328		Ireland	72
12	Finland	260	30	Turkey	64
13	Switzerland	257	31	Moldova	63
14	Denmark	220	32	Portugal	58
15	Estonia	219	33	Albania	48
	Russia	219	34	Azerbaijan	34
17	Croatia	195	35	Slovenia	32
18	Hungary	186	36	Ukraine	28

Biosphere reserves
Number, latest

#	Country	Value	#	Country	Value
1	Russia	20	15	Belarus	2
2	Bulgaria	17		Finland	2
3	Spain	16		Greece	2
4	Germany	14		Ireland	2
5	United Kingdom	13	19	Croatia	1
6	France	8		Denmark	1
	Poland	8		Estonia	1
8	Czech Republic	6		Latvia	1
9	Hungary	5		Netherlands	1
	Italy	5		Portugal	1
	Ukraine	5		Serbia & Montenegro	1
12	Austria	4		Sweden	1
	Slovakia	4		Switzerland	1
14	Romania	3			

Protected wetlands
Number, latest

#	Country	Value	#	Country	Value
1	United Kingdom	140	12	Netherlands	18
2	Italy	46	13	France	15
3	Ireland	45	14	Finland	11
4	Denmark	38		Slovakia	11
	Spain	38	16	Austria	10
6	Russia	35		Czech Republic	10
7	Germany	31		Estonia	10
8	Sweden	30		Greece	10
9	Norway	23		Portugal	10
10	Ukraine	22	21	Turkey	9
11	Hungary	19			

CONTENTS

CONTENTS

Notes

In this fifth edition of *The Economist Pocket Europe in Figures* we present a detailed picture of Europe today: how its countries compare and how they have changed over recent decades. The contents list on the previous pages gives a full list of the hundreds of subjects covered in the 11 main sections. Some 48 countries are considered.

The research for this book was carried out in 2001 using the most up-to-date and most authoritative sources available. The sources used are listed at the end of the book.

The extent and quality of the statistics available varies from country to country. Every care has been taken to specify the broad definitions on which the data are based and to indicate cases where data quality or technical difficulties are such that interpretation of the figures is likely to be seriously affected. Nevertheless, figures from individual countries will often differ from standard international statistical definitions. Availability of data also varies, particularly for the transition economies.

Serbia and Montenegro make up the Federal Republic of Yugoslavia. Macedonia is officially known as the Former Yugoslav Republic of Macedonia. Data for Cyprus normally refer to Greek Cyprus only. Data for the European Union (EU) refer to its 15 members following enlargement of the Union on January 1 1995. The euro zone's 12 members are all of the EU15 except Denmark, Sweden and the United Kingdom.

The all-important factor in a book of this kind is to be able to make reliable comparisons between countries. Although this is never quite possible for the reasons stated above, the best route, which this book takes, is to compare data for the same year or period and to use actual, not estimated, figures wherever possible.

Most countries' national accounts are now compiled on a GDP basis so, for simplicity, the term GDP has been used interchangeably with GNP.

Statistics for principal exports and principal imports are normally based on customs statistics. These are generally compiled on different definitions to the visible exports and imports figures shown in the balance of payments sections.

Figures may not add exactly to totals, or percentages to 100, because of rounding or statistical adjustment. Sums of money have generally been converted to US dollars at the official exchange rate ruling at the time to which the figures refer.

Definitions of the statistics are given on the relevant page or in the glossary on pages 12–14, which also explains various other terms.

Glossary

Balance of payments The record of a country's transactions with the rest of the world. The current account of the balance of payments consists of visible trade (goods), invisible trade (income and expenditure for services such as banking, insurance, tourism and shipping, together with profits earned overseas and interest payments) and current transfers (remittances from those working abroad, payments to international organisations, famine relief). Imports include the cost of "carriage, insurance and freight" (cif) from the exporting country to the importing.The value of exports does not include these elements and is recorded "free on board" (fob). Balance of payments statistics are generally adjusted so that both exports and imports are shown fob; the cif element is included in invisibles.

Big Mac index As published by *The Economist* it is based on the theory of purchasing-power parity, the notion that a dollar should buy the same amount in all countries; in the long run, the exchange rate between two currencies should move towards the rate that would equalise the price of an identical basket of goods and services in each country. Our "basket" is a McDonald's Big Mac, which is produced "locally" in 110 countries.

Crude birth rate The number of live births per 1,000 population. The crude rate will automatically be high if a large proportion of the population is of child-bearing age.

Crude death rate The number of deaths in one year per 1,000 population. Also affected by the population's age structure.

Current prices These are in nominal terms and do not take into account the effect of inflation.

Enrolment Gross enrolment ratios may exceed 100% because some pupils are younger or older than the standard primary or secondary school age.

ECSC European Coal and Steel Community, established by the Treaty of Paris, signed April 18th 1951 and effective 1952.

Ecu European currency unit. An accounting measure used within the EU and composed of a weighted basket of the currencies of 12 EU members. Replaced by the euro on January 1st, 1999.

EEC European Economic Community, established by the Treaty of Rome, signed March 25th 1957, effective 1958. The European Atomic Energy Community (Euratom) came into effect at the same time.

EMU Economic and monetary union. Stages for implementation were proposed in the Delors report which followed the 1988 Hanover European Council meeting. The Maastricht treaty agreed in December 1991 laid out a timetable for progress towards EMU and the adoption of a single currency.

EC European Community. Merger of ECSC, EEC and Euratom signed April 8th 1965, effective 1967.

EU European Union. Following the treaty agreed at Maastricht in December 1991 the EC was formally incorporated into a new and broader European Union. Until 1995 it had 12 members: Belgium, Denmark, France, Germany, Greece, Ireland, Italy, Luxembourg, Netherlands, Portugal, Spain and the United Kingdom. From January 1st 1995 membership increased to 15 as Austria, Finland and Sweden joined the Union.

Euro Introduced on January 1st, 1999, replacing the ecu. The euro zone's 12 members are all of the EU 15 except Denmark, Sweden and the United Kingdom. Greece joined on January 1, 2001.

Fertility rate The average number of children born to a woman who completes her childbearing years.

Foreign direct investment The purchase of assets in another country by a company or individual plus reinvested earnings and intra-company loans.

G7 The Group of Seven. Members are Canada, France, Germany, Italy, Japan, the United Kingdom and the United States.

GDP Gross domestic product. It is the sum of all output produced by economic activity within that country. GNP (gross national product) includes net income from abroad eg. rent, profits. For simplicity, the term GDP has been used interchangeably with GNP.

Government Finance and tax data may refer to central government only or to general government which includes central state and local government and the social security sectors.

Infant mortality rate The annual number of deaths of infants under one year of age per 1,000 live births.

Inflation The annual rate at which prices are increasing or decreasing. The most common measure is the change in the consumer price index.

Internet host A domain name that has an Internet address associated with it (eg www.economist.com). This would be any computer system connected to the Internet.

Invisible trade Exports and imports of such items you cannot drop on your foot, that is, services such as shipping, insurance and banking plus profits, dividends and interest received by or from overseas residents.

Life expectancy The average length of time a newborn baby can expect to live.

Market capitalisation The value of a company or companies calculated by multiplying the number of issued shares by their market price at a given time.

Marginal tax rate   The rate of tax paid on an extra unit of income.

Median age   Divides the age distribution into two halves. Half of the population is above and half below the median age.

Migration rate   The number of people per 1,000 population emigrating (minus figure) or immigrating (plus figure) to the relevant country.

Money supply   A measure of the "money" available to buy goods and services. Various definitions of money supply exist. The measures used here are based on definitions used by the IMF and may differ from measures used nationally. Narrow money consists of cash in circulation and demand deposits; broad money also includes savings and foreign currency deposits.

OECD   Organisation for Economic Co-operation and Development. The "rich countries' club" established in 1961. Now has 29 members: Australia, Austria, Belgium, Canada, Czech Republic, Denmark, Finland, France, Germany, Greece, Hungary, Iceland, Ireland, Italy, Japan, Luxembourg, Mexico, Netherlands, New Zealand, Norway, Poland, Portugal, South Korea, Spain, Sweden, Switzerland, Turkey, United Kingdom, United States.

Population density   The total number of inhabitants divided by the surface area.

Real terms   Figures are adjusted to allow for inflation.

Reserves   The stock of gold and foreign currency held by a country to finance any calls that may be made for the settlement of foreign debt. Also used to buy and sell foreign currency to control fluctuations.

Trade-weighted exchange rates   This measures a currency's depreciation (figures below 100) or appreciation (figures over 100) from a base date against a trade-weighted basket of the country's main trading partners.

Visible trade   Exports and imports of things you can drop on your foot such as bricks, brass and bombs.

LAND
AND THE
ENVIRONMENT

Land and land use

Biggest countries
Land area, sq km

1	Russia	17,075,400		26	Lithuania	65,200
2	Turkey	779,450		27	Latvia	64,589
3	Ukraine	603,700		28	Croatia	56,540
4	France	551,500		29	Bosnia	51,130
5	Spain	504,780		30	Slovakia	49,500
6	Sweden	449,960		31	Estonia	45,125
7	Germany	356,910		32	Denmark	43,070
8	Finland	338,130		33	Switzerland	41,290
9	Norway	323,900		34	Netherlands	37,330
10	Poland	312,680		35	Moldova	33,700
11	Italy	301,270		36	Belgium	33,100
12	United Kingdom	244,880		37	Armenia	29,000
13	Romania	237,500		38	Albania	28,750
14	Belarus	207,600		39	Macedonia	25,715
15	Greece	131,990		40	Slovenia	20,250
16	Bulgaria	110,910		41	Cyprus	9,251
17	Iceland	103,000		42	Luxembourg	2,586
18	Hungary	93,030		43	Andorra	468
19	Portugal	92,390		44	Malta	320
20	Serbia & Montenegro	88,361		45	Liechtenstein	160
21	Azerbaijan	86,600		46	San Marino	61
22	Austria	83,850		47	Monaco	2
23	Czech Republic	78,370		48	Vatican	0.44
24	Ireland	70,280				
25	Georgia	69,700			**Total Europe**	23,933,278

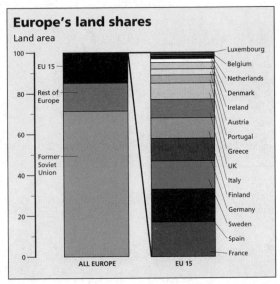

Europe's land shares
Land area

ALL EUROPE

EU 15

EU 15
Rest of Europe
Former Soviet Union

Luxembourg
Belgium
Netherlands
Denmark
Ireland
Austria
Portugal
Greece
UK
Italy
Finland
Germany
Sweden
Spain
France

How agricultural?

Agricultural land as % of land area

1	Ireland	81		Luxembourg	45
2	Moldova	80	25	Armenia	44
3	Ukraine	73		Portugal	44
4	United Kingdom	71	27	Croatia	43
5	Greece	68	28	Albania	41
6	Denmark	65		Austria	41
	Romania	65		Malta	41
8	Poland	61	31	Latvia	40
9	Spain	60		Liechtenstein	40
10	Bulgaria	59		Switzerland	40
11	Italy	56	34	Bosnia	39
12	France	55		Slovenia	39
13	Czech Republic	54	36	Georgia	38
	Lithuania	54	37	Estonia	36
15	Netherlands	53	38	Hungary	31
16	Turkey	52	39	Iceland	23
17	Macedonia	51	40	Cyprus	17
	Slovakia	51		San Marino	17
19	Andorra	49	42	Russia	12
	Germany	49	43	Finland	8
21	Azerbaijan	48		Sweden	8
22	Belarus	45	45	Norway	3
	Belgium	45			

How forested?

Forested area as % of land area

1	Finland	76		Lithuania	31
2	Sweden	68	24	Poland	29
3	Slovenia	54		Romania	29
4	Latvia	46	26	France	27
	Russia	46		Norway	27
6	Estonia	44	28	Turkey	26
7	Slovakia	41	29	Italy	23
8	Austria	39	30	Belgium	21
	Bosnia	39		Luxembourg	21
	Macedonia	39	32	Greece	20
11	Albania	38	33	Hungary	19
	Bulgaria	38	34	Ukraine	18
	Croatia	38	35	Armenia	15
14	Portugal	36	36	Cyprus	13
15	Andorra	35		Moldova	13
	Liechtenstein	35	38	Azerbaijan	11
17	Belarus	34	39	Denmark	10
	Czech Republic	34		United Kingdom	10
	Georgia	34	41	Netherlands	8
20	Spain	32	42	Ireland	5
	Switzerland	32	43	Iceland	1
22	Germany	31			

Natural facts

National high points
Metres

1	Russia	Elbrus	5,642
2	Georgia	Mount Shkhara	5,203
3	Turkey	Mount Ararat	5,165
4	France	Mont Blanc	4,808
5	Italy	Monte Bianco	4,808
6	Switzerland	Dufourspitze	4,634
7	Azerbaijan	Bazar-Dyuzi	4,480
8	Armenia	Transcaucasia	4,090
9	Austria	Grossglockner	3,797
10	Spain	Pico de Teide	3,715
11	Germany	Zugspitze	2,962
12	Andorra	Pia de l'Estany	2,951
13	Bulgaria	Musala	2,925
14	Greece	Mount Olympus	2,917
15	Slovenia	Triglan	2,863
16	Albania	Korab	2,764
17	Macedonia	Korab	2,764
18	Serbia & Montenegro	Daravica	2,656
19	Slovakia	Gerlachovsky	2,655
20	Liechtenstein	Grauspitz	2,599
21	Romania	Negoiu	2,548
22	Poland	Mount Rysy	2,499
23	Norway	Glittertind	2,470
24	Bosnia	Maglic	2,396
25	Portugal	Ponta do Pico	2,351
26	Iceland	Hvannadalshnúkur	2,119
27	Sweden	Kebnekaise	2,111
28	Ukraine	Mount Goverla	2,061
29	Cyprus	Mount Olympus	1,951
30	Croatia	Troglav	1,913
31	Czech Republic	Sniezka	1,602
32	United Kingdom	Ben Nevis	1,342
33	Finland	Haltiatunturi	1,328
34	Ireland	Carrauntoohil	1,038
35	Hungary	Kékestetö	1,014
36	San Marino	Monte Titano	793
37	Belgium	Signal de Botranges	694
38	Luxembourg	Buurgplaatz	559
39	Moldova	Mount Balaneshty	429
40	Belarus	Dzyarzhynskaya	346
41	Netherlands	Vaalserberg	321
42	Estonia	Suur Munamagi	318
43	Latvia	Uidzeme	312
44	Lithuania	Jouzapine	294
45	Malta	Dingli Cliffs	253
46	Denmark	Yding Skovhoj	173

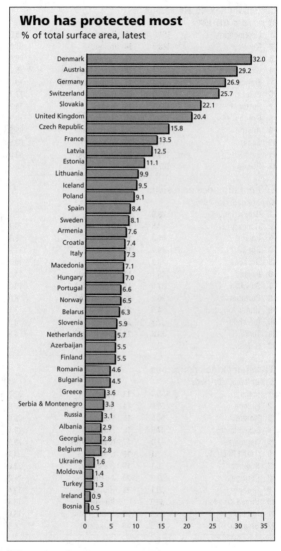

Who has protected most
% of total surface area, latest

Denmark	32.0
Austria	29.2
Germany	26.9
Switzerland	25.7
Slovakia	22.1
United Kingdom	20.4
Czech Republic	15.8
France	13.5
Latvia	12.5
Estonia	11.1
Lithuania	9.9
Iceland	9.5
Poland	9.1
Spain	8.4
Sweden	8.1
Armenia	7.6
Croatia	7.4
Italy	7.3
Macedonia	7.1
Hungary	7.0
Portugal	6.6
Norway	6.5
Belarus	6.3
Slovenia	5.9
Netherlands	5.7
Azerbaijan	5.5
Finland	5.5
Romania	4.6
Bulgaria	4.5
Greece	3.6
Serbia & Montenegro	3.3
Russia	3.1
Albania	2.9
Georgia	2.8
Belgium	2.8
Ukraine	1.6
Moldova	1.4
Turkey	1.3
Ireland	0.9
Bosnia	0.5

Notes
Protected areas are areas of at least 1,000 hectares that fall into the following categories: scientific or nature reserves; national parks; natural monuments or landscapes with some unique aspects; wildlife sanctuaries; other protected landscapes or seascapes.
Biosphere reserves are those internationally recognised supporting, self-sustaining and self-regulating ecological systems.

Air pollution

Carbon monoxide emissions
Kg per head, late-1990s

1	Luxembourg	194.8	13	Denmark	105.6
2	Norway	148.9	14	Ireland	91.0
3	Iceland	144.0	15	Finland	89.9
4	Belgium	141.4	16	Czech Republic	85.1
	France	141.4	17	United Kingdom	79.0
6	Italy	135.3	18	Germany	77.7
7	Portugal	133.1	19	Turkey	74.2
8	Greece	130.8	20	Hungary	70.9
9	Austria	123.2	21	Switzerland	65.5
10	Spain	111.5	22	Slovakia	62.5
11	Sweden	109.4	23	Netherlands	52.9
12	Russia	107.9			

Sulphur dioxides emissions
Kg per head, late-1990s

1	Czech Republic	68.0	13	Italy	23.1
2	Hungary	64.5	14	Denmark	20.7
3	Poland	61.3	15	Finland	19.5
4	Spain	49.1	16	Germany	17.9
5	Greece	48.2	17	France	16.2
6	Ireland	45.1	18	Luxembourg	14.3
7	Slovakia	37.5	19	Sweden	10.3
8	Portugal	36.2	20	Netherlands	8.0
9	United Kingdom	34.5	21	Austria	7.1
10	Iceland	32.3	22	Norway	6.9
11	Turkey	29.8	23	Switzerland	4.5
12	Belgium	23.7			

Nitrogen oxides emissions
Kg per head, late-1990s

1	Iceland	105.9	13	Spain	31.7
2	Finland	50.6	14	Italy	30.9
3	Norway	50.5	15	Poland	29.9
4	Luxembourg	47.5	16	France	29.1
5	Denmark	47.0	17	Netherlands	28.5
6	Czech Republic	41.1	18	Slovakia	23.1
7	Sweden	38.1	19	Germany	22.0
8	Portugal	37.6	20	Austria	21.2
9	Greece	35.1	21	Hungary	19.4
10	United Kingdom	35.0		Russia	19.4
11	Ireland	33.9	23	Switzerland	18.0
12	Belgium	32.9	24	Turkey	14.5

Emissions of volatile organic compounds
Kg per head, late-1990s

1	Norway	81.6	13	Spain	29.6
2	Austria	47.7	14	Ireland	28.7
3	Sweden	47.2	15	Denmark	28.3
4	Luxembourg	42.8	16	Switzerland	27.3
5	France	42.0	17	Czech Republic	26.4
	Greece	42.0	18	Russia	22.1
7	Italy	41.3	19	Germany	22.0
8	Iceland	36.3	20	Netherlands	21.4
9	United Kingdom	35.9	21	Poland	19.8
10	Finland	35.4	22	Slovakia	16.9
11	Portugal	34.7	23	Hungary	14.9
12	Belgium	29.8			

Emissions of carbon dioxide

	m tonnes, 1997			*Per head, tonnes, 1997*	
1	Russia	1,444.5	1	Norway	15.6
2	Germany	851.5	2	Estonia	13.1
3	United Kingdom	527.1	3	Czech Republic	12.2
4	Italy	424.7	4	Finland	11.0
5	Ukraine	370.5	5	Denmark	10.9
6	Poland	357.0	6	Belgium	10.5
7	France	349.8		Netherlands	10.5
8	Spain	257.7	8	Germany	10.4
9	Turkey	216.0	9	Ireland	10.2
10	Netherlands	163.6	10	Russia	9.8
11	Czech Republic	125.2	11	Poland	9.2
12	Romania	111.3	12	United Kingdom	8.9
13	Belgium	106.5	13	Greece	8.3
14	Greece	87.2	14	Austria	7.8
15	Norway	68.5		Slovenia	7.8
16	Austria	62.6	16	Italy	7.4
17	Belarus	62.3	17	Ukraine	7.3
18	Hungary	59.6	18	Slovakia	7.1
19	Denmark	57.7	19	Spain	6.6
20	Finland	56.6	20	Belarus	6.1
21	Portugal	53.8		Bulgaria	6.1
22	Bulgaria	50.3	22	France	6.0
23	Serbia & Montenegro	50.2		Switzerland	6.0
24	Sweden	48.6	24	Hungary	5.9
25	Switzerland	42.6	25	Macedonia	5.5
26	Slovakia	38.1		Sweden	5.5
27	Ireland	37.3	27	Portugal	5.4
28	Azerbaijan	32.0	28	Romania	4.9
29	Croatia	20.1	29	Serbia & Montenegro	4.7
30	Estonia	19.1	30	Croatia	4.4
31	Slovenia	15.5	31	Azerbaijan	4.1
32	Lithuania	15.1		Lithuania	4.1
33	Macedonia	10.9	33	Turkey	3.5
34	Moldova	10.4	34	Latvia	3.3

Waste and recycling

Total waste generation by sector
Agriculture, '000 tonnes, latest available

1	France	377,000	7	Norway	18,000
2	Spain	114,000	8	Netherlands	17,000
3	United Kingdom	80,000	9	Greece	7,780
4	Hungary	62,000	10	Czech Republic	5,460
5	Ireland	31,000	11	Slovakia	4,500
6	Finland	22,000			

Mining and quarrying, '000 tonnes, latest available

1	Poland	82,670	9	Czech Republic	5,000
2	France	75,000	10	Greece	3,900
3	United Kingdom	74,000	11	Ireland	2,200
4	Spain	70,000	12	Belgium	810
5	Sweden	47,000	13	Hungary	790
6	Germany	16,830	14	Slovakia	790
7	Finland	15,000	15	Portugal	470
8	Norway	7,600	16	Netherlands	330

Manufacturing, '000 tonnes, latest available

1	France	101,000	12	Netherlands	8,810
2	Germany	63,090	13	Slovakia	6,720
3	United Kingdom	56,000	14	Greece	6,680
4	Czech Republic	38,570	15	Ireland	3,780
5	Turkey	28,110	16	Norway	2,880
6	Italy	22,210	17	Denmark	2,740
7	Poland	22,200	18	Switzerland	1,500
8	Sweden	13,970	19	Luxembourg	1,440
9	Spain	13,830	20	Portugal	420
10	Belgium	13,730	21	Iceland	10
11	Finland	11,400			

Energy production, '000 tonnes, latest available

1	Germany	19,590	9	Netherlands	1,400
2	Poland	18,030	10	Finland	1,350
3	Czech Republic	17,060	11	Italy	1,330
4	United Kingdom	13,000	12	Belgium	1,140
5	Greece	9,300	13	Hungary	1,080
6	Turkey	8,680	14	Sweden	680
7	Slovakia	2,900	15	Portugal	390
8	Denmark	1,780	16	Ireland	350

Nuclear waste
Tonnes of heavy metal, 1998

1	France	1,165	6	Spain[a]	97
2	United Kingdom[a]	785	7	Finland	72
3	Germany	430	8	Switzerland	64
4	Sweden[a]	232	9	Hungary	53
5	Belgium	141	10	Czech Republic	45

a Provisional.

Municipal waste
Municipal, '000 tonnes, 1997

1	Russia	50,000	13	Austria	4,110
2	Germany	36,976	14	Greece	3,900
3	France	28,800	15	Portugal	3,800
4	United Kingdom	28,000	16	Czech Republic	3,200
5	Italy	26,605		Sweden	3,200
6	Turkey	20,253	18	Denmark	2,951
7	Spain	15,307	19	Norway	2,721
8	Poland	12,183	20	Finland	2,100
9	Netherlands	8,716	21	Ireland	2,032
10	Hungary	5,000	22	Slovakia	1,800
11	Belgium	4,852	23	Luxembourg	193
12	Switzerland	4,277	24	Iceland	150

Kg generated per person, 1997

1	Norway	630		Italy	460
2	Switzerland	600		Luxembourg	460
3	Denmark	560	15	Finland	410
	Iceland	560	16	Spain	390
	Ireland	560	17	Portugal	380
	Netherlands	560	18	Greece	370
7	Austria	510	19	Sweden	360
8	Hungary	500	20	Russia	340
9	Belgium	480		Slovakia	340
	France	480	22	Turkey	330
	United Kingdom	480	23	Poland	320
12	Germany	460	24	Czech Republic	310

Recovery rates
%, 1997

	Paper and cardboard			Glass	
1	Germany	70	1	Switzerland	91
2	Austria	69	2	Austria	88
3	Switzerland	63	3	Netherlands	82
4	Netherlands	62	4	Germany	79
	Sweden	62	5	Norway	76
6	Finland[a]	57		Sweden	76
7	Denmark	50	7	Belgium	75
8	Hungary[b]	49		Iceland[c]	75
9	Norway	44	9	Denmark	70
10	Spain	42	10	Finland	62
11	France	41	11	France	52
12	Portugal	40	12	Poland	44
	United Kingdom	40	13	Slovakia	40
14	Turkey	36	14	Ireland	38
15	Slovakia	34	15	Spain	37
16	Czech Republic	33	16	Italy	34
17	Italy	31			

a 1995 b 1996 c 1992

Weather

Hot spots
Highest average temperatures, July, °C

1	Cyprus	Nicosia	37
2	Spain	Seville	36
3	Greece	Trikkala	35
4	Armenia	Erivan	34
5	Turkey	Izmir	33
6	Albania	Tirane	31
	Bulgaria	Plovdiv	31
	Georgia	Tbilisi	31
	Macedonia	Skopje	31
	Russia	Astrakhan	31
11	Italy	Palermo	30
	Romania	Bucharest	30
13	Croatia	Dubrovnik	29
	France	Marseille	29
	Malta	Valletta	29
16	Hungary	Budapest	28
	Portugal	Faro	28
	Serbia	Belgrade	28
	Ukraine	Simferopol	28

Cold spots
Lowest average temperatures, January, °C

1	Russia	Perm	-20
2	Finland	Inari	-18
	Turkey	Kars	-18
4	Norway	Spitzbergen	-15
5	Sweden	Piteaa	-14
6	Estonia	Tallina	-11
	Lithuania	Vilnius	-11
	Switzerland	Santis	-11
9	Spain	Madrid	-10
	Ukraine	Kiev	-10
	Latvia	Riga	-10
12	Armenia	Erivan	-9
	Austria	Klagenfurt	-9
14	Moldova	Kishinev	-8
15	Romania	Bucharest	-7
	Slovakia	Kosice	-7
	Poland	Przemysl	-7
18	Hungary	Debrecen	-6
19	Czech Republic	Brno	-5
	France	Embrun	-5
	Germany	Munich	-5

Disaster spots

Country	Disaster	Killed	Date
Spain	Landslide	84	1996
Poland	Cold wave	64	1998
Poland	Flood	55	1997
Belarus	Storm	54	1999
Slovakia	Storm	54	1998
Cyprus	Heat wave	52	1998
Poland	Cold wave	50	1997
Austria	Slide	38	1999
Azerbaijan	Earthquake	31	2000
Germany	Cold wave	30	1997
Czech Republic	Flood	29	1997
France	Cold wave	23	1997
Romania	Flood	23	1998
Romania	Flood	20	1997
Ukraine	Flood	18	1998
Austria	Slide	13	2000
Russia	Flood	13	1998
Azerbaijan	Flood	11	1997
Azerbaijan	Slide	11	2000
Portugal	Flood	11	1997
Portugal	Flood	10	1996
United Kingdom	Storm	8	1998

a February.

Part II

POPULATION

Population

From biggest to smallest

Population, m

2000			2015		
1	Russia	146.5	1	Russia	133.3
2	Germany	82.0	2	Germany	80.7
3	Turkey	64.3	3	Turkey	79.0
4	France	60.8	4	France	61.9
5	United Kingdom	59.1	5	United Kingdom	60.6
6	Italy	57.6	6	Italy	55.2
7	Ukraine	49.9	7	Ukraine	43.3
8	Spain	39.4	8	Spain	39.0
9	Poland	38.7	9	Poland	38.0
10	Romania	22.5	10	Romania	21.4
11	Netherlands	15.8	11	Netherlands	16.4
12	Serbia & Montenegro	10.6	12	Greece	10.5
13	Greece	10.5	13	Belgium	10.3
14	Belarus	10.2		Serbia & Montenegro	10.3
	Belgium	10.2	15	Czech Republic	10.0
	Czech Republic	10.2		Portugal	10.0
17	Hungary	10.1	17	Belarus	9.7
18	Portugal	10.0	18	Hungary	9.3
19	Sweden	8.9	19	Azerbaijan	8.7
20	Bulgaria	8.2	20	Sweden	8.6
21	Austria	8.0	21	Austria	7.8
	Azerbaijan	8.0	22	Switzerland	7.0
23	Switzerland	7.1	23	Bulgaria	6.8
24	Georgia	5.4	24	Denmark	5.4
	Slovakia	5.4		Slovakia	5.4
26	Denmark	5.3	26	Finland	5.2
27	Finland	5.2	27	Georgia	4.8
28	Croatia	4.5	28	Norway	4.7
	Norway	4.5	29	Croatia	4.6
30	Moldova	4.3	30	Ireland	4.4
31	Bosnia	3.9	31	Bosnia	4.3
32	Armenia	3.8	32	Moldova	4.1
33	Ireland	3.7	33	Armenia	3.8
	Lithuania	3.7	34	Lithuania	3.5
35	Albania	3.3	35	Albania	3.4
36	Latvia	2.4	36	Latvia	2.2
37	Macedonia	2.0	37	Macedonia	2.0
38	Estonia	1.4	38	Slovenia	1.9
39	Slovenia	1.2	39	Estonia	1.2
40	Cyprus	0.8	40	Cyprus	0.9
41	Luxembourg	0.4	41	Luxembourg	0.5
42	Malta	0.4	42	Malta	0.4
	Iceland	0.3	43	Iceland	0.3
			44	Liechtenstein	0.04
				Monaco	0.04
	Euro-11	293.1	46	San Marino	0.03
	EU15	377.0	47	Andorra	0.01

Fastest growth
Annual average population growth, %

	1995–2000			2000–2005	
1	Bosnia	3.02	1	Turkey	1.32
2	Turkey	1.62	2	Luxembourg	1.20
3	Luxembourg	1.28	3	Bosnia	1.13
4	Cyprus	1.05	4	Ireland	0.96
	Ireland	1.05	5	Cyprus	0.77
6	Azerbaijan	0.91	6	Iceland	0.67
7	Iceland	0.87	7	Albania	0.63
8	Macedonia	0.71	8	Azerbaijan	0.59
9	Malta	0.63	9	Malta	0.40
10	Netherlands	0.52	10	Norway	0.37
11	Norway	0.50	11	France	0.36
12	France	0.37	12	Netherlands	0.35
13	Denmark	0.35	13	Macedonia	0.30
14	Greece	0.30	14	United Kingdom	0.18
15	United Kingdom	0.27	15	Denmark	0.16
16	Finland	0.25	16	Portugal	0.13
17	Belgium	0.22	17	Belgium	0.09
18	Portugal	0.20	18	Slovakia	0.08
19	Switzerland	0.15	19	Finland	0.07
20	Armenia	0.14	20	Armenia	0.06

Slowest growth
Annual average population growth, %

	1995–2000			2000–2005	
1	Estonia	-1.26	1	Estonia	-1.14
2	Bulgaria	-1.12	2	Bulgaria	-0.98
3	Ukraine	-0.78	3	Ukraine	-0.94
4	Latvia	-0.77	4	Russia	-0.64
5	Hungary	-0.49	5	Latvia	-0.56
6	Russia	-0.36	6	Georgia	-0.53
7	Georgia	-0.34	7	Hungary	-0.50
8	Albania	-0.32	8	Belarus	-0.40
9	Belarus	-0.28	9	Moldova	-0.26
10	Romania	-0.22		Romania	-0.26
11	Moldova	-0.20	11	Lithuania	-0.24
12	Czech Republic	-0.11	12	Serbia & Montenegro	-0.15
13	Lithuania	-0.10	13	Italy	-0.13
14	Slovenia	-0.02		Sweden	-0.13
15	Poland	0.01	15	Slovenia	-0.12
	Serbia & Montenegro	0.01	16	Austria	-0.10
17	Sweden	0.03		Czech Republic	-0.10
18	Austria	0.08	18	Poland	-0.09
	Italy	0.08	19	Switzerland	-0.06
20	Croatia	0.09	20	Germany	-0.04

Population density

Most crowded countries
Population per sq km

1955			1975		
1	Malta	994	1	Malta	963
2	Belgium	291	2	Netherlands	334
3	Netherlands	263	3	Belgium	321
4	United Kingdom	210	4	United Kingdom	230
5	Germany	197	5	Germany	221
6	Italy	161	6	Italy	184
7	Switzerland	121	7	Switzerland	154
8	Czech Republic	118	8	Luxembourg	140
	Luxembourg	118	9	Czech Republic	127
10	Hungary	106	10	Denmark	117
11	Denmark	103	11	Moldova	114
12	Portugal	93	12	Hungary	113
13	Poland	84	13	Poland	105
14	Austria	83	14	Portugal	98
15	France	79	15	Slovakia	97
16	Moldova	78	16	France	96
17	Slovakia	77	17	Armenia	95
18	Slovenia	76	18	Austria	90
19	Romania	74	19	Romania	89
20	Croatia	70	20	Slovenia	86

Most crowded EU regions
No. of people per sq km, 1998

1	Copenhagen/Frederiksberg	Denmark	5,972
2	Brussels	Belgium	5,913
3	London	United Kingdom	4,538
4	Berlin	Germany	3,835
5	Bremen	Germany	1,660
6	Ile de France	France	910
7	Attiki	Greece	906
8	West Netherlands	Netherlands	844
9	Madrid	Spain	629
10	Cologne	Germany	576
11	South Netherlands	Netherlands	488
12	North-West England	United Kingdom	486
13	Arnsberg	Germany	477
14	Flemish Region	Belgium	438
15	Campania	Italy	426
16	Saarland	Germany	419
17	South-East England	United Kingdom	419
18	West Midlands	United Kingdom	410
19	Karlsruhe	Germany	385
20	Lombardy	Italy	377

_2000[a]_			_2025[a]_		
1	Monaco	16,500	1	Monaco	19,500
2	Malta	1,234	2	Malta	1,322
3	San Marino	442	3	San Marino	524
4	Netherlands	382	4	Netherlands	399
5	Belgium	336	5	Andorra	389
6	United Kingdom	244	6	Belgium	335
7	Germany	230	7	United Kingdom	251
8	Liechtenstein	206	8	Liechtenstein	244
9	Italy	191	9	Luxembourg	223
10	Andorra	185	10	Germany	221
11	Switzerland	173	11	Italy	179
12	Luxembourg	169	12	Switzerland	163
13	Czech Republic	130	13	Albania	128
14	Moldova	127	14	Armenia	125
	Armenia	127		Denmark	125
16	Denmark	124	16	Czech Republic	123
17	Poland	123	17	Moldova	120
18	Portugal	113	18	Poland	119
19	Slovakia	110	19	France	115
20	Albania	109	20	Turkey	111
	France	109		Portugal	111

Least crowded EU regions

No. of people per sq km, 1998

1	Ovre Norrland	Sweden	3
2	Mellersta Norrland	Sweden	5
3	Norra Mellansverige	Sweden	13
4	Manner-Suomi	Finland	17
	Aland	Finland	17
6	Smaland med oarna	Sweden	24
7	Central Spain	Spain	25
8	Ostra Mellansverige	Sweden	39
9	Central Greece	Greece	49
10	North-East Spain	Spain	57
11	South-West France	France	59
12	North Greece	Greece	60
	Vastsverige	Sweden	60
14	Sonderjylland	Denmark	64
15	Scotland	United Kingdom	65
16	Sudosterreich	Austria	68
17	Sardinia	Italy	69
18	Bassin Parisien	France	72
	Central Portugal	Portugal	72
20	Storstrom	Denmark	76
	Bornholm	Denmark	76

a Some countries not available for earlier years.

City living

Capital facts

Country	Capital city	Ranking	Population, '000
Albania	Tirana	39	279
Andorra	Andorra-La-Veila	45	25
Armenia	Yerevan	21	1,284
Austria	Vienna	12	2,070
Azerbaijan	Baku	14	1,936
Belarus	Minsk	16	1,772
Belgium	Brussels	26	1,122
Bosnia	Sarajevo	33	522
Bulgaria	Sofia	23	1,192
Croatia	Zagreb	27	1,060
Cyprus	Nicosia	40	193
Czech Republic	Prague	22	1,226
Denmark	Copenhagen	19	1,388
Estonia	Tallinn	36	397
Finland	Helsinki	24	1,167
France	Paris	1	9,624
Georgia	Tbilisi	20	1,310
Germany	Berlin	6	3,324
Greece	Athens	8	3,116
Hungary	Budapest	15	1,825
Iceland	Reykjavik	41	168
Ireland	Dublin	28	985
Italy	Rome	9	2,688
Latvia	Riga	30	775
Liechtenstein	Vaduz	46	7
Lithuania	Vilnius	32	579
Luxembourg	Luxembourg-Ville	43	79
Macedonia	Skopje	34	485
Malta	Valletta	42	102
Moldova	Kishinev	31	655
Monaco	Monaco	44	33
Netherlands	Amsterdam	25	1,144
Norway	Oslo	29	978
Poland	Warsaw	11	2,269
Portugal	Lisbon	5	3,826
Romania	Bucharest	13	2,054
Russia	Moscow	2	9,321
San Marino	San Marino	47	4
Serbia & Montenegro	Belgrade	18	1,482
Slovakia	Bratislava	35	460
Slovenia	Ljubljana	38	295
Spain	Madrid	4	4,072
Sweden	Stockholm	17	1,583
Switzerland	Berne	37	344
Turkey	Ankara	7	3,203
Ukraine	Kiev	10	2,670
United Kingdom	London	3	7,640
Vatican	Vatican City	48	1

Note: Estimates of city populations taken from latest UN statistics for agglomerations.

Most urbanised countries
% of population living in urban areas

1970			2000		
1	Monaco	100	1	Monaco	100
	Vatican	100		Vatican	100
3	Andorra	96	3	Belgium	97
4	Belgium	94	4	Andorra	93
5	United Kingdom	89	5	Iceland	92
6	Iceland	87	6	Luxembourg	91
7	Netherlands	86	7	Malta	90
8	Sweden	81	8	Netherlands	89
9	Denmark	80		San Marino	89
	Germany	80		United Kingdom	89

Least urbanised countries
% of population living in urban areas

1970			2000		
1	Liechtenstein	20	1	Liechtenstein	23
2	Portugal	26	2	Albania	42
3	Bosnia	27	3	Bosnia	43
4	Albania	32	4	Moldova	46
	Moldova	32	5	Slovenia	50
6	Slovenia	37	6	Serbia & Montenegro	52
7	Turkey	38	7	Romania	56
8	Serbia & Montenegro	39		Cyprus	56
9	Croatia	40	9	Azerbaijan	57
10	Slovakia	41		Slovakia	57

City population
Annual rate of growth, 1995–2000, %

1	Bursa, Turkey	4.42
2	Gaziantep, Turkey	4.30
3	Istanbul, Turkey	3.56
4	Adana, Turkey	3.49
5	Porto, Portugal	3.48
6	Izmir, Turkey	3.20
7	Oslo, Norway	2.62
8	Lisbon, Portugal	2.58
9	Ankara, Turkey	2.36
10	Helsinki, Finland	1.99
11	Zagreb, Croatia	1.54
12	Dusseldorf, Germany	1.32
13	Zurich, Switzerland	1.20
14	Tyneside, UK	0.98
15	Minsk, Belarus	0.92
16	Baku, Azerbaijan	0.91
17	Liverpool, UK	0.84
18	Dublin, Ireland	0.79
19	Amsterdam, Netherlands	0.75
20	Lyon, France	0.59

EU city population density
Population per sq km, 1998

1	Paris, France	20,090
2	Brussels, Belgium	5,913
3	Portsmouth, UK	4,713
4	London, UK	4,568
5	Blackpool, UK	4,313
6	Liverpool, UK	4,091
7	Munich, Germany	3,855
8	Vienna, Austria	3,852
9	Nottingham, UK	3,844
10	Berlin, Germany	3,835
11	Birmingham, UK	3,817
12	Herne, Germany	3,449
13	Kingston-Upon-Hull, UK	3,212
14	Coventry, UK	3,153
15	Brighton and Hove, UK	3,112
16	Derby, UK	3,023
17	Essen, Germany	2,880
18	Stuttgart, Germany	2,815
19	Dusseldorf, Germany	2,625
20	Nuremberg, Germany	2,620

Sex and age

Most male populations
No. of men per 100 women, 2000

1	Albania	105
2	Belgium	103
3	Turkey	102
4	Iceland	101
5	Cyprus	100
	Macedonia	100
7	Ireland	99
	Serbia & Montenegro	99
9	Bosnia	98
	Denmark	98
	Malta	98
	Netherlands	98
	Norway	98
	Sweden	98
	Switzerland	98
16	Azerbaijan	97
	Greece	97
	Luxembourg	97
	United Kingdom	97
20	Germany	96
	Romania	96
	Spain	96

Most female populations
No. of men per 100 women, 2000

1	Latvia	86
2	Belarus	87
	Estonia	87
	Ukraine	87
5	Russia	88
6	Lithuania	89
7	Georgia	91
	Hungary	91
9	Moldova	92
10	Portugal	93
11	Armenia	94
	Croatia	94
	Italy	94
14	Austria	95
	Bulgaria	95
	Czech Republic	95
	Finland	95
	France	95
	Poland	95
	Slovakia	95
	Slovenia	95

Oldest populations
% aged 65 and over

2000			2050		
1	Italy	24.1	1	Spain	44.1
2	Greece	23.4	2	Slovenia	42.4
3	Germany	23.2	3	Italy	42.3
4	Sweden	22.4	4	Austria	41.0
5	Belgium	22.1	5	Greece	40.7
6	Spain	21.8	6	Czech Republic	40.1
7	Bulgaria	21.7	7	Armenia	39.5
8	Switzerland	21.3	8	Switzerland	38.9
9	Latvia	20.9	9	Bulgaria	38.6
10	Portugal	20.8	10	Germany	38.1
11	Austria	20.7		Ukraine	38.1
12	United Kingdom	20.6	12	Bosnia	37.7
13	France	20.5		Sweden	37.7
	Ukraine	20.5	14	Latvia	37.5
15	Croatia	20.2	15	Lithuania	37.3
	Estonia	20.2	16	Russia	37.2
17	Denmark	20.0	17	Slovakia	36.8
18	Finland	19.9	18	Hungary	36.2
19	Hungary	19.7	19	Estonia	35.9
20	Norway	19.6	20	Belarus	35.8
				Georgia	35.8

Median[a] age

Oldest, 2000			Oldest, 2020		
1	Italy	40.6	1	Italy	48.1
2	Germany	40.0	2	Germany	45.6
3	Sweden	39.9		Spain	45.6
4	Greece	39.4	4	Greece	45.4
	Finland	39.4	5	Netherlands	44.2
6	Belgium	39.3		Switzerland	44.2
7	Denmark	39.0	7	Austria	43.9
8	Croatia	38.8	8	Belgium	43.8
	Bulgaria	38.8	9	Slovenia	43.5
10	EU15	38.3	10	Euro-11	43.2
	Switzerland	38.3	11	EU15	43.1
12	United Kingdom	38.2	12	Denmark	42.8
13	Hungary	38.1		Portugal	42.8
	Slovenia	38.1	14	Czech Republic	42.4
15	Euro-11	38.0	15	Finland	42.3
				Sweden	42.3

Youngest, 2000			Youngest, 2020		
1	Turkey	25.6	1	Turkey	30.6
2	Albania	26.7	2	Albania	30.9
3	Azerbaijan	27.0	3	Azerbaijan	32.2
4	Armenia	30.4	4	Armenia	34.8
5	Moldova	31.6	5	Macedonia	35.5
6	Macedonia	32.2	6	Moldova	35.6
7	Ireland	32.3	7	Cyprus	36.1
8	Iceland	32.9	8	Georgia	36.3
9	Cyprus	33.3		Iceland	36.3
10	Slovakia	34.0	10	Ireland	36.7
11	Georgia	34.1	11	Serbia & Montenegro	37.4
12	Romania	34.9	12	Malta	38.6
13	Bosnia	35.1		Russia	38.6
	Poland	35.1	14	Slovakia	39.0
15	Serbia & Montenegro	35.6	15	Poland	39.2

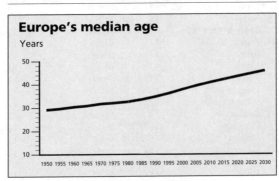

Europe's median age

Years

a Age at which there are an equal number of people above and below.

Matters of breeding

Crude birth rate: countries compared
No. of live births per 1,000 population, 1995–2000

#	Country	Rate		#	Country	Rate
1	Turkey	23.4		24	Bosnia	10.5
2	Albania	21.2			Poland	10.5
3	Azerbaijan	16.1		26	EU15	10.4
4	Iceland	15.4		27	Romania	10.3
5	Macedonia	14.7			Switzerland	10.3
6	Ireland	14.2		29	Lithuania	10.2
7	Cyprus	13.9		30	Austria	10.1
8	Norway	13.1			Euro-11	10.1
9	Luxembourg	12.8		32	Sweden	10.0
10	Malta	12.6		33	Hungary	9.8
11	Denmark	12.4		34	Greece	9.5
	France	12.4		35	Germany	9.3
	Serbia & Montenegro	12.4		36	Belarus	9.2
14	Moldova	12.3			Spain	9.2
15	United Kingdom	12.0		38	Italy	9.1
16	Netherlands	11.9			Slovenia	9.1
17	Croatia	11.7		40	Ukraine	8.9
	Georgia	11.7		41	Czech Republic	8.8
19	Finland	11.3			Russia	8.8
	Portugal	11.3		43	Estonia	8.7
21	Armenia	11.2		44	Bulgaria	8.0
22	Belgium	10.8		45	Latvia	7.8
	Slovakia	10.8				

Fertility rate: countries compared
Average no. of children per woman, 1995–2000

#	Country	Rate	#	Country	Rate
1	Turkey	2.7		Austria	1.4
2	Albania	2.6		Hungary	1.4
3	Azerbaijan	2.0		Lithuania	1.4
	Cyprus	2.0		Poland	1.4
	Iceland	2.0		Portugal	1.4
6	Ireland	1.9		Slovakia	1.4
	Macedonia	1.9		Switzerland	1.4
	Malta	1.9		Euro-11	1.4
9	Norway	1.8	32	Belarus	1.3
	Serbia & Montenegro	1.8		Bosnia	1.3
11	Croatia	1.7		Germany	1.3
	Denmark	1.7		Greece	1.3
	Finland	1.7		Romania	1.3
	France	1.7	37	Estonia	1.2
	Luxembourg	1.7		Italy	1.2
	United Kingdom	1.7		Russia	1.2
17	Belgium	1.6		Slovenia	1.2
	Georgia	1.6		Ukraine	1.2
	Moldova	1.6	42	Bulgaria	1.1
20	Netherlands	1.5		Czech Republic	1.1
	Sweden	1.5		Latvia	1.1
	EU15	1.5		Spain	1.1
23	Armenia	1.4			

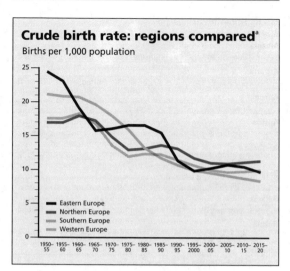

Crude birth rate: regions compared[a]

Births per 1,000 population

- Eastern Europe
- Northern Europe
- Southern Europe
- Western Europe

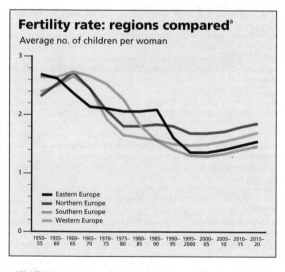

Fertility rate: regions compared[a]

Average no. of children per woman

- Eastern Europe
- Northern Europe
- Southern Europe
- Western Europe

a UN definitions are:
Eastern Europe – Belarus; Bulgaria; Czech Republic; Hungary; Moldova; Poland; Romania; Russia; Slovakia; Ukraine
Northern Europe – Denmark; Estonia; Finland; Iceland; Ireland; Latvia; Lithuania; Norway; Sweden; United Kingdom
Southern Europe – Albania; Bosnia; Croatia; Greece; Italy; Macedonia; Malta; Portugal; Serbia & Montenegro; Slovenia; Spain
Western Europe – Austria; Belgium; France; Germany; Luxembourg; Netherlands; Switzerland

Who lives where

Ethnic breakdown
% of total population

Albania

Albanian 95	Greek 3	Other 2

Andorra

Spanish 43	Andorran 33	Portuguese 11	Other 13

Armenia

Armenian 93	Azeri 3	Russian 2	Other 2

Austria

Austrian 98	Other 2

Azerbaijan

Azeri 90	Russian 3	Armenian 2	Other 5

Belgium

Fleming 58	Walloon 31	Other 11

Belarus

Belarussian 78	Russian 13	Polish 4	Other 4

Bosnia

Bosniak 44	Serbian 31	Croatian 17	Other 8

Bulgaria

Bulgarian 83	Turkish 9	Other 8

Croatia

Croatian 78	Serbian 12	Muslim 1	Other 9

Cyprus

Greek 78	Turkish 18	Other 4

Czech Republic

Czech 81	Moravian 13	Slovakian 3	Other 3

Denmark

Danish 95	Other 5

Estonia

Estonian 65	Russian 28	Ukrainian 3	Other 4

Finland

Finnish 93	Swedish 6	Other 1

France

French 91	Other 9

Georgia

Georgian 70	Armenian 8	Russian 6	Other 16

Germany

German 92	Turkish 2	Other 6

Greece

Greek 98	Other 2

Hungary

Hungarian 90	Gypsy 4	German 3	Other 3

Iceland

Icelandic 98	Other 2

Ireland

Irish 94	Other 6

Italy

Italian 98	Other 2

Latvia

| Latvian 57 | Russian 30 | Belarussian 4 | Other 9 |

Liechtenstein

| German 88 | Italian 3 | | Other 9 |

Lithuania

| Lithuanian 81 | Russian 9 | Polish 7 | Other 3 |

Luxembourg

| Luxembourger 73 | Portuguese 9 | Italian 5 | Other 13 |

Macedonia

| Macedonian 67 | Albanian 23 | Turkish 4 | Other 6 |

Malta

| Maltese 95 | English 2 | | Other 3 |

Moldova

| Moldovan 65 | Ukrainian 14 | Russian 13 | Other 8 |

Monaco

| French 47 | Monegasque 16 | Italian 16 | Other 21 |

Netherlands

| Dutch 91 | | | Other 9 |

Norway

| Norwegian 97 | | | Other 3 |

Poland

| Polish 98 | German 1 | | Other 1 |

Portugal

| Portugese 98 | | | Other 2 |

Romania

| Romanian 89 | Hungarian 7 | | Other 4 |

Russia

| Russian 82 | Tatar 4 | Ukrainian 3 | Other 11 |

San Marino

| Sanmarinesi 87 | Italian 12 | | Other 1 |

Serbia and Montenegro

| Serbian 63 | Albanians 17 | Montenegrian 5 | Other 15 |

Slovakia

| Slovakian 86 | Hungarian 11 | Gypsy 1 | Other 2 |

Slovenia

| Slovene 88 | Croatian 3 | Serbian 2 | Other 7 |

Spain

| Spanish 73 | Catalan 16 | Galician 8 | Other 3 |

Sweden

| Swedish 91 | | | Other 9 |

Switzerland

| German 65 | French 18 | Italian 10 | Other 7 |

Turkey

| Turkish 80 | Kurdish 20 | | |

Ukraine

| Ukrainian 73 | Russian 22 | | Other 5 |

United Kingdom

| English 82 | Scottish 10 | Welsh 2 | Other 6 |

Migration

The recent picture
Net migration rate, per 1,000 population, 1999 estimated

Albania	-2.93	Liechtenstein	5.90
Armenia	-8.26	Lithuania	-1.58
Austria	1.32	Luxembourg	7.78
Azerbaijan	-5.76	Macedonia	-0.83
Belarus	3.13	Malta	1.24
Belgium	1.01	Moldova	-0.92
Bosnia	33.42	Monaco	4.17
Bulgaria	-0.66	Netherlands	1.99
Croatia	1.81	Norway	1.62
Cyprus	0.44	Poland	-0.40
Czech Republic	0.91	Portugal	-1.51
Denmark	3.22	Romania	-0.87
Estonia	-3.08	Russia	2.05
Finland	0.40	San Marino	4.23
France	0.53	Slovakia	0.29
Georgia	-4.69	Slovenia	0.23
Germany	2.12	Spain	0.66
Greece	4.04	Sweden	1.68
Hungary	0.50	Switzerland	0.49
Iceland	-2.17	Turkey	0.00
Ireland	-1.31	Ukraine	0.63
Italy	0.17	United Kingdom	1.11
Latvia	-1.25		

Average annual migration rate, per 1,000 population, 1995–2000 projection

Albania	-19.1	Latvia	-9.5
Armenia	-8.7	Lithuania	-1.4
Austria	4.9	Luxembourg	8.6
Azerbaijan	-5.6	Macedonia	-2.0
Belarus	0.4	Malta	1.9
Belgium	1.3	Moldova	-2.3
Bosnia	27.1	Netherlands	1.3
Bulgaria	-1.8	Norway	2.3
Croatia	0.0	Poland	-0.4
Cyprus	3.9	Portugal	0.5
Czech Republic	0.6	Romania	-1.3
Denmark	2.1	Russia	2.7
Estonia	-7.8	Serbia & Montenegro	-1.9
Finland	1.0	Slovakia	0.0
France	0.7	Slovenia	0.5
Georgia	-15.7	Spain	0.5
Germany	2.9	Sweden	3.4
Greece	3.3	Switzerland	4.3
Hungary	0.0	Turkey	1.0
Iceland	0.0	Ukraine	0.4
Ireland	0.8	United Kingdom	0.7
Italy	1.2		

Looking back

	1960–69	
	Av. ann. migration rate per 1,000 pop.	Av. ann. net migration, '000s
Austria	0.75	5.45
Belgium	1.65	15.62
Denmark	0.20	0.10
Finland	-3.30	-15.06
France	4.20	204.78
Germany	2.55	193.88
Greece	-4.50	-38.48
Iceland	-1.50	-0.29
Ireland	-6.25	-17.98
Italy	-1.80	-93.80
Liechtenstein	12.30	0.23
Luxembourg	4.55	1.51
Malta	-14.18	-4.51
Netherlands	0.55	6.76
Norway	0.00	0.00
Portugal	-13.90	-126.89
Spain	-2.20	-70.59
Sweden	2.25	17.40
Switzerland	2.85	16.69
United Kingdom	0.55	29.98

	1970–79		1980–89	
	Av. ann. migration rate per 1,000 pop.	Av. ann. net migration, '000s	Av. ann. migration rate per 1,000 pop.	Av. ann. net migration, '000s
Austria	1.05	7.96	1.75	13.23
Belgium	0.80	7.84	0.05	0.49
Denmark	0.85	4.30	0.70	3.58
Finland	-0.60	-2.83	0.65	3.19
France	1.40	73.78	0.95	52.41
Germany	1.20	94.41	2.10	163.10
Greece	1.65	14.93	2.10	20.86
Iceland	-2.70	-0.59	0.20	0.05
Ireland	3.25	10.33	-5.70	-20.25
Italy	-0.35	-19.40	-0.25	-14.15
Liechtenstein	13.00	0.31	2.15	0.06
Luxembourg	7.50	2.72	3.50	1.28
Malta	-3.46	-1.07	0.29	0.10
Netherlands	2.30	31.40	1.45	21.01
Norway	0.90	3.61	1.40	5.81
Portugal	2.25	20.46	-2.00	-19.81
Spain	-0.05	-1.78	-0.30	-11.52
Sweden	1.45	11.88	1.75	14.61
Switzerland	-2.00	-12.68	3.20	20.92
United Kingdom	-0.40	-22.57	0.40	22.75

Who speaks what

First language most spoken in Europe

		No. of people million	% of pop. of Europe			No. of people million	% of pop. of Europe
1	Russian	170.00	21.7	19	Swedish	9.26	1.2
2	German	98.00	12.5	20	Lombard	9.11	1.2
3	French	62.76	8.0	21	Bulgarian	8.97	1.1
4	English	61.91	7.9	22	Tatar	8.00	1.0
5	Turkish	59.00	7.5	23	Azerbaijani	7.06	0.9
6	Polish	44.00	5.6	24	Nap.-Calab.	7.05	0.9
7	Italian	42.30	5.4	25	Slovak	5.11	0.7
8	Ukrainian	41.20	5.3	26	Albanian	5.10	0.7
9	Spanish	28.30	3.6	27	Danish	5.07	0.6
10	Romanian	26.00	3.3	28	Finnish	5.02	0.6
11	Serbo-Croat	21.00	2.7	29	Sicilian	4.67	0.6
12	Dutch	20.00	2.6	30	Catalan	4.31	0.6
13	Hungarian	14.50	1.9	31	Armenian	4.30	0.5
14	Greek	12.00	1.5	32	Norwegian	4.28	0.5
15	Kurdish	11.62	1.5	33	Georgian	4.21	0.5
16	Portuguese	11.55	1.5	34	Galician	3.19	0.4
17	Czech	10.53	1.3	35	Lithuanian	3.04	0.4
18	Belarussian	10.20	1.3	36	Venetian	2.21	0.3

Learning second languages

Pupils studying at upper secondary level, 1998–99, %

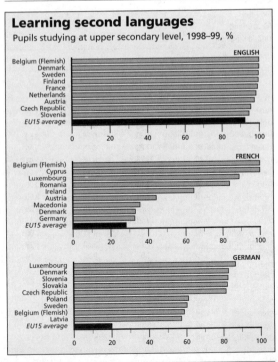

Part III

THE ECONOMY

Economic strength

Largest economies
GDP, $bn at market exchange rates

1999

1	Germany	2,111.9		21	Hungary	48.4
2	United Kingdom	1,441.8		22	Ukraine	38.7
3	France[a]	1,432.3		23	Romania	34.0
4	Italy	1,171.0		24	Belarus	26.8
5	Spain	595.9		25	Serbia & Montenegro[b]	20.6
6	Russia	401.4		26	Croatia	20.4
7	Netherlands	393.7		27	Slovenia	20.0
8	Switzerland	258.6		28	Slovakia	19.7
9	Belgium	248.4		29	Luxembourg	18.5
10	Sweden	238.7		30	Bulgaria	12.4
11	Austria	208.2		31	Lithuania	10.6
12	Turkey	185.7		32	Cyprus	9.1
13	Denmark	174.3		33	Iceland	8.2
14	Poland	155.2		34	Latvia	6.3
15	Norway	152.9		35	Estonia	5.2
16	Finland	129.7		36	Bosnia	4.4
17	Greece	125.1		37	Azerbaijan	4.0
18	Portugal	113.7		38	Albania	3.7
19	Ireland	93.4		39	Macedonia	3.5
20	Czech Republic	53.1			Malta	3.5

1990

1	Germany	1,504		13	Denmark	129
2	France	1,195		14	Norway	115
3	Italy	1,094		15	Greece	83
4	United Kingdom	984		16	Portugal	67
5	Spain	492		17	Poland	59
6	Netherlands	284		18	Ireland	45
7	Sweden	230		19	Romania	38
8	Switzerland	228		20	Hungary	33
9	Belgium	194		21	Luxembourg	9
10	Austria	158		22	Iceland	6
11	Turkey	150			Cyprus	6
12	Finland	135		24	Malta	2

1980

1	Western Germany	758.5		11	Turkey	61.6
2	France	601.6		12	Denmark	61.5
3	United Kingdom	476.9		13	Ex-Yugoslavia	56.7
4	Italy	359.2		14	Norway	52.4
5	Spain	195.7		15	Romania	50.9
6	Netherlands	155.7		16	Finland	46.4
7	Sweden	114.2		17	Greece	39.9
8	Belgium	109.6		18	Portugal	22.4
9	Switzerland	101.4		19	Hungary	20.7
10	Austria	70.6		20	Ireland	16.3

a Including French Guiana, Guadeloupe, Martinique and Réunion. b Estimate.

Largest economies
GDP, $bn at PPP exchange rates

1999

#	Country	Value	#	Country	Value
1	Germany	1,930	21	Finland	117
2	France	1,349	22	Hungary	111
3	United Kingdom	1,322	23	Ireland	84
4	Italy	1,268	24	Belarus	69
5	Russia	1,022	25	Slovakia	56
6	Spain	704	26	Bulgaria	42
7	Turkey	415	27	Croatia	32
8	Netherlands	386		Slovenia	32
9	Poland	324	29	Lithuania	24
10	Belgium	263	30	Azerbaijan	20
11	Switzerland	205	31	Luxembourg	18
12	Austria	199	32	Cyprus	15
13	Sweden	196		Latvia	15
14	Ukraine	168	34	Georgia	14
15	Greece	166	35	Estonia	12
16	Portugal	158	36	Albania	11
17	Denmark	136	37	Armenia	9
18	Romania	134		Macedonia	9
19	Czech Republic	132		Moldova	9
20	Norway	126	40	Iceland	8

1990

#	Country	Value	#	Country	Value
1	France	1,006.9	13	Austria	135.4
2	Italy	928.2	14	Portugal	104.1
3	United Kingdom	924.8	15	Greece	100.8
4	Russia	913.8	16	Czech Republic	97.3
5	Spain	477.3	17	Romania	94.5
6	Turkey	257.7	18	Denmark	90.4
7	Netherlands	238.9	19	Finland	83.0
8	Ukraine	221.1	20	Norway	70.2
9	Belgium	179.1	21	Hungary	67.1
10	Poland	176.2	22	Belarus	60.1
11	Switzerland	151.8	23	Bulgaria	42.3
12	Sweden	143.8	24	Ireland	41.4

1980

#	Country	Value	#	Country	Value
1	France	523.5	13	Romania	61.8
2	Italy	489.2	14	Greece	56.5
3	Russia	473.2	15	Portugal	51.3
4	United Kingdom	468.8	16	Denmark	48.6
5	Spain	233.4	17	Finland	40.1
6	Netherlands	126.4	18	Hungary	37.8
7	Poland	112.5	19	Norway	36.4
8	Turkey	102.2	20	Bulgaria	20.9
9	Belgium	97.7	21	Ireland	19.1
10	Switzerland	81.1	22	Georgia	18.3
11	Sweden	77.5	23	Armenia	9.0
12	Austria	70.8	24	Latvia	7.2

Strongest growth
Average annual change in GDP
1990–99

1	Bosnia	35.2	17	Belgium	1.7
2	Ireland	6.9	18	Sweden	1.6
3	Poland	4.5	19	France	1.5
4	Norway	3.8	20	Italy	1.4
	Turkey	3.8	21	Germany	1.3
6	Albania	3.2	22	Hungary	1.0
7	Netherlands	2.7	23	Czech Republic	0.8
8	Portugal	2.5	24	Switzerland	0.6
	United Kingdom	2.5	25	Croatia	0.2
10	Denmark	2.4	26	Macedonia	-0.8
	Finland	2.4		Romania	-0.8
	Slovenia	2.4	28	Estonia	-1.3
13	Greece	2.2	29	Bulgaria	-2.7
	Spain	2.2	30	Belarus	-3.0
15	Austria	1.9	31	Armenia	-3.2
16	Slovakia	1.8	32	Lithuania	-4.0

1980–90

1	Turkey	5.3		United Kingdom	3.2
2	Bulgaria	4.0	9	Portugal	2.9
3	Latvia	3.4	10	Norway	2.8
4	Armenia	3.3		Russia	2.8
	Finland	3.3	12	Denmark	2.4
6	Ireland	3.2		France	2.4
	Spain	3.2		Italy	2.4

1970–79

1	Malta	10.8		Italy	3.7
2	Iceland	6.5	12	Cyprus	3.3
3	Hungary	5.5	13	Belgium	3.2
4	Greece	5.0		Finland	3.2
5	Portugal	4.9		Netherlands	3.2
6	Norway	4.8	16	Germany	2.9
7	Ireland	4.7	17	Denmark	2.6
8	France	4.1	18	United Kingdom	2.4
9	Spain	3.8	19	Sweden	2.0
10	Austria	3.7	20	Switzerland	1.1

EU GDP: who contributes what
%, 1999

1	Germany	24.9	9	Austria	2.5
2	United Kingdom	17.0	10	Denmark	2.1
3	France	16.9	11	Finland	1.5
4	Italy	13.8		Greece	1.5
5	Spain	7.0	13	Portugal	1.3
6	Netherlands	4.6	14	Ireland	1.1
7	Belgium	2.9	15	Luxembourg	0.2
8	Sweden	2.8			

Living standards

Human development index
1998

1	Norway	93.4	22	Czech Republic	84.3
2	Iceland	92.7	23	Slovakia	82.5
3	Sweden	92.6	24	Hungary	81.7
4	Belgium	92.5	25	Poland	81.4
	Netherlands	92.5	26	Estonia	80.1
6	United Kingdom	91.8	27	Croatia	79.5
7	Finland	91.7	28	Lithuania	78.9
	France	91.7	29	Belarus	78.1
9	Switzerland	91.5	30	Bulgaria	77.2
10	Denmark	91.1	31	Latvia	77.1
	Germany	91.1		Russia	77.1
12	Austria	90.8	33	Romania	77.0
	Luxembourg	90.8	34	Macedonia	76.3
14	Ireland	90.7	35	Georgia	76.2
15	Italy	90.3	36	Ukraine	74.4
16	Spain	89.9	37	Turkey	73.2
17	Cyprus	88.6	38	Azerbaijan	72.2
18	Greece	87.5	39	Armenia	72.1
19	Malta	86.5	40	Albania	71.3
20	Portugal	86.4	41	Moldova	70.0
21	Slovenia	86.1			

1990

1	Norway	97.8	16	Spain	91.6
2	Switzerland	97.7	17	Cyprus	91.2
3	Sweden	97.6	18	Greece	90.1
4	France	96.9	19	Ex-Czechoslovakia	89.7
5	Netherlands	96.8	20	Hungary	89.3
6	United Kingdom	96.2	21	Poland	87.4
7	Iceland	95.8	22	Ex-Soviet Union	87.3
8	Germany	95.5	23	Bulgaria	86.5
9	Finland	95.3	24	Ex-Yugoslavia	85.7
10	Denmark	95.3	25	Malta	85.4
11	Belgium	95.0	26	Portugal	85.0
12	Austria	95.0	27	Albania	79.1
13	Luxembourg	92.9	28	Romania	73.3
14	Italy	92.2	29	Turkey	67.1
15	Ireland	92.1			

Note: GDP or GDP per head is often taken as a measure of how developed a country is but its usefulness is limited as it refers only to economic welfare. In 1990 the UN Development Programme published its first estimate of a Human Development Index, which combined statistics on two other indicators – adult literacy and life expectancy – with income levels to give a better, though still far from perfect, indicator of human development. In 1991 average years of schooling was combined with adult literacy to give a knowledge variable. The index is shown here scaled from 0 to 100; countries scoring over 80 are considered to have high human development, those scoring from 50–79 have medium human development.

GDP per head
$
1999

1	Luxembourg	42,930	23	Czech Republic	5,170
2	Switzerland	36,310	24	Hungary	4,810
3	Norway	34,340	25	Croatia	4,580
4	Denmark	32,780	26	Poland	4,010
5	Iceland	29,590	27	Slovakia	3,650
6	Sweden	26,950	28	Estonia	3,630
7	Germany	25,750	29	Turkey	2,890
8	Austria	25,740	30	Lithuania	2,870
9	Finland	25,090	31	Russia	2,740
10	Ireland	25,060	32	Belarus	2,630
11	Netherlands	24,910	33	Latvia	2,580
12	United Kingdom	24,390	34	Serbia & Montenegro[a]	1,940
13	Belgium	24,300	35	Macedonia	1,710
14	France	23,560	36	Romania	1,520
15	Euro area	22,280	37	Bulgaria	1,510
16	Italy	20,310	38	Bosnia	1,130
17	Spain	15,120	39	Albania	1,090
18	Cyprus	11,960	40	Ukraine	770
19	Greece	11,870	41	Azerbaijan	500
20	Portugal	11,380		Georgia	500
21	Slovenia	10,100	43	Armenia	480
22	Malta	9,210	44	Moldova	270

1980

1	Switzerland	19,620	11	Finland	10,710
2	Luxembourg	17,010	12	United Kingdom	8,580
3	Sweden	15,410	13	Italy	7,900
4	Norway	15,360	14	Spain	5,740
5	Iceland	15,230	15	Ireland	5,650
6	Denmark	14,420	16	Greece	5,510
7	Belgium	13,190	17	Cyprus	3,590
8	Netherlands	12,980	18	Malta	3,370
9	France	12,680	19	Portugal	2,910
10	Austria	10,930	20	Hungary	2,060

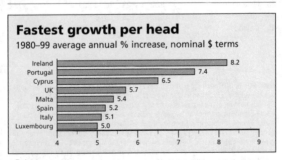

Fastest growth per head
1980–99 average annual % increase, nominal $ terms

Ireland	8.2
Portugal	7.4
Cyprus	6.5
UK	5.7
Malta	5.4
Spain	5.2
Italy	5.1
Luxembourg	5.0

a Estimate.

GDP per head in PPP

$	1980	1990	1995	1999
Albania	...	2,653	2,782	3,240
Armenia	...	3,166	1,894	2,360
Austria	9,754	18,153	22,017	24,600
Azerbaijan	...	4,791	1,942	2,450
Belgium	10,293	18,404	22,630	25,710
Bulgaria	2,699	4,920	5,426	5,070
Croatia	...	6,728	5,768	7,260
Cyprus	5,163	12,810	16,884	19,080
Czech Republic	...	12,368	12,401	12,840
Denmark	9,655	17,404	22,678	25,600
Estonia	...	7,775	6,440	8,190
Finland	8,591	16,708	18,119	22,600
France	9,594	17,193	20,410	23,020
Georgia	6,157	8,304	2,626	2,540
Germany	...	...	21,378	23,510
Greece	6,632	11,137	13,266	15,800
Hungary	5,069	8,612	8,941	11,050
Iceland	11,148	19,403	22,120	27,210
Ireland	5,241	10,093	14,991	22,460
Italy	9,099	16,764	20,209	22,000
Latvia	4,063	8,117	4,939	6,220
Lithuania	...	8,328	5,558	6,490
Luxembourg	11,832	28,167	35,801	41,230
Macedonia	...	...	4,147	4,590
Malta	3,608	8,160	11,115	...
Moldova	2,537	...	2,273	2,100
Netherlands	9,469	16,818	20,842	24,410
Norway	9,632	17,842	24,378	28,140
Poland	3,331	5,033	6,499	8,390
Portugal	5,200	10,774	13,491	15,860
Romania	4,111	6,114	6,387	5,970
Russia	...	9,855	6,960	6,990
Slovakia	...	8,653	8,480	10,430
Slovenia	...	...	13,122	16,050
Spain	6,378	12,332	15,032	17,850
Sweden	9,753	17,013	19,228	22,150
Switzerland	13,853	24,254	26,574	28,760
Turkey	2,360	4,711	5,873	6,440
Ukraine	...	6,517	3,674	3,360
United Kingdom	8,435	15,946	19,422	22,220

Richest and poorest EU regions
GDP per head in PPP as % of EU average, 1998

Richest			Poorest		
1	Inner London	243	1	Ipeiros	42
2	Hamburg	186	2	Extremadura	50
3	Luxembourg	176		Réunion	50
4	Brussels	169	4	Azores	52
				Guadeloupe	52

Agriculture's contribution

Agricultural output
As % of GDP
1999 or latest year available

1	Albania	54		Slovenia	5
2	Armenia	33	21	Czech Republic	4
3	Georgia	22		Denmark	4
4	Greece	21		Finland	4
	Moldova	21		Poland	4
6	Azerbaijan	19		Portugal	4
7	Bulgaria	18		Slovakia	4
	Turkey	18	27	Italy	3
9	Romania	16		Netherlands	3
10	Ukraine	14		Spain	3
11	Belarus	13		Switzerland	3
12	Macedonia	11	31	France	2
13	Lithuania	10		Norway	2
14	Croatia	9		Sweden	2
15	Ireland	8		United Kingdom	2
16	Russia	7	35	Austria	1
17	Estonia	6		Belgium	1
	Hungary	6		Bosnia	1
19	Latvia	5		Germany	1

1980

1	Albania	34	10	Ex-Czechoslovakia	7
2	Greece	27	11	Denmark	6
3	Turkey	26		Italy	6
4	Georgia	24	13	Austria	4
5	Armenia	18		France	4
6	Bulgaria	14		Norway	4
7	Finland	12		Sweden	4
	Latvia	12	17	Netherlands	3
9	Russia	9	18	United Kingdom	2

1965

1	Turkey	34		Denmark	9
2	Greece	24	9	France	8
3	Ex-Yugoslavia	23		Norway	8
4	Finland	16	11	Sweden	6
5	Spain	15	12	Belgium	5
6	Italy	11	13	Germany	4
7	Austria	9	14	United Kingdom	3

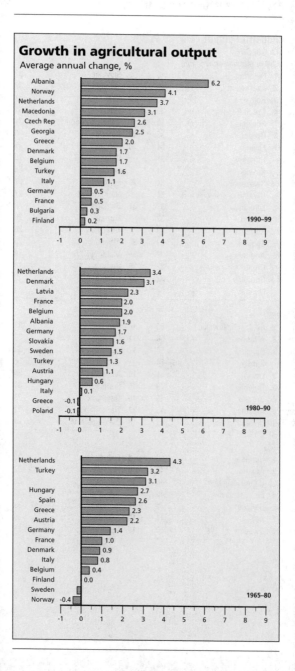

Growth in agricultural output

Average annual change, %

1990–99

Albania	6.2
Norway	4.1
Netherlands	3.7
Macedonia	3.1
Czech Rep	2.6
Georgia	2.5
Greece	2.0
Denmark	1.7
Belgium	1.7
Turkey	1.6
Italy	1.1
Germany	0.5
France	0.5
Bulgaria	0.3
Finland	0.2

1980–90

Netherlands	3.4
Denmark	3.1
Latvia	2.3
France	2.0
Belgium	2.0
Albania	1.9
Germany	1.7
Slovakia	1.6
Sweden	1.5
Turkey	1.3
Austria	1.1
Hungary	0.6
Italy	0.1
Greece	-0.1
Poland	-0.1

1965–80

Netherlands	4.3
Turkey	3.2
	3.1
Hungary	2.7
Spain	2.6
Greece	2.3
Austria	2.2
Germany	1.4
France	1.0
Denmark	0.9
Italy	0.8
Belgium	0.4
Finland	0.0
Sweden	
Norway	-0.4

Industry's contribution

Industrial output
As % of GDP
1999 or latest year available

1	Belarus	46		Slovakia	32
2	Azerbaijan	43		Sweden	32
3	Romania	40	22	Italy	31
4	Czech Republic	39		Latvia	31
	Slovenia	39		United Kingdom	31
6	Greece	36	25	Austria	30
7	Finland	34	26	Denmark	29
	Hungary	34		Belgium	28
	Russia	34		Macedonia	28
	Switzerland	34	29	Estonia	27
	Ukraine	34		Netherlands	27
12	Lithuania	33	31	Bulgaria	26
	Poland	33		France	26
	Portugal	33		Turkey	26
	Spain	33	34	Albania	25
16	Armenia	32	35	Moldova	24
	Croatia	32	36	Georgia	13
	Germany	32	37	Ireland	9
	Norway	32			

1980

1	Ex-Czechoslovakia	63	10	Italy	39
2	Armenia	58	11	Sweden	37
3	Bulgaria	54	12	Austria	36
	Russia	54		Georgia	36
5	Latvia	51	14	Norway	35
6	Finland	49	15	France	34
7	Greece	48	16	Denmark	33
8	Albania	45	17	Netherlands	32
9	United Kingdom	43	18	Ex-Yugoslavia	23

1965

1	Germany	53	8	France	39
2	Austria	46	9	Finland	37
	United Kingdom	46	10	Denmark	36
4	Ex-Yugoslavia	42		Spain	36
5	Belgium	41	12	Norway	33
	Italy	41	13	Greece	26
7	Sweden	40	14	Turkey	25

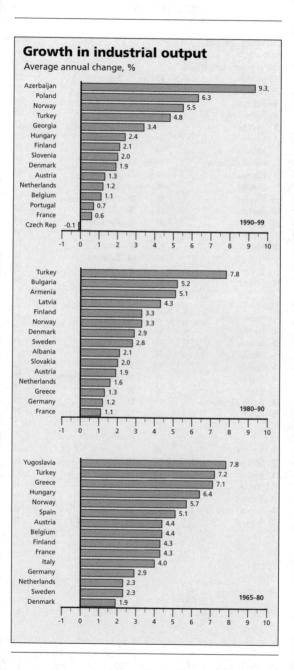

Growth in industrial output

Average annual change, %

1990–99

Azerbaijan	9.3.
Poland	6.3
Norway	5.5
Turkey	4.8
Georgia	3.4
Hungary	2.4
Finland	2.1
Slovenia	2.0
Denmark	1.9
Austria	1.3
Netherlands	1.2
Belgium	1.1
Portugal	0.7
France	0.6
Czech Rep	-0.1

1980–90

Turkey	7.8
Bulgaria	5.2
Armenia	5.1
Latvia	4.3
Finland	3.3
Norway	3.3
Denmark	2.9
Sweden	2.8
Albania	2.1
Slovakia	2.0
Austria	1.9
Netherlands	1.6
Greece	1.3
Germany	1.2
France	1.1

1965–80

Yugoslavia	7.8
Turkey	7.2
Greece	7.1
Hungary	6.4
Norway	5.7
Spain	5.1
Austria	4.4
Belgium	4.4
Finland	4.3
France	4.3
Italy	4.0
Germany	2.9
Netherlands	2.3
Sweden	2.3
Denmark	1.9

Services' contribution

Services' output
As % of GDP
1999 or latest year available

1	Ireland	83		Latvia	62
2	France	72	20	Hungary	60
3	Belgium	71		Macedonia	60
4	Netherlands	70	22	Russia	58
5	Austria	68	23	Czech Republic	57
6	Denmark	67		Lithuania	57
	Italy	67		Slovenia	57
	United Kingdom	67	26	Turkey	56
9	Estonia	66	27	Bulgaria	55
	Norway	66		Moldova	55
	Sweden	66	29	Azerbaijan	52
12	Georgia	65	30	Ukraine	51
13	Slovakia	64	31	Romania	44
	Switzerland	64	32	Greece	43
15	Poland	63	33	Belarus	40
	Portugal	63	34	Germany	36
	Spain	63	35	Armenia	35
18	Finland	62	36	Albania	21

1980

1	Netherlands	64	10	Georgia	40
2	France	62	11	Finland	39
3	Norway	61	12	Russia	37
	Denmark	61		Latvia	37
5	Austria	60	14	Bulgaria	32
6	Sweden	59	15	Ex-Czechoslovakia	30
7	Italy	55	16	Armenia	25
8	United Kingdom	54	17	Greece	24
9	Turkey	51	18	Albania	21

1965

1	Norway	59		Spain	49
2	Denmark	55	9	Italy	48
3	Belgium	53	10	Finland	47
	France	53	11	Austria	45
	Sweden	53	12	Germany	43
6	United Kingdom	51	13	Turkey	41
7	Greece	49	14	Ex-Yugoslavia	35

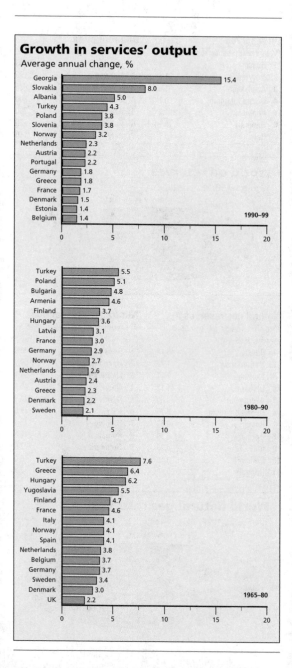

Growth in services' output

Average annual change, %

1990–99

Georgia	15.4
Slovakia	8.0
Albania	5.0
Turkey	4.3
Poland	3.8
Slovenia	3.8
Norway	3.2
Netherlands	2.3
Austria	2.2
Portugal	2.2
Germany	1.8
Greece	1.8
France	1.7
Denmark	1.5
Estonia	1.4
Belgium	1.4

1980–90

Turkey	5.5
Poland	5.1
Bulgaria	4.8
Armenia	4.6
Finland	3.7
Hungary	3.6
Latvia	3.1
France	3.0
Germany	2.9
Norway	2.7
Netherlands	2.6
Austria	2.4
Greece	2.3
Denmark	2.2
Sweden	2.1

1965–80

Turkey	7.6
Greece	6.4
Hungary	6.2
Yugoslavia	5.5
Finland	4.7
France	4.6
Italy	4.1
Norway	4.1
Spain	4.1
Netherlands	3.8
Belgium	3.7
Germany	3.7
Sweden	3.4
Denmark	3.0
UK	2.2

Energy

Oil reserves
Proved reserves, bn tonnes, 1999

1	Russia	6.7
2	Norway	1.4
3	Azerbaijan	1.0
4	United Kingdom	0.7
5	Romania	0.2
6	Denmark	0.1
	Italy	0.1

Oil production
'000 barrels daily, 1999

1	Russia	6,180
2	Norway	3,195
3	United Kingdom	2,895
4	Denmark	300
5	Azerbaijan	280
6	Romania	130
7	Italy	110

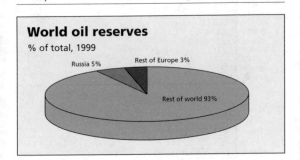

World oil reserves
% of total, 1999

Russia 5%
Rest of Europe 3%
Rest of world 93%

Natural gas reserves
Proved reserves, trillion cubic metres, 1999

1	Russia	48.14
2	Netherlands	1.77
3	Norway	1.17
4	Ukraine	1.12
5	Azerbaijan	0.85
6	United Kingdom	0.76
7	Romania	0.37
8	Germany	0.34
9	Italy	0.23
10	Denmark	0.10
11	Hungary	0.08

Natural gas production
M tonnes of oil equivalent, 1999

1	Russia	495.9
2	United Kingdom	89.7
3	Netherlands	54.1
4	Norway	45.9
5	Germany	16.1
6	Italy	15.9
7	Ukraine	15.1
8	Romania	12.4
9	Denmark	7.0
10	Azerbaijan	5.0
11	Hungary	2.7

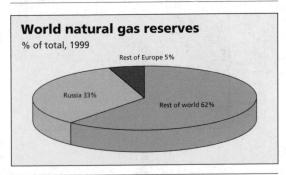

World natural gas reserves
% of total, 1999

Rest of Europe 5%
Russia 33%
Rest of world 62%

Coal reserves
Proved reserves
M tonnes, 1999

1	Russia	157,010
2	Germany	67,000
3	Ukraine	34,356
4	Poland	14,309
5	Czech Republic	6,177
6	Hungary	4,461
7	Romania	3,611
8	Greece	2,874
9	Bulgaria	2,711
10	United Kingdom	1,500
11	Turkey	1,075
12	Spain	660

Coal production
M tonnes of oil equivalent, 1999

1	Russia	112.6
2	Poland	73.1
3	Germany	59.6
4	Ukraine	42.3
5	Turkey	24.4
6	United Kingdom	22.8
7	Czech Republic	21.3
8	Spain	11.6
9	Greece	8.4
10	Bulgaria	4.6
11	Romania	4.3
12	Hungary	4.0

World coal reserves
% of total, 1999

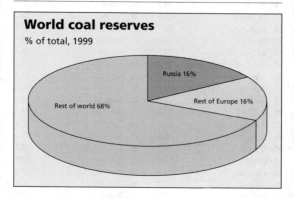

Russia 16%
Rest of Europe 16%
Rest of world 68%

Nuclear power consumption
M tonnes of oil equivalent, 1999

1	France	101.5	9	Switzerland	6.4
2	Germany	43.8	10	Finland	6.0
3	Russia	31.2	11	Bulgaria	3.9
4	United Kingdom	24.8	12	Hungary	3.6
5	Ukraine	18.5	13	Czech Republic	3.4
6	Sweden	18.1		Slovakia	3.4
7	Spain	15.2	15	Romania	1.3
8	Belgium[a]	12.6	16	Netherlands	0.9

a Includes Luxembourg.

Who produces most
M tonnes of coal equivalent, 1997

1	Russia	1,365.4
2	United Kingdom	381.9
3	Norway	303.4
4	Germany	195.0
5	France	168.4
6	Poland	136.1
7	Ukraine	117.4
8	Netherlands	101.3
9	Italy	44.1
10	Czech Republic	43.4
11	Romania	39.7
12	Spain	39.3
13	Sweden	34.9
14	Turkey	29.0
15	Denmark	26.5
16	Azerbaijan	20.9
17	Hungary	19.1
18	Belgium	17.1
19	Serbia & Montenegro	16.2
20	Switzerland	13.8
21	Greece	13.1
22	Finland	13.0
23	Bulgaria	12.8
24	Austria	8.3
25	Slovakia	6.6
26	Croatia	5.7
27	Lithuania	4.9
28	Estonia	4.8
29	Ireland	4.2
30	Belarus	3.8
	Slovenia	3.8

Who uses most
M tonnes of coal equivalent, 1997

1	Russia	832.2
2	Germany	467.1
3	France	322.2
4	United Kingdom	320.1
5	Italy	238.1
6	Ukraine	220.9
7	Poland	142.3
8	Spain	132.9
9	Netherlands	118.5
10	Turkey	85.6
11	Belgium	72.8
12	Sweden	57.5
13	Czech Republic	57.0
14	Romania	55.8
15	Finland	38.0
16	Greece	36.7
17	Austria	35.7
	Hungary	35.7
19	Belarus	35.2
20	Norway	34.7
21	Switzerland	32.8
22	Bulgaria	27.8
23	Denmark	24.5
24	Portugal	23.4
25	Slovakia	22.6
26	Serbia & Montenegro	20.7
27	Ireland	17.2
28	Azerbaijan	15.9
29	Lithuania	12.1
30	Croatia	10.2
31	Slovenia	8.8

Highest consumption per head
Kg of coal equivalent, 1997

1	Luxembourg	10,914	16	Switzerland	4,498
2	Norway	7,886	17	Slovenia	4,414
3	Netherlands	7,588	18	Austria	4,408
4	Iceland	7,497	19	Ukraine	4,327
5	Finland	7,390	20	Slovakia	4,212
6	Belgium	7,191	21	Macedonia	4,206
7	Sweden	6,491	22	Italy	4,147
8	Germany	5,692	23	Poland	3,677
9	Russia	5,636	24	Hungary	3,511
10	Czech Republic	5,529	25	Greece	3,476
11	France	5,507	26	Belarus	3,401
12	Estonia	5,452	27	Spain	3,354
13	United Kingdom	5,446	28	Bulgaria	3,309
14	Ireland	4,694	29	Lithuania	3,273
15	Denmark	4,653	30	Cyprus	3,049

Biggest importers

M tonnes of coal equivalent, 1997

1	Germany	326.5
2	Italy	223.1
3	France	210.0
4	Netherlands	151.2
5	Spain	121.4
6	Ukraine	112.7
7	United Kingdom	105.2
8	Belgium	99.1
9	Turkey	63.6
10	Poland	43.6
11	Sweden	42.9
12	Belarus	38.7
13	Greece	32.3
14	Finland	30.9
15	Austria	30.7
16	Russia	28.0
17	Czech Republic	27.9
	Portugal	27.9
19	Romania	25.1
20	Switzerland	25.0
21	Denmark	24.8
22	Hungary	23.1
23	Slovakia	21.1
24	Bulgaria	18.8
25	Ireland	15.6
26	Lithuania	12.8
27	Norway	8.7
28	Croatia	8.0
29	Moldova	6.8
30	Serbia & Montenegro	6.5

Biggest exporters

M tonnes of coal equivalent, 1997

1	Russia	524.2
2	Norway	271.7
3	United Kingdom	147.9
4	Netherlands	119.7
5	France	33.8
6	Germany	30.8
7	Poland	30.1
8	Belgium	29.4
9	Italy	28.2
10	Denmark	21.8
11	Sweden	15.5
12	Czech Republic	11.4
13	Spain	7.8
14	Ukraine	6.8
15	Lithuania	5.9
16	Finland	5.5
17	Belarus	5.0
18	Romania	4.1
	Switzerland	4.1
20	Greece	3.9
21	Slovakia	3.2
22	Portugal	3.1
23	Hungary	3.0
24	Bulgaria	2.8
25	Azerbaijan	2.4
26	Austria	2.3
27	Croatia	2.0
28	Ireland	1.8
29	Turkey	1.4
30	Estonia	1.3

Leading electricity generators

M tonnes of coal equivalent, 1997

1	France	156.25	16	Czech Republic	4.90
2	Germany	65.95	17	Austria	4.59
3	Russia	60.02	18	Lithuania	4.57
4	United Kingdom	37.28	19	Slovakia	4.55
5	Sweden	34.55	20	Romania	4.16
6	Ukraine	30.78	21	Slovenia	2.25
7	Spain	25.08	22	Portugal	1.69
8	Belgium	16.93	23	Serbia & Montenegro	1.50
9	Switzerland	13.78	24	Greece	1.33
10	Norway	13.64	25	Iceland	1.10
11	Italy	10.54	26	Netherlands	0.97
12	Finland	9.28	27	Armenia	0.77
13	Bulgaria	6.97	28	Georgia	0.74
14	Hungary	5.22	29	Albania	0.66
15	Turkey	5.00	30	Croatia	0.65

Current account balances

Recent picture
Current account balance, 1999

	As % of GDP				$m
1	Switzerland	11.3	1	France	36,580
2	Luxembourg	7.1	2	Switzerland	29,119
3	Russia	6.3	3	Russia	25,302
4	Finland	5.5	4	Netherlands	17,275
5	Belgium	4.7	5	Belgium	11,685
6	Netherlands	4.4	6	Finland	7,141
7	Ukraine	4.3	7	Italy	6,304
8	Norway	3.9	8	Sweden	5,982
9	France	2.6	9	Norway	5,961
10	Sweden	2.5	10	Denmark	2,580
11	Denmark	1.5	11	Ukraine	1,658
12	Ireland	0.6	12	Luxembourg	1,314
13	Italy	0.5	13	Ireland	595
14	Turkey	-0.7	14	Moldova	-34
15	Germany	-0.9	15	Macedonia	-109
16	Belarus	-1.0	16	Albania	-155
17	United Kingdom	-1.1	17	Georgia	-198
18	Czech Republic	-1.9	18	Malta	-221
19	Spain	-2.1	19	Cyprus	-234
20	Cyprus	-2.6	20	Belarus	-257
21	Austria	-2.8	21	Estonia	-295
22	Moldova	-2.9	22	Armenia	-307
23	Macedonia	-3.1	23	Azerbaijan	-600
24	Serbia & Montenegro[a]	-3.4		Iceland	-600
25	Romania	-3.8	25	Latvia	-647
26	Slovenia	-3.9	26	Bulgaria	-685
27	Greece[b]	-4.0	27	Serbia & Montenegro[a]	-703
28	Albania	-4.2	28	Slovenia	-782
29	Hungary	-4.3	29	Bosnia	-884
30	Bulgaria	-5.5	30	Czech Republic	-1,032
31	Estonia	-5.6	31	Slovakia	-1,155
32	Slovakia	-5.9	32	Lithuania	-1,194
33	Malta	-6.4	33	Romania	-1,297
34	Georgia	-7.2	34	Turkey	-1,364
35	Iceland	-7.3	35	Croatia	-1,522
36	Croatia	-7.5	36	Hungary	-2,101
37	Poland	-8.0	37	Greece[b]	-4,860
38	Portugal	-8.9	38	Austria	-5,747
39	Latvia	-10.3	39	Portugal	-10,169
40	Lithuania	-11.2	40	Poland	-12,487
41	Azerbaijan	-15.0	41	Spain	-12,621
42	Armenia	-16.6	42	United Kingdom	-15,980
43	Bosnia	-20.2	43	Germany	-19,310
	Euro area[c]	-0.1		Euro area[c]	-6,050

a 1998
b 1997
c Excludes transactions between member states.

Looking back
Current account balance as % GDP

Top 10, 1990

1	Poland	5.20
2	Norway	3.46
3	Netherlands	3.25
4	Switzerland	3.07
5	Germany[a]	2.58
6	Belgium & Lux	1.89
7	Hungary	1.15
8	Denmark	1.06
9	Austria	0.74
10	Portugal	-0.27

Bottom 10, 1990

1	Romania	-8.51
2	Russia[b]	-7.10
3	Slovakia	-7.00
4	Bulgaria	-6.30
5	Finland	-5.15
6	Greece	-4.32
7	Spain	-3.66
8	Cyprus	-3.42
9	United Kingdom	-3.40
10	Sweden	-3.00

Top 10, 1980

1	Malta	3.42
2	Norway	1.87
3	United Kingdom	1.27
4	Cyprus	-0.01
5	Switzerland	-0.20
6	Netherlands	-0.58
7	France	-0.63
8	Western Germany	-1.64
9	Italy	-2.34
10	Iceland	-2.35

Bottom 10, 1980

1	Ireland	-11.07
2	Romania	-7.06
3	Poland	-6.02
4	Greece	-5.50
5	Austria	-5.03
6	Portugal	-4.24
7	Belgium & Lux	-4.18
8	Denmark	-3.70
9	Sweden	-3.47
10	Finland	-2.73

Top 10, 1970

1	Belgium & Lux	2.78
2	Switzerland	1.71
3	United Kingdom	1.60
4	Italy	0.80
5	Hungary	0.63
6	Western Germany	0.46
7	Iceland	0.42
8	Spain	0.21
9	Cyprus	0.00
10	France	-0.14

Bottom 10, 1970

1	Ireland	-5.00
2	Greece	-4.24
3	Denmark	-3.44
4	Finland	-2.20
5	Norway	-2.17
6	Malta	-2.11
7	Netherlands	-1.75
8	Sweden	-0.80
9	Austria	-0.52
10	Turkey	-0.34

Top 5, 1960

1	Malta	8.69
2	Spain	3.78
3	Netherlands	3.13
4	Western Germany	1.53
5	Switzerland	1.09

Bottom 5, 1960

1	Iceland	-4.10
2	Norway	-2.47
3	Greece	-1.57
4	Austria	-1.42
5	United Kingdom	-1.00

a Includes Eastern Germany from July 1990.
b Convertible currencies only.

Biggest visible traders

Recent picture
Exports plus imports, 1999

	Average as % of GDP				$bn
1	Malta	61.4	1	Germany	1,013.9
2	Belgium	60.6	2	United Kingdom	580.2
3	Ireland	58.8	3	France	577.1
4	Estonia	55.3	4	Italy	441.3
5	Slovakia	54.6	5	Netherlands	372.2
6	Luxembourg	51.8	6	Belgium	300.9
7	Czech Republic	51.2	7	Spain	251.2
8	Hungary	47.4	8	Switzerland	182.7
9	Netherlands	47.3	9	Sweden	159.4
10	Slovenia	46.2	10	Austria	132.5
11	Moldova	45.8	11	Russia	115.5
12	Macedonia	40.0	12	Ireland	109.8
13	Latvia	38.4	13	Denmark	92.9
14	Bulgaria	36.7	14	Norway	80.7
15	Bosnia	36.2	15	Poland	75.2
16	Lithuania	36.2	16	Finland	72.3
17	Switzerland	35.3	17	Turkey	69.1
18	Ukraine	33.8	18	Portugal	65.5
19	Sweden	33.4	19	Czech Republic	54.4
20	Austria	31.8	20	Hungary	45.9
21	Azerbaijan	30.7	21	Greece	35.2
22	Croatia	29.6	22	Ukraine	26.1
23	Portugal	28.8	23	Slovakia	21.5
24	Finland	27.9	24	Luxembourg	19.2
25	Denmark	26.7	25	Slovenia	18.5
26	Romania	26.6	26	Romania	18.1
27	Iceland	26.4	27	Belarus	12.5
	Norway	26.4	28	Croatia	12.1
29	Armenia	26.3	29	Bulgaria	9.1
30	Poland	24.2	30	Lithuania	7.7
31	Germany	24.0	31	Estonia	5.8
32	Cyprus	23.7	32	Latvia	4.8
33	Belarus	23.3	33	Cyprus	4.3
34	Georgia	21.8		Iceland	4.3
35	Spain	21.1	35	Malta	4.2
36	France	20.1	36	Bosnia	3.2
	United Kingdom	20.1	37	Serbia & Montenegro	2.9
38	Italy	18.8	38	Macedonia	2.8
39	Turkey	18.6	39	Azerbaijan	2.5
40	Albania	16.5	40	Albania	1.2
41	Russia	14.4		Georgia	1.2
42	Greece	14.1	42	Moldova	1.1
43	Serbia & Montenegro	7.1	43	Armenia	1.0
	Euro area[a]	12.6		Euro area[a]	1,644.9

a Excludes transactions between member states.

Looking back

Exports plus imports, $m

1990

1	France	451,024	11	Austria	90,411
2	Germany	410,104	12	Denmark	67,361
3	United Kingdom	408,149	13	Norway	61,278
4	Italy	352,454	14	Finland	53,572
5	Germany	346,153	15	Ireland	44,412
6	Netherlands	257,873	16	Portugal	41,680
7	Belgium & Lux	237,405	17	Turkey	35,261
8	Spain	143,357	18	Ex-Yugoslavia	33,179
9	Switzerland	133,465	19	Greece	27,882
10	Sweden	111,804	20	Poland	22,040

1980

1	Western Germany	380,862	11	Denmark	36,089
2	France	250,896	12	Norway	35,488
3	United Kingdom	225,679	13	Poland	30,881
4	Italy	178,845	14	Finland	29,785
5	Netherlands	173,438	15	Romania	25,052
6	Belgium & Lux	136,400	16	Ex-Yugoslavia	24,054
7	Switzerland	65,973	17	Ireland	19,551
8	Sweden	64,344	18	Hungary	17,857
9	Spain	54,798	19	Greece	15,701
10	Austria	41,933	20	Portugal	13,949

1970

1	Western Germany	64,175	11	Spain	7,135
2	United Kingdom	41,294	12	Austria	6,406
3	France	36,998	13	Norway	6,157
4	Netherlands	28,917	14	Finland	4,944
5	Italy	28,179	15	Ex-Yugoslavia	4,553
6	Belgium & Lux	22,854	16	Romania	3,968
7	Sweden	13,802	17	Hungary	3,603
8	Switzerland	11,441	18	Ireland	2,742
9	Denmark	7,763	19	Greece	2,601
10	Poland	7,156	20	Portugal	2,502

1960

1	United Kingdom	23,637	6	Belgium & Lux	7,640
2	Western Germany	21,588	7	Sweden	5,467
3	France	13,149	8	Switzerland	4,066
4	Netherlands	8,559	9	Denmark	3,301
5	Italy	8,391	10	Austria	2,536

Visible trade balances

Recent picture
Visible trade balance, 1999

	As % of GDP				$m
1	Ireland	25.9	1	Germany	72,000
2	Finland	9.0	2	Russia	36,219
	Russia	9.0	3	Ireland	24,178
4	Norway	6.9	4	Italy	20,384
5	Sweden	6.6	5	France	19,390
6	Netherlands	4.6	6	Netherlands	17,954
7	Denmark	3.9	7	Sweden	15,714
8	Germany	3.4	8	Finland	11,655
9	Belgium	2.9	9	Norway	10,527
10	Italy	1.7	10	Belgium	7,255
11	France	1.4	11	Denmark	6,758
12	Ukraine	0.6	12	Switzerland	724
13	Switzerland	0.3	13	Ukraine	244
14	Austria	-1.8	14	Moldova	-123
15	Belarus	-2.2	15	Iceland	-308
16	United Kingdom	-2.9	16	Azerbaijan	-408
17	Romania	-3.2	17	Macedonia	-410
18	Czech Republic	-3.6	18	Armenia	-474
19	Iceland	-3.8	19	Georgia	-534
20	Hungary	-4.5	20	Malta	-593
21	Spain	-4.9	21	Belarus	-599
22	Slovakia	-5.6	22	Albania	-663
	Turkey	-5.6	23	Estonia	-878
24	Slovenia	-6.2	24	Latvia	-1,027
25	Serbia & Montenegro	-7.2	25	Bulgaria	-1,081
26	Bulgaria	-8.7	26	Romania	-1,092
27	Poland	-9.7	27	Slovakia	-1,109
28	Azerbaijan	-10.2	28	Slovenia	-1,245
29	Moldova	-10.6	29	Lithuania	-1,405
30	Macedonia	-11.7	30	Serbia & Montenegro	-1,479
31	Portugal	-12.4	31	Czech Republic	-1,902
32	Greece	-12.5	32	Bosnia	-1,988
33	Lithuania	-13.2	33	Hungary	-2,191
34	Luxembourg	-13.3	34	Cyprus	-2,309
35	Croatia	-16.1	35	Luxembourg	-2,475
36	Latvia	-16.4	36	Croatia	-3,299
37	Estonia	-16.8	37	Austria	-3,650
38	Malta	-17.2	38	Turkey	-10,447
39	Albania	-18.0	39	Portugal	-14,157
40	Georgia	-19.5	40	Poland	-15,072
41	Cyprus	-25.4	41	Greece	-15,618
42	Armenia	-25.7	42	Spain	-29,208
43	Bosnia	-45.3	43	United Kingdom	-42,340
	Euro area[a]	1.4		Euro area[a]	88,680

a Excludes transactions between member states.

Looking back
Visible trade balance as % of GDP

Top 10, 1990			Bottom 10, 1990		
1	Ireland	8.80	1	Cyprus	-27.98
2	Norway	6.73	2	Malta	-24.22
3	Poland	6.09	3	Greece	-12.35
4	Netherlands	4.25	4	Portugal	-9.94
5	Germany	3.83	5	Romania	-8.74
6	Denmark	3.78	6	Turkey	-6.35
7	Hungary	1.62	7	Spain	-5.93
8	Sweden	1.61	8	Austria	-4.40
9	Iceland	1.27	9	Bulgaria	-4.17
10	Belgium & Lux	0.87	10	United Kingdom	-3.33

Top 10, 1980			Bottom 10, 1980		
1	Norway	3.29	1	Malta	-30.57
2	Western Germany	0.98	2	Portugal	-15.72
3	United Kingdom	0.62	3	Greece	-13.80
4	Iceland	0.61	4	Ireland	-11.53
5	Cyprus	-0.03	5	Austria	-8.44
6	Netherlands	-0.06	6	Spain	-5.54
7	Hungary	-0.65	7	Switzerland	-5.17
8	Finland	-1.33	8	Romania	-4.85
9	Sweden	-1.76	9	Italy	-3.51
10	France	-2.12	10	Belgium & Lux	-3.27

Top 10, 1970			Bottom 10, 1970		
1	Western Germany	3.07	1	Malta	-41.40
2	Belgium & Lux	1.80	2	Ireland	-10.91
3	Sweden	0.91	3	Norway	-10.32
4	Iceland	0.54	4	Greece	-9.00
5	France	0.18	5	Switzerland	-5.09
6	United Kingdom	0.00	6	Spain	-5.07
7	Cyprus	-0.02	7	Denmark	-4.80
8	Italy	-0.38	8	Austria	-4.67
9	Finland	-1.62	9	Netherlands	-2.70
10	Hungary	-1.84	10	Turkey	-1.89

Top 5, 1960			Bottom 5, 1960		
1	Western Germany	2.91	1	Malta	-47.82
2	Spain	0.40	2	Cyprus	-17.23
3	Belgium & Lux	0.12	3	Norway	-10.18
4	Finland	-0.04	4	Ireland	-10.05
5	Sweden	-0.81	5	Greece	-7.13

Biggest invisible traders

Recent picture
Invisible trade, total credits and debits, 1999

	Average % of GDP				$m
1	Luxembourg	285.9	1	United Kingdom	537,180
2	Malta	65.2	2	Germany	401,920
3	Ireland	55.8	3	France	273,150
4	Belgium	41.2	4	Italy	223,512
5	Cyprus	27.7	5	Belgium	204,748
6	Estonia	26.5	6	Netherlands	193,643
7	Netherlands	24.6	7	Switzerland	119,866
8	Switzerland	23.2	8	Spain	118,673
9	Moldova	21.6	9	Luxembourg	106,027
10	Austria	19.6	10	Ireland	104,217
11	United Kingdom	18.6	11	Sweden	85,683
12	Sweden	17.9	12	Austria	81,430
13	Latvia	16.6	13	Denmark	53,076
14	Croatia	16.3	14	Norway	45,949
15	Bulgaria	16.2	15	Russia	37,311
16	Czech Republic	15.8	16	Turkey	33,588
17	Denmark	15.2	17	Finland	27,278
18	Norway	15.0	18	Portugal	25,375
19	Iceland	14.7	19	Poland	20,227
20	Hungary	13.5	20	Greece[a]	17,985
21	Georgia	13.1	21	Czech Republic	16,834
22	Armenia	12.6	22	Hungary	13,108
23	Slovakia	11.6	23	Ukraine	7,226
24	Portugal	11.2	24	Croatia	6,675
25	Lithuania	11.1	25	Cyprus	5,042
26	Slovenia	10.7	26	Slovakia	4,579
27	Finland	10.5	27	Malta	4,500
28	Azerbaijan	10.1	28	Slovenia	4,279
29	Spain	10.0	29	Bulgaria	4,007
30	France	9.5	30	Romania	3,865
	Germany	9.5	31	Estonia	2,777
	Italy	9.5	32	Iceland	2,411
	Macedonia	9.5	33	Lithuania	2,365
34	Ukraine	9.3	34	Latvia	2,077
35	Turkey	9.0	35	Belarus	1,292
36	Greece[a]	7.4	36	Azerbaijan	809
37	Albania	7.2	37	Georgia	717
38	Poland	6.5	38	Macedonia	661
39	Romania	5.7	39	Albania	528
40	Russia	4.6	40	Moldova	501
41	Belarus	2.4	41	Armenia	466
	Euro area[b]	7.8		Euro area[b]	1,015,540

a 1997
b Excludes transactions between member states.

Looking back

Invisible trade, total credits and debits, $m

1990			1980		
1	United Kingdom	387,040	1	United Kingdom	176,733
2	France	367,691	2	France	114,816
3	Germany[a]	248,320	3	Germany[a]	102,430
4	Belgium & Lux	183,770	4	Belgium & Lux	62,545
5	Italy	153,636	5	Netherlands	59,289
6	Netherlands	114,273	6	Italy	49,524
7	Switzerland	78,711	7	Switzerland	29,321
8	Spain	63,158	8	Spain	22,133
9	Austria	56,708	9	Austria	21,159
10	Sweden	54,635	10	Norway	19,508
11	Denmark	40,778	11	Sweden	18,362
12	Norway	35,615	12	Denmark	15,199
13	Finland	23,091	13	Finland	7,131
14	Ireland	18,458	14	Poland	6,676
15	Turkey	15,429	15	Greece	6,152
16	Portugal	11,918	16	Ireland	5,492
17	Greece	11,899	17	Portugal	4,485
18	Poland	10,639	18	Hungary	3,688
19	Hungary	7,271	19	Romania	3,031
20	Cyprus	3,116	20	Turkey	2,500
21	Malta	1,636	21	Cyprus	1,821
22	Romania	1,586	22	Malta	935
23	Iceland	1,492	23	Iceland	683

1970			1960		
1	United Kingdom	20,961	1	United Kingdom	11,034
2	France	14,267	2	Germany[a]	6,000
3	Italy	13,588	3	Italy	3,043
4	Netherlands	8,188	4	Netherlands	2,131
5	Belgium & Lux	6,185	5	Belgium & Lux	1,764
6	Poland	5,417	6	Sweden	1,539
7	Switzerland	5,179	7	Norway	1,486
8	Norway	3,698	8	Switzerland	1,438
9	Sweden	3,427	9	Denmark	805
10	Austria	2,393	10	Spain	614
11	Denmark	2,205	11	Austria	576
12	Germany[a]	1,951	12	Finland	402
13	Spain	1,782	13	Greece	387
14	Ireland	1,277	14	Ireland	286
15	Finland	1,016	15	Turkey	237
16	Greece	847	16	Malta	101
17	Hungary	608	17	Cyprus	86
18	Turkey	508	18	Iceland	58
19	Cyprus	188			
20	Iceland	177			
21	Malta	151			

a Western only up to June 1990.

Invisible trade balances

The recent picture
Invisible trade balance
1999

		As % of GDP				$m
1	Luxembourg	22.2	1	United Kingdom		33,060
2	Cyprus	21.9	2	Switzerland		32,546
3	Switzerland	12.6	3	France		30,170
4	Malta	11.8	4	Spain		13,435
5	Estonia	9.0	5	Belgium		8,990
6	Croatia	6.2	6	Netherlands		5,871
7	Georgia	5.1	7	Luxembourg		4,123
8	Albania	4.9	8	Turkey		3,908
9	Latvia	4.6	9	Greece[a]		3,005
10	Belgium	3.6	10	Cyprus		1,989
11	Greece[a]	2.5	11	Croatia		1,276
12	Spain	2.3	12	Ukraine		708
	United Kingdom	2.3	13	Estonia		470
14	France	2.1	14	Malta		407
	Turkey	2.1	15	Poland		371
16	Ukraine	1.8	16	Czech Republic		362
17	Slovenia	1.7	17	Slovenia		340
18	Netherlands	1.5	18	Latvia		287
19	Moldova	1.0	19	Belarus		233
20	Belarus	0.9	20	Albania		182
21	Bulgaria	0.8	21	Georgia		140
22	Czech Republic	0.7	22	Bulgaria		97
23	Lithuania	0.4	23	Portugal		51
24	Poland	0.2	24	Lithuania		48
25	Austria	0.0	25	Moldova		12
	Portugal	0.0	26	Armenia		-7
27	Denmark	-0.2	27	Austria		-54
28	Armenia	-0.4	28	Macedonia		-119
29	Hungary	-0.5	29	Slovakia		-245
30	Italy	-0.7	30	Hungary		-258
31	Slovakia	-1.2	31	Azerbaijan		-273
32	Norway	-1.9	32	Iceland		-283
33	Finland	-2.3	33	Denmark		-324
34	Romania	-2.4	34	Romania		-831
35	Sweden	-2.6	35	Norway		-2,957
36	Russia	-2.9	36	Finland		-3,014
37	Germany	-3.0	37	Sweden		-6,133
38	Macedonia	-3.4	38	Italy		-8,700
39	Iceland	-3.5	39	Russia		-11,459
40	Azerbaijan	-6.8	40	Ireland		-24,869
41	Ireland	-26.6	41	Germany		-63,980
	Euro area[b]	-0.7		Euro area[b]		-47,100

a 1997
b Excludes transactions between member states.

Looking back
Invisible trade balance as % of GDP

Top 10, 1990			Bottom 10, 1990		
1	Cyprus	24.09	1	Ireland	-14.50
2	Malta	18.05	2	Poland	-5.14
3	Switzerland	7.28	3	Finland	-4.97
4	Austria	5.14	4	Russia	-4.87
5	Greece	2.26	5	Sweden	-3.70
6	Belgium & Lux	2.16	6	Iceland	-3.42
7	Spain	1.70	7	Hungary	-2.85
8	Turkey	1.62	8	Bulgaria	-2.60
9	Portugal	1.48	9	Denmark	-2.40
10	France	0.96	10	Norway	-1.99

Top 10, 1980			Bottom 10, 1980		
1	Malta	29.39	1	Ireland	-5.78
2	Switzerland	6.09	2	Poland	-4.16
3	Greece	5.59	3	Iceland	-2.92
4	Austria	3.50	4	Romania	-2.21
5	Spain	2.13	5	Hungary	-2.17
6	France	2.11	6	Finland	-1.18
7	United Kingdom	1.50	7	Western Germany	-1.03
8	Italy	0.93	8	Sweden	-0.73
9	Netherlands	0.24	9	Denmark	-0.70
10	Belgium & Lux	0.13	10	Norway	-0.52

Top 10, 1970			Bottom 10, 1970		
1	Malta	22.23	1	Sweden	-1.25
2	Switzerland	8.38	2	Western Germany	-1.19
3	Norway	8.25	3	Turkey	-1.03
4	Austria	4.09	4	Finland	-0.53
5	Spain	3.50	5	Iceland	-0.04
6	Ireland	3.26	6	Cyprus	0.01
7	United Kingdom	1.96	7	France	0.29
8	Denmark	1.64	8	Hungary	0.76
9	Belgium & Lux	1.58	9	Italy	0.97
10	Greece	1.29	10	Netherlands	1.06

Top 5, 1960			Bottom 5, 1960		
1	Malta	43.44	1	Finland	-0.87
2	Cyprus	8.38	2	Turkey	-0.59
3	Norway	8.02	3	Western Germany	-0.25
4	Ireland	6.60	4	Sweden	0.28
5	Netherlands	4.14	5	Belgium & Lux	0.74

Who exports to whom

Most important export destinations

Exports to main partners and to EU 15 countries as % of total exports

1999	Main ptnrs	EU 15	1999	Main ptnrs	EU 15
Albania		93.7	**Denmark**		65.9
Italy	67.3		Germany	20.0	
Greece	14.3		Sweden	11.4	
Armenia		41.8	**Estonia**		62.7
Belgium	36.3		Finland	19.4	
Iran	14.8		Sweden	18.8	
Austria		63.0	**Finland**		56.9
Germany	35.0		Germany	13.0	
Italy	8.6		Sweden	9.9	
Azerbaijan		45.6	**France**		61.7
Italy	33.7		Germany	15.7	
Russia	8.9		United Kingdom	10.2	
Belarus		10.6	**Georgia**		28.9
Russia	59.4		Turkey	23.3	
Ukraine	6.3		Russia	12.4	
Belgium		73.8	**Germany**		56.9
Germany	17.9		France	11.5	
France	17.4		United States	10.2	
Bosnia		61.7	**Greece**		49.0
Italy	27.5		Germany	15.0	
Croatia	17.7		Italy	12.9	
Bulgaria		54.2	**Hungary**		74.7
Italy	14.4		Germany	38.3	
Germany	10.3		Austria	9.7	
Croatia		49.5	**Iceland**		64.1
Italy	18.3		United Kingdom	19.7	
Germany	15.9		Germany	13.1	
Cyprus		40.5	**Ireland**		64.4
United Kingdom	16.5		United Kingdom	21.7	
Greece	9.0		United States	15.5	
Czech Republic		69.2	**Italy**		57.4
Germany	42.1		Germany	16.5	
Slovakia	8.2		France	13.0	

1970	Main ptnrs	EU 15	1970	Main ptnrs	EU 15
Austria		56.3	**Germany, Western**[a]		59.4
Western Germany	23.7		France	12.4	
Switzerland	10.4		Netherlands	10.6	
Belgium & Lux		78.1	**Greece**		56.6
Western Germany	24.1		Western Germany	20.2	
France	19.9		Italy	10.0	
Denmark		63.3	**Iceland**		40.3
United Kingdom	18.6		United States	30.0	
Sweden	16.6		United Kingdom	13.2	
Finland		63.7	**Ireland**		73.1
United Kingdom	17.4		United Kingdom	60.8	
Sweden	15.1		United States	9.2	
France		59.6	**Italy**		55.3
Western Germany	20.4		Western Germany	21.6	
Italy	11.0		France	12.8	

1999	Main ptnrs	EU 15	1999	Main ptnrs	EU 15
Latvia		62.6	**Russia**		33.2
Germany	16.9		United States	8.9	
United Kingdom	16.4		Germany	8.5	
Lithuania		50.1	**Serbia & Montenegro**		76.8
Germany	16.0		Germany	24.1	
Latvia	12.8		Italy	23.7	
Luxembourg		86.3	**Slovakia**		59.5
Germany	25.1		Germany	27.7	
France	21.2		Czech Republic	18.1	
Macedonia		44.8	**Slovenia**		66.2
Germany	21.4		Germany	30.8	
United States	12.2		Italy	13.8	
Malta		48.7	**Spain**		71.1
United States	21.3		France	19.5	
Singapore	15.9		Germany	13.2	
Moldova		21.0	**Sweden**		56.2
Russia	36.9		Germany	10.6	
United States	14.3		United Kingdom	9.3	
Netherlands		78.6	**Switzerland**		61.3
Germany	26.8		Germany	22.6	
Belgium	12.3		United States	12.4	
Norway		73.9	**Turkey**		54.0
United Kingdom	17.4		Germany	20.6	
Germany	11.3		United States	9.2	
Poland		70.6	**Ukraine**		18.4
Germany	36.1		Russia	20.7	
Italy	6.6		China	6.3	
Portugal		82.7	**United Kingdom**		53.2
Germany	19.9		United States	15.1	
Spain	17.8		Germany	11.1	
Romania		65.7			
Italy	23.4				
Germany	17.7				

1970	Main ptnrs	EU 15	1970	Main ptnrs	EU 15
Netherlands		76.9	**Sweden**		71.6
Western Germany	32.6		United Kingdom	12.5	
Belgium & Lux	13.9		Western Germany	11.7	
Norway		78.6	**Switzerland**		60.4
United Kingdom	17.9		Western Germany	14.8	
Western Germany	17.9		Italy	9.4	
Portugal		52.6	**Turkey**		52.6
United Kingdom	20.3		Western Germany	19.9	
Angola	12.5		United States	9.5	
Spain		52.3	**United Kingdom**		44.7
United States	14.2		United States	11.7	
Western Germany	11.8		Western Germany	6.2	

a Trade between Western and Eastern Germany is excluded.

Who imports from where

Most important sources of imports
Imports from main partners and from EU 15 countries as % of total imports

1999	Main ptnrs	EU 15	1999	Main ptnrs	EU 15
Albania		80.1	**Denmark**		66.8
Italy	38.0		Germany	21.7	
Greece	27.7		Sweden	12.3	
Armenia		22.0	**Estonia**		57.8
Russia	21.5		Finland	22.8	
Belgium	10.1		Russia	13.5	
Austria		72.4	**Finland**		62.7
Germany	45.6		Germany	15.9	
Italy	7.2		Sweden	14.4	
Azerbaijan		22.2	**France**		65.9
Russia	21.9		Germany	19.0	
Turkey	13.8		Italy	9.4	
Belarus		17.6	**Georgia**		21.5
Russia	61.2		Turkey	13.9	
Germany	10.6		Azerbaijan	8.7	
Belgium		69.8	**Germany**		53.4
Germany	17.7		France	10.5	
Netherlands	16.6		United States	8.3	
Bosnia		43.8	**Greece**		65.7
Croatia	23.0		Italy	15.1	
Slovenia	15.4		Germany	14.8	
Bulgaria		50.0	**Hungary**		63.5
Russia	19.9		Germany	29.2	
Germany	15.2		Austria	8.9	
Croatia		56.7	**Iceland**		55.9
Germany	18.6		Germany	11.8	
Italy	16.0		United States	10.9	
Cyprus		52.9	**Ireland**		57.3
United Kingdom	11.4		United Kingdom	36.3	
United States	10.8		United States	16.1	
Czech Republic		64.0	**Italy**		60.8
Germany	33.9		Germany	19.0	
Slovakia	6.1		France	12.6	

1970	Main ptnrs	EU 15	1970	Main ptnrs	EU 15
Austria		68.5	**Germany, Western**[a]		57.4
Western Germany	41.3		France	12.7	
Switzerland	7.4		Netherlands	12.2	
Belgium & Lux		69.2	**Greece**		56.9
Western Germany	23.4		Western Germany	18.6	
France	17.1		Japan	12.7	
Denmark		53.4	**Iceland**		63.6
Western Germany	18.8		Western Germany	15.1	
Sweden	15.9		United Kingdom	14.2	
Finland		61.9	**Ireland**		72.9
Western Germany	16.5		United Kingdom	51.7	
Sweden	16.1		Western Germany	6.8	
France		58.9	**Italy**		51.0
Western Germany	22.1		Western Germany	19.8	
Belgium & Lux	11.2		France	13.2	

1999	Main ptnrs	EU 15	1999	Main ptnrs	EU 15
Latvia		53.7	**Russia**		36.7
Germany	15.2		Germany	13.9	
Russia	10.5		Belarus	10.7	
Lithuania		46.5	**Serbia & Montenegro**		64.2
Russia	20.0		Italy	18.5	
Germany	16.5		Germany	17.4	
Luxembourg		83.6	**Slovakia**		51.7
Belgium	34.2		Germany	26.2	
Germany	25.4		Czech Republic	16.7	
Macedonia		40.0	**Slovenia**		68.8
Germany	13.6		Germany	20.2	
Greece	9.1		Italy	16.9	
Malta		65.4	**Spain**		68.0
France	19.1		France	18.2	
Italy	16.7		Germany	16.0	
Moldova		26.8	**Sweden**		61.7
Russia	23.9		Germany	16.3	
Ukraine	12.9		United Kingdom	9.5	
Netherlands		55.6	**Switzerland**		77.8
Germany	17.8		Germany	31.0	
United States	9.4		France	12.0	
Norway		68.8	**Turkey**		52.6
Sweden	15.4		Germany	14.5	
Germany	13.1		Italy	7.8	
Poland		65.0	**Ukraine**		20.3
Germany	25.2		Russia	47.2	
Italy	9.4		Germany	8.0	
Portugal		76.9	**United Kingdom**		47.7
Spain	24.5		United States	13.1	
Germany	14.6		Germany	12.3	
Romania		60.6			
Italy	19.7				
Germany	17.2				

1970	Main ptnrs	EU 15	1970	Main ptnrs	EU 15
Netherlands		66.8	**Sweden**		64.3
Western Germany	27.1		Western Germany	18.9	
Belgium & Lux	16.8		United Kingdom	13.8	
Norway		68.4	**Switzerland**		78.7
Sweden	20.1		Western Germany	30.5	
Western Germany	14.3		France	12.3	
Portugal		57.1	**Turkey**		45.3
Western Germany	15.1		United States	18.2	
United Kingdom	13.9		Western Germany	17.3	
Spain		44.7	**United Kingdom**		36.7
United States	18.9		United States	13.0	
Western Germany	12.6		Canada	7.6	

a Trade between Western and Eastern Germany is excluded.

Top traders by sector

Food

		As % of world exports/imports		
	Value, $bn 1999	1980	1990	1999
Exporters				
1 United States	51.97	17.6	13.5	11.9
2 **France**	36.25	8.0	10.5	8.3
3 **Netherlands**	27.74	6.6	8.3	6.4
4 **Germany**	23.31	4.5	6.3	5.3
5 **Belgium**	17.57	2.7[a]	3.5[a]	4.0
6 Canada	16.57	3.5	3.5	3.8
7 **United Kingdom**	16.39	3.5	4.1	3.8
8 **Spain**	15.83	1.7	2.6	3.6
EU15	189.18	34.8[b]	45.7	43.3
Intra-exports	138.27	23.5[b]	33.7	31.7
Extra-exports	50.91	11.3[b]	12.0	11.7
Importers				
1 United States	48.64	8.8	8.9	10.3
2 Japan	46.95	7.2	10.1	10.0
3 **Germany**	36.05	9.7	10.6	7.6
4 **United Kingdom**	29.02	6.6	6.8	6.1
5 **France**	26.29	5.9	6.7	5.6
6 **Italy**	21.15	5.5	6.4	4.5
7 **Netherlands**	17.88	4.9	4.7	3.8
8 **Belgium**	16.15	3.3[a]	3.4[a]	3.4

Textiles

		As % of world exports/imports		
	Value, $bn 1999	1980	1990	1999
Exporters				
1 China[d]	13.04	4.6	6.9	8.8
2 **Germany**	11.89	11.4	13.5	8.0
3 **Italy**	11.78	7.6	9.1	8.0
4 South Korea	11.62	4.0	5.8	7.9
5 Taiwan	10.99	3.2	5.9	7.4
6 United States	9.51	6.8	4.8	6.4
7 **France**	7.03	6.2	5.8	4.8
EU15	60.6[c]	46.3[b]	48.6	40.1[c]
Intra-exports	37.68[c]	29.1[b]	34.1	25.3[c]
Extra-exports	22.92[c]	17.1[b]	14.5	15.2[c]
Importers				
1 United States	14.31	4.5	6.2	9.2
2 China[d]	11.08	1.9	4.9	7.1
3 **Germany**	9.89	12.1	11.0	6.4
4 **United Kingdom**	7.41	6.2	6.5	4.8
5 **France**	6.92	7.2	7.0	4.4
6 **Italy**	5.83	4.6	5.7	3.7
7 Mexico[de]	4.83	0.2	0.9	3.1

Clothing

	Value, $bn 1999	As % of world exports/imports 1980	1990	1999
Exporters				
1 China	30.08	4.0	9.0	16.2
2 **Italy**	13.24	11.3	11.0	7.1
3 Hong Kong[f]	9.57	11.5	8.6	5.1
4 United States	8.27	3.1	2.4	4.4
5 Mexico[d]	7.81	0.0	0.5	4.2
6 **Germany**	7.44	7.1	7.3	4.0
7 Turkey	6.52	0.3	3.1	3.5
8 **France**	5.69	5.6	4.3	3.1
EU15	51.17[c]	38.0[b]	37.7	28.5[c]
Intra-exports	35.37[c]	25.9[b]	27.2	19.7[c]
Extra-exports	15.80[c]	12.1[b]	10.5	8.8[c]
Importers				
1 United States	58.79	16.4	24.1	30.0
2 **Germany**	20.77	19.7	18.2	10.6
3 Japan	16.40	3.6	7.8	8.4
4 **United Kingdom**	12.53	6.8	6.2	6.4
5 **France**	11.58	6.2	7.5	5.9
6 **Italy**	5.84	1.9	2.3	3.0
7 **Netherlands**	5.14	6.8	4.3	2.6
8 **Belgium**	4.87	4.2[a]	3.1[a]	2.5

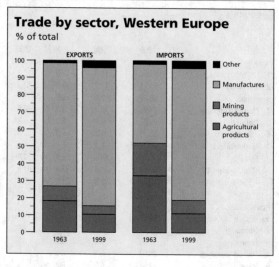

Trade by sector, Western Europe
% of total

EXPORTS   IMPORTS

Other
Manufactures
Mining products
Agricultural products

1963   1999   1963   1999

a Includes Luxembourg.   b EU12.   c 1998
d Includes significant shipments through processing zones.
e Imports are valued fob.   f Domestic exports, ie excluding re-exports.

Automotive products

	Value, $bn 1999	As % of world exports/imports		
		1980	1990	1999
Exporters				
1 **Germany**	93.15	21.0	21.9	17.0
2 Japan	82.64	19.8	20.8	15.0
3 United States	62.92	11.9	10.2	11.5
4 Canada	60.53	6.9	8.9	11.0
5 **France**	39.69	9.9	8.2	7.2
6 **Spain**	27.00	1.8	3.7	4.9
7 **United Kingdom**	26.46	5.8	4.4	4.8
8 Mexico[d]	25.25	0.3	1.5	4.6
EU15	267.67[c]	49.4[b]	53.8	51.0[c]
Intra-exports	189.31[c]	28.5[b]	39.5	36.1[c]
Extra-exports	78.36[c]	20.9[b]	14.3	14.9[c]
Importers				
1 United States	155.72	20.3	24.7	27.5
2 **Germany**	46.13	6.2	9.6	8.2
3 Canada[e]	45.25	8.7	7.7	8.0
4 **United Kingdom**	40.10	5.7	7.1	7.1
5 **France**	30.41	5.4	6.7	5.4
6 **Spain**	27.12	0.9	3.2	4.8
7 **Italy**	26.74	5.5	5.6	4.7
8 **Belgium**	21.70	5.2[a]	5.7[a]	3.8

Chemicals

	Value, $bn 1999	As % of world exports/imports		
		1980	1990	1999
Exporters				
1 United States	71.98	14.8	13.3	13.7
2 **Germany**	69.71	17.2	17.9	13.3
3 **France**	40.37	9.4	9.6	7.7
4 **United Kingdom**	34.64	8.7	8.0	6.6
5 **Belgium**	32.90	5.3[a]	5.6[a]	6.3
6 Japan	30.69	4.7	5.3	5.8
7 **Netherlands**	25.96	8.0	6.8	4.9
EU15	282.76	58.4	56.0	53.8
Intra-exports	172.56	35.0	37.9	32.8
Extra-exports	110.20	23.3	21.1	21.0
Importers				
1 United States	64.07	6.2	7.7	11.7
2 **Germany**	47.47	9.2	10.3	7.6
3 **France**	35.89	8.4	8.2	6.6
4 **United Kingdom**	30.07	5.1	6.3	5.5
5 **Italy**	27.84	5.5	6.5	5.1
6 **Belgium**	26.17	4.0[a]	4.4[a]	4.8
7 China[d]	24.03	2.0	2.2	4.4

Machinery and transport equipment

		As % of world exports/imports		
	Value, $bn			
	1999	1980	1990	1999
Exporters				
1 United States	369.3	16.4	15.1	16.1
2 Japan	286.5	14.5	16.7	12.5
3 Germany	264.2	16.3	17.2	11.5
4 France	130.7	7.0	6.5	5.7
5 United Kingdom	128.3	7.6	6.2	6.0
6 Canada	101.7	3.2	3.9	4.4
7 Italy	88.6	4.8	5.2	3.9
EU15	910.4c	43.0b	47.8	42.0c
Intra-exports	539.3c	20.9b	29.8	24.9c
Extra-exports	371.0c	22.1b	18	17.1c
Importers				
1 United States	489.2	12.1	17.5	20.7
2 Germany	169.8	6.6	9.4	7.2
3 United Kingdom	146.5	5.7	6.9	6.2
5 Canadae	114.9	5.1	4.8	4.9
4 France	114.5	5.5	6.5	4.8
6 Japan	85.3	1.6	2.9	3.6
7 Italy	75.8	3.8	4.4	3.2

Office machines and telecoms equipment

		As % of world exports/imports		
	Value, $bn			
	1999	1980	1990	1999
Exporters				
1 United States	125.66	20.2	17.3	16.3
2 Japan	91.27	21.1	22.4	11.9
3 Taiwan	45.1	3.2	4.7	5.9
4 Malaysiad	44.27	1.4	2.7	5.8
5 United Kingdom	44.04	6.4	6.5	5.7
6 South Korea	42.92	2.0	4.8	5.6
7 Singapore	38.62	2.5	4.9	5.0
EU15	202.35c	32.6b	31.1	29.7c
Intra-exports	133.41c	19.3b	22.0	19.6c
Extra-exports	68.93c	13.3b	9.1	10.1c
Importers				
1 United States	176.84	15.9	21.1	22.3
2 United Kingdom	51.74	7.0	8.0	6.5
3 Germany	50.39	9.4	9.8	6.4
4 Japan	44.05	2.6	3.7	5.6
5 Netherlands	34.37	3.9	4.1	4.3
6 France	30.68	6.4	6.0	3.9
7 Chinad	30.49	...	...	3.8

See page 75 for footnotes.

Inflation

Snapshots
Consumer price inflation, %

2000

1	Belarus[a]	293.7
2	Turkey	54.9
3	Romania[a]	45.8
4	Moldova	31.3
5	Ukraine[a]	22.7
6	Russia	20.8
7	Georgia[a]	19.1
8	Slovakia	12.0
9	Slovenia	10.9
10	Bulgaria	10.4
11	Poland	10.2
12	Hungary	9.7
13	Ireland	5.6
14	Croatia	5.4
15	Iceland	5.1
16	Czech Republic	4.9
17	Estonia	4.0
18	Finland	3.4
	Spain	3.4
20	Greece	3.1
	Luxembourg	3.1
22	Norway	3.0
23	Denmark	2.9
	Portugal	2.9
	United Kingdom	2.9
26	Latvia	2.7
27	Netherlands	2.6
28	Belgium	2.5
	Italy	2.5
30	Austria	2.4
31	Malta[a]	2.1
32	Germany	2.0
33	Cyprus[a]	1.7
	France	1.7

1990

1	Ex-Yugoslavia	583.1
2	Poland	555.4
3	Turkey	60.3
4	Hungary	29.0
5	Greece	20.4
6	Iceland	15.5
7	Portugal	13.4
8	Sweden	10.5
9	Ex-Czechoslovakia	10.0
10	United Kingdom	9.5
11	Spain	6.7
12	Italy	6.5
13	Finland	6.1
14	Switzerland	5.4
15	Cyprus	4.5
16	Romania	4.2
17	Norway	4.1
18	Luxembourg	3.7
19	Belgium	3.5
20	France	3.4
21	Austria	3.3
	Ireland	3.3
23	Malta	3.0
24	Germany	2.7
25	Denmark	2.6
26	Netherlands	2.5

1980

1	Turkey	110.2
2	Iceland	58.5
3	Ex-Yugoslavia	30.9
4	Greece	24.9
5	Italy	21.3
6	Ireland	18.2
7	United Kingdom	18.0
8	Portugal	16.6
9	Malta	15.7
10	Spain	15.6
11	Sweden	13.7
12	Cyprus	13.5
	France	13.5
14	Denmark	12.3

1970

1	Iceland	13.1
2	Norway	10.6
3	Ex-Yugoslavia	9.5
4	Ireland	8.2
5	Sweden	7.0
6	Turkey	6.9
7	Denmark	6.5
8	United Kingdom	6.4
9	France	5.8
10	Spain	5.7
11	Italy	4.8
12	Luxembourg	4.6
13	Portugal	4.5
14	Austria	4.4

Highest averages

Average annual consumer price inflation, %

1990–2000

1	Belarus[b]	353.4	14	Estonia	70.6
2	Georgia[b]	323.0	15	Latvia	64.2
3	Ukraine[b]	279.2	16	Albania	34.7
4	Armenia	265.5	17	Slovenia	33.5
5	Azerbaijan[b]	209.7	18	Poland	27.0
6	Russia	166.4	19	Hungary	20.1
7	Moldova	135.9	20	Slovakia	15.0
8	Romania[b]	113.9	21	Czech Republic	13.4
9	Bulgaria	108.8	22	Greece	9.2
10	Macedonia[b]	98.2	23	Portugal	4.9
11	Croatia	92.6	24	Spain	3.9
12	Lithuania	91.1	25	Cyprus[b]	3.8
13	Turkey	76.1	26	Italy	3.7

1980–90

1	Poland	69.9	10	Norway	7.6
2	Turkey	45.8		Sweden	7.6
3	Iceland	33.4	12	Finland	6.7
4	Greece	19.0	13	United Kingdom	6.6
5	Portugal	17.1	14	France	6.3
6	Hungary	10.7	15	Denmark	5.9
7	Italy	9.6	16	Cyprus	4.9
8	Spain	9.3	17	Belgium	4.5
9	Ireland	7.7	18	Luxembourg	4.4

1970–80

1	Iceland	34.0	10	Denmark	9.9
2	Turkey	27.7	11	France	9.7
3	Portugal	18.1	12	Sweden	9.1
4	Spain	15.3	13	Norway	8.4
5	Greece	14.4	14	Cyprus	7.9
6	Italy	13.9	15	Belgium	7.4
7	Ireland	13.7	16	Netherlands	7.3
	United Kingdom	13.7	17	Malta	6.7
9	Finland	11.2	18	Luxembourg	6.6

1960–70

1	Iceland	11.6	10	France	4.0
2	Spain	6.2		Sweden	4.0
3	Denmark	5.9		Turkey	4.0
4	Finland	5.0	13	Italy	3.6
5	Ireland	4.7		Austria	3.6
6	Norway	4.5	15	Switzerland	3.3
7	Netherlands	4.3	16	Belgium	3.0
8	Portugal	4.2	17	Germany	2.6
9	United Kingdom	4.1		Luxembourg	2.6

a 1999   b 1990–99

Exchange rates

Currency units per dollar

	1960	1965	1970	1975	1980
Austria	26.04	25.89	25.88	18.51	13.81
Belgium & Lux	49.70	49.64	49.68	39.53	31.52
Cyprus	0.36	0.36	0.42	0.39	0.36
Denmark	6.91	6.89	7.49	6.18	6.02
Finland	3.21	3.22	4.18	3.85	3.84
France	4.90	4.90	5.55	4.49	4.52
Germany	4.17	4.01	3.65	2.62	1.96
Greece	30.00	30.00	30.00	35.65	46.54
Hungary			60.00	43.51	32.21
Iceland	0.38	0.43	0.88	1.71	6.24
Ireland	0.36	0.36	0.42	0.49	0.53
Italy	620.60	624.70	623.00	683.60	930.50
Malta	0.36	0.36	0.42	0.40	0.35
Netherlands	3.77	3.61	3.60	2.69	2.13
Norway	7.15	7.15	7.14	5.59	5.18
Poland			–	–	–
Portugal	28.83	28.83	28.75	27.47	53.04
Romania			6.00	20.00	18.00
Spain	60.15	59.99	69.72	59.77	79.25
Sweden	5.18	5.18	5.17	4.39	4.37
Switzerland	4.31	4.32	4.32	2.62	1.76
Turkey	9.02	9.04	9.00	15.20	90.10
United Kingdom	0.36	0.36	0.42	0.49	0.42

Changing values

Currencies change against the dollar, %
End 1990[a]–end 2000

1	Latvia	37.03	17	Ireland	-33.84
2	Lithuania	-5.23	18	Portugal	-37.99
3	Switzerland	-20.56	19	Sweden	-40.22
4	United Kingdom	-22.41	20	Finland	-43.18
5	Estonia	-23.25	21	Slovakia	-45.34
6	Iceland	-23.65	22	Italy	-45.69
7	Czech Republic	-25.95	23	Spain	-45.97
8	France	-27.23	24	Greece	-56.89
9	Austria	-27.78	25	Slovenia	-75.07
10	Denmark	-27.94	26	Poland	-77.07
11	Belgium & Lux	-28.54	27	Hungary	-78.42
12	Netherlands	-28.64	28	Albania	-94.62
13	Germany	-29.11	29	Russia	-98.51
14	Cyprus	-30.28	30	Turkey	-99.56
15	Malta	-31.87	31	Romania	-99.81
16	Norway	-33.21	32	Bulgaria	-99.87

a Or earliest available.
Note: Andorra uses the Spanish peseta; Liechtenstein uses the Swiss franc; the Luxembourg franc is at parity with the Belgian franc, which, in turn, is also legal tender in Luxembourg; Monaco uses the French franc; San Marino and the Vatican use the Italian lira.

1985	1990	1995	December 2000 per $	December 2000 per euro
17.28	10.68	10.09	14.79	13.76
50.36	30.98	29.42	43.35	40.35
0.54	0.43	0.46	0.62	0.57
8.97	5.78	5.55	8.02	7.46
5.42	3.63	4.36	6.39	5.95
7.56	5.13	4.90	7.05	6.56
2.46	1.49	1.43	2.10	1.96
147.76	157.63	237.04	365.62	340.75
47.35	61.45	139.47	284.73	265.08
42.06	55.39	65.23	72.55	79.56
0.80	0.56	0.62	0.85	0.79
1,678.50	1,130.20	1,584.70	2,080.91	1,936.58
0.42	0.30	0.35	0.44	0.41
2.77	1.69	1.60	2.37	2.20
7.58	5.91	6.32	8.85	8.23
0.01	0.95	2.47	4.14	3.88
157.49	133.60	149.41	215.46	200.52
15.73	34.71	2,578.00	25,926.00	24,340.00
154.15	96.61	121.41	178.82	166.41
7.62	5.70	6.66	9.54	8.83
2.08	1.30	1.15	1.64	1.52
576.90	2,930.10	59,650.00	673,385.00	629,311.00
0.69	0.52	0.65	0.67	0.62

Currency units per dollar

	1992 per $	1995 per $	December 2000 per $	December 2000 per euro
Albania	102.90	94.24	142.64	134.02
Armenia	2.07	402.00	552.18	513.66
Azerbaijan	48.60	4,440.00	4,378.00	4,072.56
Belarus	15.00	11,500.00	1,217.50	1,138.36
Bosnia			2.08	1.93
Bulgaria	24.49	70.70	2.10	1.96
Croatia	0.80	5.32	8.16	7.59
Czech Republic	28.90	26.60	37.81	35.33
Estonia	12.91	11.46	16.82	15.66
Georgia		1.25	1.98	1.84
Latvia	0.84	0.54	0.61	0.53
Lithuania	3.79	4.00	4.00	3.75
Macedonia		37.98	66.33	61.70
Moldova	0.41	4.50	12.38	11.52
Russia	0.42	4.64	28.16	26.90
Serbia & Montenegro			13.65	12.82
Slovakia	28.90	29.57	51.22	44.01
Slovenia	98.70	125.99	227.38	213.57
Ukraine	0.01	1.79	5.43	5.10

Burgernomics

Over/under valuation of national currencies (as measured by *The Economist*'s Big Mac index, see Glossary, page 12, for explanation) in April 2001, compared to that of the US$, %

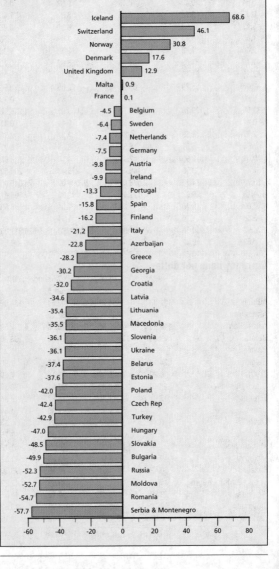

Iceland	68.6
Switzerland	46.1
Norway	30.8
Denmark	17.6
United Kingdom	12.9
Malta	0.9
France	0.1
Belgium	-4.5
Sweden	-6.4
Netherlands	-7.4
Germany	-7.5
Austria	-9.8
Ireland	-9.9
Portugal	-13.3
Spain	-15.8
Finland	-16.2
Italy	-21.2
Azerbaijan	-22.8
Greece	-28.2
Georgia	-30.2
Croatia	-32.0
Latvia	-34.6
Lithuania	-35.4
Macedonia	-35.5
Slovenia	-36.1
Ukraine	-36.1
Belarus	-37.4
Estonia	-37.6
Poland	-42.0
Czech Rep	-42.4
Turkey	-42.9
Hungary	-47.0
Slovakia	-48.5
Bulgaria	-49.9
Russia	-52.3
Moldova	-52.7
Romania	-54.7
Serbia & Montenegro	-57.7

GOVERNMENT FINANCE

General government revenue

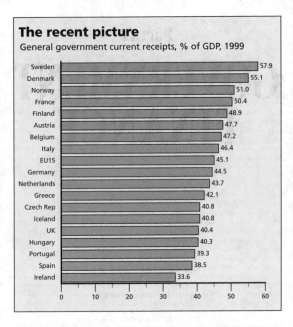

The recent picture

General government current receipts, % of GDP, 1999

Sweden	57.9
Denmark	55.1
Norway	51.0
France	50.4
Finland	48.9
Austria	47.7
Belgium	47.2
Italy	46.4
EU15	45.1
Germany	44.5
Netherlands	43.7
Greece	42.1
Czech Rep	40.8
Iceland	40.8
UK	40.4
Hungary	40.3
Portugal	39.3
Spain	38.5
Ireland	33.6

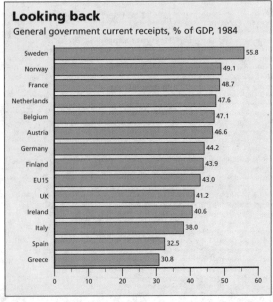

Looking back

General government current receipts, % of GDP, 1984

Sweden	55.8
Norway	49.1
France	48.7
Netherlands	47.6
Belgium	47.1
Austria	46.6
Germany	44.2
Finland	43.9
EU15	43.0
UK	41.2
Ireland	40.6
Italy	38.0
Spain	32.5
Greece	30.8

General government spending

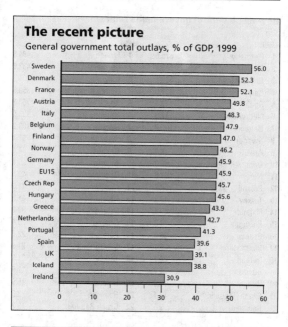

The recent picture
General government total outlays, % of GDP, 1999

Sweden	56.0
Denmark	52.3
France	52.1
Austria	49.8
Italy	48.3
Belgium	47.9
Finland	47.0
Norway	46.2
Germany	45.9
EU15	45.9
Czech Rep	45.7
Hungary	45.6
Greece	43.9
Netherlands	42.7
Portugal	41.3
Spain	39.6
UK	39.1
Iceland	38.8
Ireland	30.9

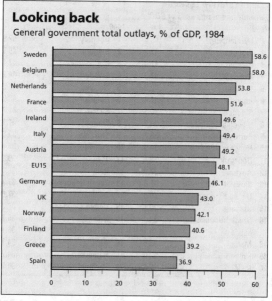

Looking back
General government total outlays, % of GDP, 1984

Sweden	58.6
Belgium	58.0
Netherlands	53.8
France	51.6
Ireland	49.6
Italy	49.4
Austria	49.2
EU15	48.1
Germany	46.1
UK	43.0
Norway	42.1
Finland	40.6
Greece	39.2
Spain	36.9

Central government revenue

How much central governments raise

$bn

1999			*1990*		
1	Germany[a]	675.6	1	France	484.6
2	France[b]	589.4	2	Germany	432.6
3	United Kingdom	526.1	3	Italy	424.7
4	Italy	477.0	4	United Kingdom	359.5
5	Spain	117.5	5	Spain	150.3
6	Netherlands	112.9	6	Netherlands	133.5
7	Belgium[a]	105.2	7	Russia[c]	103.2
8	Sweden	95.7	8	Sweden	101.7
9	Austria	78.4	9	Belgium	84.4
10	Denmark	66.3	10	Austria	55.1
11	Norway[a]	61.6	11	Denmark[d]	49.5
12	Poland	50.7	12	Norway	49.0
13	Turkey	47.3	13	Finland	41.9
14	Finland[a]	41.4	14	Poland[e]	38.8
15	Portugal[a]	38.8	15	Greece	23.4
16	Greece	38.0	16	Portugal	22.6
17	Switzerland	25.1	17	Switzerland	21.9
18	Ireland	24.7	18	Turkey	21.0
	Russia	24.7	19	Hungary	17.5
20	Hungary	18.6	20	Ireland	15.9
21	Czech Republic	18.1	21	Romania	13.3
22	Romania[b]	9.5	22	Czech Republic[f]	13.2

...and relative revenue

Revenue and grants as % of GDP

1999			*1990*		
1	Luxembourg[b]	45.8	1	Hungary	52.9
2	France[b]	42.9	2	Bulgaria	49.8
3	Belgium[a]	42.4	3	Netherlands	47.1
4	Norway[a]	42.3	4	Sweden	44.2
5	Croatia	42.2	5	Norway	43.2
6	Italy	41.4	6	Belgium	43.0
7	Sweden	40.6	7	Slovakia[g]	41.7
8	Slovenia	39.9	8	France	41.1
9	Portugal[a]	39.7	9	Slovenia[h]	39.8
10	Hungary	38.5	10	Poland[e]	39.4
11	Denmark	38.4	11	Malta	39.3
12	Austria	37.9	12	Italy	38.9
13	Slovakia	37.0	13	Czech Republic[f]	37.7
14	United Kingdom	36.8	14	Denmark[d]	37.5
15	Bulgaria	36.1	15	United Kingdom	37.2
16	Czech Republic	34.1	16	Ireland	36.7
	Latvia	34.1	17	Luxembourg	36.1
18	Malta	33.5	18	Austria	34.7
19	Finland[a]	33.0		Romania	34.7
20	Iceland	32.9	20	Portugal	34.2

Central government spending

How much central governments spend
$bn

1999			*1990*		
1	Germany[a]	701.6	1	Italy	523.1
2	France[b]	649.4	2	France	508.7
3	United Kingdom	524.9	3	Germany	443.3
4	Italy	494.5	4	United Kingdom	372.6
5	Spain	124.2	5	Spain	166.4
6	Belgium[a]	109.6	6	Netherlands	146.4
7	Sweden	95.4	7	Russia[c]	126.8
8	Austria	80.0	8	Belgium	94.4
9	Turkey	70.4	9	Sweden	93.7
10	Denmark	63.5	10	Austria	60.8
11	Poland	54.8	11	Denmark[d]	52.0
12	Norway[a]	54.6	12	Norway	47.7
13	Netherlands	50.2	13	Greece	43.9
14	Greece	44.3	14	Finland	41.5
15	Portugal[a]	43.3	15	Poland[e]	41.0
16	Finland[a]	43.1	16	Portugal	26.9
17	Switzerland	27.2	17	Turkey	26.2
18	Russia	26.6	18	Switzerland	20.7
19	Ireland	23.5	19	Ireland	17.9
20	Hungary	20.5	20	Hungary	17.2
21	Czech Republic	19.4	21	Czech Republic[f]	13.1
22	Romania[b]	11.1	22	Romania	12.9

...and relative spending
Spending and lending minus repayments as % of GDP

1999			*1990*		
1	France[b]	46.7	1	Bulgaria	58.1
2	Belgium[a]	44.2	2	Greece	53.0
	Croatia	44.2	3	Hungary	52.1
4	Norway[a]	44.0	4	Netherlands	51.5
5	Italy	43.0	5	Italy	49.1
6	Malta	42.8	6	Belgium	48.6
7	Hungary	42.1	7	Malta	44.5
8	Portugal[a]	41.0	8	Slovakia[g]	43.2
9	Austria	40.6		Sweden	43.2
	Slovenia	40.6	10	Norway	42.7
11	Sweden	40.4	11	France	42.4
12	Slovakia	40.3	12	Poland[e]	41.6
13	Luxembourg[b]	40.1	13	Russia[c]	39.9
14	Latvia	38.1	14	Slovenia[h]	39.5
15	Denmark	37.9		Denmark[d]	39.4
16	Turkey	37.4	16	Austria	39.2
17	United Kingdom	36.8		Ireland	39.2
18	Czech Republic	35.7	18	Portugal	38.8
19	Greece	35.4	19	United Kingdom	36.5
20	Bulgaria	34.6	20	Czech Republic[f]	35.4

a 1998 b 1997 c 1995 d 1991 e 1994 f 1993 g 1996 h 1992

Spending on what?

General public services

Central government spending, % of total

1986			1999		
1	Turkey	31.6	1	Georgia	10.6
2	Greece	19.8	2	Luxembourg[d]	10.2
3	Luxembourg	13.6	3	Bulgaria	9.6
4	Malta	9.8	4	Denmark	8.6
	Netherlands[a]	9.8	5	Slovenia	8.2
6	Switzerland[b]	9.5	6	Malta[e]	7.9
7	Cyprus	7.8	7	Russia	6.7
8	Finland	7.7	8	Estonia	6.6
9	Ireland	7.4	9	Netherlands[e]	6.4
	Denmark	7.4	10	Sweden	6.2
11	Italy	6.9	11	Cyprus[f]	6.1
12	Estonia[a]	6.2		Slovakia	6.1
	Portugal	6.2	13	Azerbaijan	6.0
14	France	5.6	14	Albania	5.8
15	Norway	5.0	15	Austria[g]	5.7
16	Austria	5.0	16	Finland[f]	5.6
17	Bulgaria[c]	4.5		Latvia	5.6
	Iceland	4.5	18	Norway[f]	5.4
19	Sweden	3.9	19	Hungary[f]	5.1
	Germany	3.9	20	Belarus	4.7
21	United Kingdom	3.6	21	Greece[f]	4.6
22	Belgium	3.1	22	Iceland[f]	4.2
23	Spain	3.0		United Kingdom	4.2
24	Croatia[a]	2.0	24	Croatia	4.0
25	Romania	0.5		Lithuania	4.0

Public order

Central government spending, % of total

1986			1999		
1	Croatia[a]	8.1	1	Georgia	11.6
2	Greece	8.0	2	Azerbaijan	11.3
3	Cyprus	7.5	3	Estonia	7.4
4	Iceland	4.8	4	Latvia	7.2
5	Switzerland[b]	4.5	5	Bulgaria	6.8
6	Luxembourg	4.2	6	Lithuania	6.6
7	Estonia[a]	3.6	7	Albania	5.8
	Netherlands[a]	3.6	8	Croatia	5.7
9	Spain	3.4	9	Cyprus[f]	5.3
10	United Kingdom	3.1	10	Russia	5.1
11	Malta	2.8	11	Moldova	4.8
12	Sweden	2.7	12	Czech Republic	4.7
13	Austria	2.5	13	Turkey	4.6
14	Denmark	2.3	14	Malta[e]	4.0
15	Bulgaria[c]	1.9		Slovakia	4.0
	Norway	1.9	16	Slovenia	3.9

Note: These figures are for central government spending. In countries such as Germany a lot of government spending is done at the regional level.

Education
Central government spending, % of total

1986			1999		
1	Bulgaria[c]	25.3	1	Iceland[f]	28.2
2	Switzerland[b]	22.1	2	Ireland[e]	13.6
3	Greece	16.6	3	Malta[e]	12.2
	Luxembourg	16.6	4	Denmark	11.9
5	Iceland	14.0	5	Cyprus[f]	11.8
6	Finland	13.9	6	Turkey	11.3
7	Turkey	12.6	7	Greece[f]	10.8
8	Belgium	12.2	8	Slovakia	10.7
9	Ireland	11.8		Slovenia	10.7
10	Cyprus	10.4	10	Finland[f]	10.4
11	Austria	9.7	11	Luxembourg[d]	10.3

Health
Central government spending, % of total

1986			1999		
1	Iceland	24.5	1	Switzerland[f]	19.8
2	Bulgaria[c]	23.3	2	Germany[h]	18.9
3	Germany	18.3	3	Slovakia	18.7
4	Croatia[a]	16.3	4	Czech Republic	17.9
5	Switzerland[b]	16.0	5	Estonia	16.7
6	France	15.5	6	Ireland[e]	16.3
7	United Kingdom	13.4	7	United Kingdom	15.4
8	Spain	12.5	8	Netherlands[e]	14.8
9	Ireland	12.4	9	Lithuania	14.7
10	Austria	12.2	10	Croatia	14.6
11	Finland	10.6	11	Slovenia	13.8

Social security
Central government spending, % of total

1986			1999		
1	Germany	49.0	1	Luxembourg[d]	52.3
2	Sweden	46.4	2	Poland	51.0
3	Austria	46.3	3	Germany[h]	50.0
4	France	44.6	4	Switzerland[f]	48.8
5	Estonia[a]	41.9	5	Austria[g]	46.3
6	Belgium	41.6	5	Sweden	46.3
7	Croatia[a]	39.0	7	Slovenia	43.6
8	Spain	36.4	8	Latvia	42.9
9	Denmark	36.4	9	Denmark	40.1
10	Italy	35.1	10	Spain[e]	39.6
	Malta	35.1	11	Norway[f]	39.0
12	Finland	34.4	12	Croatia	38.6
13	Norway	33.0	13	Czech Republic	37.8
14	United Kingdom	31.9	14	Netherlands[e]	37.4
15	Netherlands[a]	25.4		Russia	37.4
			16	United Kingdom	36.5

a 1991   b 1990   c 1988   d 1995   e 1997   f 1998   g 1994   h 1996

Debt: rich countries

Total debt
General government gross financial liabilities as % of GDP

		1999	1990	1980
1	Italy	116.6	103.7	58.1
2	Belgium	115.9	125.2	78.2
3	Greece	104.6	89.0	22.9
4	Spain	72.4	48.5	18.3
5	Austria	65.2	57.9	37.3
6	France	65.0	39.5	30.9
7	Sweden	63.5	42.9	44.3
8	Netherlands	62.6	75.6	46.9
9	Germany	60.6	42.0	31.1
10	United Kingdom	57.0	39.1	54.0
11	Portugal	55.9	65.3	32.8
12	Denmark	55.1	65.8	44.7
13	Ireland	50.1	92.6	72.7
14	Finland	46.6	14.5	14.1

Net debt
General government net financial liabilities as % of GDP

		1999	1990	1980
1	Belgium	107.4	115.5	68.7
2	Italy	104.4	83.7	53.0
3	Netherlands	49.9	35.4	24.6
4	Austria	48.5	38.4	20.0
5	Spain	45.9	31.5	6.1
6	France	43.0	16.1	-3.3
7	Germany	42.3	17.8	9.3
8	United Kingdom	37.1	18.6	36.2
9	Denmark	31.3	33.0	14.2
10	Iceland	24.6	19.5	3.3
11	Sweden	8.1	-7.8	-13.9
12	Finland	-28.2	-35.7	-30.7

Interest payments
General government net interest payments as % of GDP

		1999	1990	1980
1	Greece	7.6	10.0	2.3
2	Belgium	6.8	9.6	5.3
3	Italy	6.4	8.9	4.2
4	Netherlands	3.8	4.1	2.4
5	Austria	3.5	3.2	1.7
6	Spain	3.4	3.0	0.3
7	Portugal	3.2	8.1	2.8
8	Sweden	3.1	0.1	-0.4
9	France	3.0	2.3	0.8
	Germany	3.0	1.9	1.3
11	Denmark	2.3	3.7	0.5
	United Kingdom	2.3	2.3	3.1
13	Iceland	2.1	–	–
14	Finland	1.5	-1.7	-1.0

Debt: poor countries

External debt
$bn, 1999

1	Russia	173.9	9	Romania	9.4
2	Turkey	101.8	10	Slovakia	9.1
3	Poland	54.3	11	Lithuania	3.6
4	Hungary	29.0	12	Estonia	2.9
5	Czech Republic	22.6	13	Latvia	2.7
6	Ukraine	14.1	14	Bosnia	2.0
7	Serbia & Montenegro	12.9	15	Georgia	1.7
8	Bulgaria	9.9	16	Macedonia	1.4

As % of GDP, 1999

1	Bulgaria	81.0	8	Croatia	47.0
2	Moldova	78.9	9	Russia	46.3
3	Hungary	62.0	10	Bosnia	43.5
4	Georgia	57.8	11	Czech Republic	43.1
5	Estonia	56.1	12	Latvia	42.8
6	Turkey	54.3	13	Macedonia	42.1
7	Slovakia	47.1	14	Ukraine	37.6

As % of exports, 1999

1	Russia	204	9	Hungary	103
2	Turkey	194	10	Albania	99
3	Armenia	190	11	Macedonia	93
4	Georgia	175		Romania	93
5	Bulgaria	163	13	Latvia	86
6	Moldova	134	14	Lithuania	82
7	Poland	132		Ukraine	82
8	Croatia	107	16	Azerbaijan	79

Interest payments
$m, 1999

1	Turkey	5,833.5	9	Slovakia	519.9
2	Russia	4,651.0	10	Bulgaria	403.0
3	Poland	2,129.8	11	Estonia	147.5
4	Czech Republic	1,478.6	12	Bosnia	145.5
5	Hungary	1,446.3	13	Lithuania	113.8
6	Ukraine	677.3	14	Latvia	109.3
7	Romania	584.1	15	Macedonia	74.7
8	Croatia	541.5	16	Belarus	65.1

As % of GDP, 1999

1	Moldova	4.4	10	Macedonia	2.2
2	Bulgaria	3.3	11	Latvia	1.8
3	Bosnia	3.2		Ukraine	1.8
4	Hungary	3.1	13	Romania	1.7
	Turkey	3.1	14	Georgia	1.6
6	Estonia	2.9	15	Poland	1.4
7	Czech Republic	2.8	16	Russia	1.2
8	Croatia	2.7	17	Lithuania	1.1
	Slovakia	2.7	18	Azerbaijan	0.8

Aid

Givers

*Official Development Assistance (ODA) from
Development Assistance Committee (DAC) countries to developing countries*
$bn

1988–89			*1999*		
1	France	5.63	1	France	5.64
2	Germany	4.84	2	Germany	5.52
3	Italy	3.40	3	United Kingdom	3.40
4	United Kingdom	2.62	4	Netherlands	3.13
5	Netherlands	2.16	5	Italy	1.81
6	Sweden	1.67	6	Denmark	1.73
7	Norway	0.95	7	Sweden	1.63
8	Denmark	0.93	8	Norway	1.37
9	Finland	0.66	9	Spain	1.36
10	Belgium	0.65	10	Switzerland	0.97
11	Switzerland	0.59	11	Belgium	0.76
12	Spain	0.40	12	Austria	0.53
13	Austria	0.29	13	Finland	0.42
14	Portugal	0.10	14	Portugal	0.28
15	Ireland	0.06	15	Ireland	0.25
16	Luxembourg	0.02	16	Greece	0.19
	Total EU	20.79		Total EU	26.56

% of GDP

1988–89			*1999*		
1	Norway	0.99	1	Denmark	0.99
2	Netherlands	0.94	2	Norway	0.94
3	Sweden	0.91	3	Netherlands	0.81
4	Denmark	0.87	4	Sweden	0.72
5	Finland	0.62	5	Luxembourg	0.68
6	France	0.59	6	France	0.40
7	Belgium	0.42	7	Switzerland	0.37
8	Italy	0.40	8	Finland	0.33
9	Switzerland	0.31	9	Belgium	0.31
	United Kingdom	0.31	10	Ireland	0.29
11	Germany	0.28	11	Germany	0.27
12	Austria	0.23	12	Portugal	0.26
13	Luxembourg	0.20	13	Austria	0.25
14	Portugal	0.19		United Kingdom	0.25
15	Ireland	0.18	15	Spain	0.24
16	Spain	0.11	16	Italy	0.16
	Total EU	0.46		Total EU	0.33

Per head, $, 1999

1	Denmark	326	9	Belgium	74
2	Norway	308	10	Germany	67
3	Luxembourg	275	11	Ireland	66
4	Netherlands	198	12	Austria	65
5	Sweden	184	13	United Kingdom	58
6	Switzerland	136	14	Spain	35
7	France	93	15	Italy	31
8	Finland	81	16	Portugal	28

Receivers

Aid (ODA) received, $m, 1999

1	Russia	1,816	9	Bulgaria	265
2	Bosnia	1,063	10	Hungary	248
3	Albania	480	11	Georgia	239
4	Ukraine	480	12	Armenia	208
5	Romania	373	13	Azerbaijan	162
6	Slovakia	318	14	Lithuania	129
6	Czech Republic	318	15	Moldova	102
8	Macedonia	273	16	Latvia	96

Aid (ODA) as % of GDP, 1999

1	Bosnia	39.40	9	Slovakia	1.65
2	Albania	15.70	10	Estonia	1.62
3	Armenia	10.88	11	Latvia	1.45
4	Moldova	9.35	12	Lithuania	1.23
5	Macedonia	7.92	13	Ukraine	1.13
6	Georgia	5.70	14	Romania	1.11
7	Azerbaijan	3.63	15	Malta	0.72
8	Bulgaria	2.19	16	Czech Republic	0.56

Aid (ODA) per head, $, 1999

1	Bosnia	274	9	Georgia	44
2	Albania	142	10	Latvia	40
3	Macedonia	135	11	Lithuania	35
4	Cyprus	66	12	Bulgaria	32
	Malta	66	13	Czech Republic	31
6	Slovakia	59	14	Hungary	25
7	Estonia	57	15	Moldova	24
8	Armenia	55	16	Azerbaijan	20

Where the EU's money goes

ODA from EU countries to multinational organisations, 1999, % of total of $11.4bn

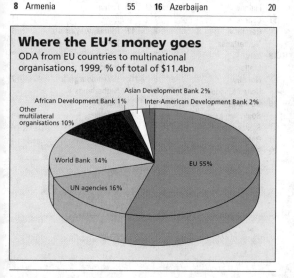

Asian Development Bank 2%
Inter-American Development Bank 2%
African Development Bank 1%
Other multilateral organisations 10%
World Bank 14%
UN agencies 16%
EU 55%

Money supply

Narrow money
Average annual % growth

1995–2000

1	Turkey[a]	102.4	16	Iceland[d]	16.1
2	Bulgaria	102.0	17	Macedonia	12.9
3	Belarus	100.5	18	Azerbaijan	12.8
4	Romania	45.6	19	Cyprus	12.2
5	Russia	42.2	20	Norway	9.5
6	Moldova[b]	37.8	21	Greece	9.4
7	Ukraine	34.6	22	Lithuania	8.6
8	Estonia	20.5	23	Euro-11	7.8
9	Armenia	18.9	24	United Kingdom	7.1
10	Georgia	18.8	25	Denmark[e]	6.5
11	Slovenia	18.7	26	Switzerland[f]	5.7
12	Hungary[c]	17.6	27	Slovakia	4.5
13	Poland	17.1	28	Czech Republic	3.6
14	Croatia	16.8		Malta	3.6
15	Latvia	16.7			

1990–95

1	Romania	95
2	Turkey	66
3	Poland	32
4	Hungary	15
5	Greece	13
6	Portugal	12
7	Iceland	10
	Ireland	10
9	Austria	9
10	Finland[g]	8
11	Cyprus	7
	Germany	7
	Netherlands	7
13	Italy	5
	Malta	5
	Norway	5
	United Kingdom	5
16	Denmark	4
	Spain	4
	Switzerland	4
21	Belgium	3
22	France	1

1980–90

1	Poland	60
2	Turkey	45
3	Iceland	38
4	Greece	20
	Norway	20
6	Portugal	17
7	Spain	14
8	Denmark	12
9	Cyprus	11
	Finland	11
	Italy	11
12	Germany, Western	9
13	France	8
	Romania	8
15	Ireland	7
	Luxembourg	7
	Netherlands	7
18	Austria	5
19	Belgium	4
	Malta	4
21	Switzerland	2

Broad money
Average annual % growth

1995–2000

1	Belarus	177.2
2	Turkey[a]	127.1
3	Bulgaria	98.7
4	Romania	78.8
5	Russia	54.2
6	Moldova[b]	42.3
7	Armenia	39.3
8	Georgia	35.6
9	Ukraine	35.2
10	Estonia	33.7
11	Croatia	31.1
12	Azerbaijan	30.8
13	Poland	29.6
14	Slovenia	25.4
15	Latvia	24.5
16	Macedonia	22.0
17	Hungary[c]	20.0
18	Iceland	14.3
19	Slovakia	14.2
20	Lithuania	12.4
21	Cyprus	11.4
22	Malta	10.0
23	Norway	8.5
24	Greece[g]	7.9
25	United Kingdom	7.1
26	Czech Republic	5.3
27	Euro-11	5.2
28	Denmark[e]	4.6
29	Switzerland[f]	1.3

1990–95

1	Romania	102
2	Turkey	93
3	Poland	40
4	Hungary	21
5	Portugal	15
6	Cyprus	14
7	Ireland	13
8	Malta	11
9	Greece	9
	Spain	9
11	Germany	7
	United Kingdom	7
13	Austria	6
	Iceland	6
15	France	4
	Italy	4
	Netherlands	4
	Norway	4
	Switzerland	4
20	Denmark	3
	Sweden	3
22	Belgium	2
	Finland[g]	2

1980–90

1	Poland	62
2	Turkey	58
3	Iceland	42
4	Greece	22
5	United Kingdom	21
6	Portugal	19
7	Cyprus	15
8	Finland	13
9	Spain	12
10	Denmark	11
	Luxembourg	11
	Norway	11
13	Italy	10
	Romania	10
15	Ireland	9
16	Austria	8
	Malta	8
	Sweden	8
19	Belgium	7
	France	7
	Germany, Western	7
	Switzerland	7
23	Netherlands	6

a 1995–November 2000
b 1998–2000
c 1995–September 2000
d 1995–November 1999
e 1995–June 2000
f 1996–2000

Reserves

Recent picture
Total reserves minus gold, $m, December 2000

1	Germany	56,890	22	Slovakia[a]	4,007
2	United Kingdom	43,890	23	Romania	3,922
3	France	37,039	24	Croatia	3,524
4	Switzerland	32,272	25	Bulgaria	3,342
5	Spain	30,989	26	Slovenia	3,196
6	Poland	26,562	27	Cyprus[a]	1,812
7	Italy	25,566	28	Malta[b]	1,631
8	Russia	24,264	29	Ukraine	1,382
9	Norway	20,164	30	Lithuania	1,312
10	Turkey	19,952	31	Estonia	921
11	Denmark	15,108	32	Latvia	851
12	Sweden	14,863	33	Azerbaijan	680
13	Austria	14,318	34	Macedonia	429
14	Greece	13,424	35	Iceland	389
15	Czech Republic	13,018	36	Albania	352
16	Hungary	11,190	37	Belarus	351
17	Belgium	9,994	38	Armenia	318
18	Netherlands	9,643	39	Moldova	230
19	Portugal	8,908	40	Georgia	109
20	Finland	7,873		Euro-11	122,195
21	Ireland	5,360		EU15	147,724

Gold
Fine troy ounces, m, December 2000

1	Germany	111.52	18	Finland	1.58
2	France	97.25	19	Slovakia[a]	1.29
3	Italy	78.83	20	Norway	1.18
4	Switzerland	77.79	21	Bulgaria	1.03
5	Netherlands	29.32	22	Cyprus[a]	0.46
6	Portugal	19.51	23	Czech Republic	0.45
7	Spain	16.83		Ukraine	0.45
8	United Kingdom	15.67	25	Latvia	0.25
9	Russia	12.36	26	Lithuania	0.19
10	Austria	12.14	27	Ireland	0.18
11	Belgium	8.30	28	Albania	0.11
12	Sweden	5.96		Macedonia	0.11
13	Greece	4.26	30	Hungary	0.10
14	Turkey	3.74	31	Luxembourg	0.08
15	Romania	3.37	32	Iceland	0.06
16	Poland	3.31		Euro-11	375.53
17	Denmark	2.00		EU15	403.42

The world picture
Gold, % of total weight, December 2000

Euro-11	42.1	Other Asia	6.0
Other European Union	3.0	Middle East	3.7
Other industrial countries	38.8	Latin America	1.9
Other Europe	3.0	Africa	1.5

a November. b June.

Looking back
Total reserves minus gold, $m
1990

1	Germany	67,902	13	Finland	9,644
2	Italy	62,927	14	Austria	9,376
3	Spain	51,228	15	Turkey	6,050
4	France	36,778	16	Ireland	5,223
5	United Kingdom	35,850	17	Poland	4,492
6	Switzerland	29,223	18	Greece	3,412
7	Sweden	17,988	19	Cyprus	1,507
8	Netherlands	17,484	20	Malta	1,432
9	Norway	15,332	21	Hungary	1,070
10	Portugal	14,485	22	Romania	524
11	Belgium	12,151	23	Iceland	436
12	Denmark	10,591	24	Luxembourg	81

1980

1	Germany	48,592	12	Denmark	3,387
2	France	27,340	13	Ireland	2,860
3	Italy	23,126	14	Finland	1,870
4	United Kingdom	20,650	15	Greece	1,346
5	Switzerland	15,656	16	Turkey	1,077
6	Spain	11,863	17	Malta	990
7	Netherlands	11,645	18	Portugal	795
8	Belgium	7,823	19	Cyprus	368
9	Norway	6,048	20	Romania	323
10	Austria	5,280	21	Iceland	174
11	Sweden	3,418	22	Poland	128

1970

1	Germany	9,630	11	Ireland	681
2	Italy	2,465	12	Portugal	602
3	Switzerland	2,401	13	Sweden	561
4	United Kingdom	1,480	14	Finland	425
5	Netherlands	1,454	15	Denmark	419
6	France	1,428	16	Turkey	304
7	Belgium	1,377	17	Cyprus	194
8	Spain	1,319		Greece	194
9	Austria	1,044	19	Malta	148
10	Norway	787.9	20	Iceland	53

Total reserves minus gold, % of total value, December 2000			
Euro-11	12.1	Other Asia	35.3
Other European Union	4.4	Middle East	5.9
Other industrial countries	25.8	Latin America	7.8
Other Europe	6.2	Africa	2.5

Interest rates

Central bank discount rates

%

End 2000

1	Belarus[a]	80.0	13	Macedonia	7.9
2	Armenia[b]	65.1	14	Cyprus	7.0
3	Romania	35.0	15	Iceland[d]	6.8
4	Bulgaria[b]	22.1	16	United Kingdom[a]	6.0
5	Poland	21.5	17	Croatia	5.9
6	Hungary[c]	14.5	18	Euro-11	5.8
7	Slovenia	11.9	18	Czech Republic	5.0
8	Albania	10.8	20	Denmark	4.8
9	Azerbaijan	10.0		Malta	4.8
10	Norway	9.0	22	Latvia	3.5
11	Slovakia	8.8	23	Switzerland	3.2
12	Greece	8.1	24	Sweden	2.0

1990

1	Poland	48.00	13	Belgium	10.50
2	Turkey	45.00		Norway	10.50
3	Ex-Yugoslavia	30.00	15	France	9.55
4	Hungary	22.00	16	Denmark	8.50
5	Iceland	21.00		Finland	8.50
6	Greece	19.00	18	Netherlands	7.25
7	Spain	14.71	19	Austria	6.50
8	Portugal	14.50		Cyprus	6.50
9	United Kingdom	14.09	21	Germany	6.00
10	Italy	12.50		Switzerland	6.00
11	Sweden	11.50	23	Malta	5.50
12	Ireland	11.25			

1980

1	Iceland	28.00	11	Spain	10.90
2	Turkey	26.00	12	Sweden	10.00
3	Greece	20.50	13	Finland	9.25
4	Portugal	18.00	14	Norway	9.00
5	Italy	16.50	15	Netherlands	8.00
6	United Kingdom	15.11	16	Germany	7.50
7	Ireland	14.00	17	Austria	6.75
8	Belgium	12.00	18	Cyprus	6.00
9	France	11.90	19	Malta	5.50
10	Denmark	11.00	20	Switzerland	3.00

a End-1997.
b End-1998.
c End-1999.
d Refinancing rate.

Money market rates

%

End 2000

1	Turkey	56.72	13	Greece[b]	6.20
2	Romania[b]	51.90	14	United Kingdom	5.71
3	Moldova	20.80	15	Denmark	4.98
4	Armenia	18.63	16	Malta[b]	4.89
5	Ukraine	18.34	17	Estonia	4.57
6	Poland	18.20	18	Euro-11	4.39
7	Georgia	18.17	19	Sweden	3.81
8	Iceland	11.61	20	Lithuania	3.60
9	Croatia	8.85	21	Switzerland	3.50
10	Czech Rep[a]	7.50	22	Bulgaria	3.02
11	Russia	7.10	23	Latvia	2.97
12	Slovenia	6.95			

1990

1	Turkey	47.60	13	Finland	7.50
2	Poland	41.70	14	Germany	7.07
3	Hungary	24.70	15	Italy	6.80
4	Greece	19.52	16	Ireland	6.29
5	Portugal	13.99	17	Belgium	6.13
6	United Kingdom	12.54	18	Luxembourg	6.00
7	Iceland	12.30	19	Cyprus	5.75
8	Spain	10.65	20	France	4.50
9	Sweden	9.93		Malta	4.50
10	Norway	9.68	22	Austria	3.41
11	Switzerland	8.28	23	Netherlands	3.31
12	Denmark	7.90			

1980

1	Iceland	38.80	12	Turkey	8.00
2	Portugal	19.00	13	Germany	7.95
3	Greece	14.50	14	Belgium	7.69
4	United Kingdom	14.13	15	France	7.25
5	Spain	13.05	16	Luxembourg	6.50
6	Italy	12.70	17	Netherlands	5.96
7	Ireland	12.00	18	Cyprus	5.75
8	Sweden	11.25	19	Austria	5.00
9	Denmark	10.80		Malta	5.00
10	Finland	9.00		Norway	5.00
11	Switzerland	8.80	22	Hungary	3.00

a Refinancing rate.
b Treasury bill rate.

Taxation

Total tax revenue
As % of GDP

1999

1	Sweden	52.1	11	Poland[a]	37.9
2	Denmark	50.6	12	Germany	37.7
3	Finland	46.5	13	Czech Republic	37.5
4	France	46.0	14	Hungary	37.0
5	Belgium	45.4	15	United Kingdom	36.6
6	Austria	44.3	16	Iceland	35.4
7	Italy	43.0	17	Spain	35.1
8	Luxembourg	42.1		Switzerland	35.1
9	Norway	41.8	19	Portugal	34.5
10	Netherlands	40.3		EU15[b]	41.9

1990

1	Sweden	55.6	11	Germany	36.7
2	Denmark	47.1	12	United Kingdom	36.3
3	Finland	44.9	13	Spain	34.4
4	Netherlands	44.6	14	Ireland	33.6
5	Luxembourg	43.9	15	Iceland	31.4
6	Belgium	43.9	16	Switzerland	30.9
7	France	43.0	17	Portugal	30.2
8	Norway	41.8	18	Greece	29.7
9	Austria	41.0	19	Turkey	20.0
10	Italy	38.9		EU15[b]	40.3

1980

1	Sweden	48.8	11	United Kingdom	35.1
2	Denmark	45.4	12	Ireland	32.6
3	Netherlands	45.2	13	Italy	30.4
4	Belgium	43.7	14	Iceland	29.2
5	Luxembourg	43.0	15	Switzerland	28.9
6	Norway	42.7	16	Portugal	24.7
7	France	41.7	17	Greece	24.3
8	Austria	40.3	18	Spain	23.9
9	Germany	38.2	19	Turkey	17.9
10	Finland	36.9		EU15[b]	36.9

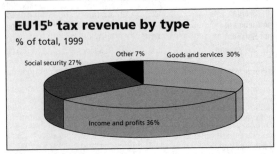

EU15[b] tax revenue by type
% of total, 1999

Social security 27%
Other 7%
Goods and services 30%
Income and profits 36%

a 1998   b Unweighted average.

=== Part V ===
LABOUR

The changing workforce

Force in numbers
Total no. in workforce, 1999, m

1	Russia	69.7	22	Bulgaria	3.1
2	Germany	39.9	23	Denmark	2.7
3	United Kingdom	29.2	24	Finland	2.6
4	Turkey	23.8		Slovakia	2.6
5	Italy	23.4	26	Norway	2.3
6	France	22.7	27	Georgia	2.0
	Ukraine	22.7	28	Lithuania	1.9
8	Spain	16.4	29	Croatia	1.8
9	Poland	15.4	30	Bosnia	1.7
10	Romania	10.8		Ireland	1.7
11	Netherlands	7.4		Moldova	1.7
12	Czech Republic	5.2	33	Albania	1.6
13	Portugal	4.8	34	Armenia	1.2
14	Belarus	4.7		Latvia	1.2
15	Belgium	4.4	36	Slovenia	1.0
	Greece	4.4	37	Macedonia	0.8
17	Sweden	4.3	38	Estonia	0.6
18	Hungary	4.1	39	Cyprus	0.4
19	Switzerland	4.0	40	Luxembourg	0.2
20	Austria	3.7	41	Iceland	0.1
	Azerbaijan	3.7		Malta	0.1

Most male workforce
Male % of workforce, 1999

1	Turkey	69	12	Armenia	58
2	Malta	68		Netherlands	58
3	Macedonia	63	14	Austria	57
4	Bosnia	62		Belgium	57
	Italy	62		Germany	57
6	Cyprus	61		Norway	57
	Greece	61	18	Czech Republic	56
	Luxembourg	61		Denmark	56
9	Spain	60		France	56
10	Albania	59		Hungary	56
	Ireland	59			

Most female workforce
Female % of workforce, 1999

1	Belarus	53	10	Iceland	47
2	Estonia	50		Lithuania	47
	Georgia	50	12	Finland	46
4	Azerbaijan	49		Romania	46
	Sweden	49		Slovakia	46
6	Bulgaria	48	15	Poland	45
	Norway	48		Switzerland	45
	Russia	48		United Kingdom	45
	Ukraine	48			

Total no. in workforce, 1985, m

1	Russia	76.2	22	Azerbaijan	2.9
2	Germany	38.1	23	Denmark	2.8
3	United Kingdom	27.8	24	Georgia	2.6
4	Ukraine	26.0		Slovakia	2.6
5	France	24.3	26	Finland	2.5
6	Italy	23.2	27	Croatia	2.2
7	Turkey	21.6	28	Moldova	2.1
8	Poland	19.0	29	Norway	2.0
9	Spain	15.0	30	Bosnia	1.8
10	Romania	10.9		Lithuania	1.8
11	Netherlands	6.2	32	Armenia	1.6
12	Czech Republic	5.4	33	Albania	1.4
13	Belarus	5.2		Latvia	1.4
14	Hungary	5.0	35	Ireland	1.3
15	Portugal	4.8	36	Slovenia	1.0
16	Bulgaria	4.6	37	Estonia	0.8
17	Sweden	4.3		Macedonia	0.8
18	Greece	4.0	39	Cyprus	0.3
19	Belgium	3.9	40	Luxembourg	0.2
20	Austria	3.5	41	Iceland	0.1
21	Switzerland	3.3		Malta	0.1

Male % of workforce, 1985

1	Malta	77	12	Macedonia	62
2	Ireland	70		Switzerland	62
3	Spain	69	14	Albania	61
4	Greece	68	15	Austria	59
5	Turkey	66		Croatia	59
6	Bosnia	65		Germany	59
	Italy	65		Portugal	59
	Luxembourg	65		United Kingdom	59
	Netherlands	65	20	France	58
10	Cyprus	64		Iceland	58
11	Belgium	63			

Female % of workforce, 1985

1	Estonia	50		Czech Republic	47
	Latvia	50		Finland	47
	Ukraine	50	13	Slovakia	46
4	Belarus	49		Slovenia	46
	Lithuania	49		Sweden	46
	Moldova	49	16	Azerbaijan	45
	Russia	49		Denmark	45
8	Armenia	48		Poland	45
	Georgia	48		Romania	45
10	Bulgaria	47	20	Hungary	44

What people do – and did

Agriculture
% of workforce employed in agriculture, latest

Male			Female		
1	Romania	37	1	Turkey	70
2	Turkey	33	2	Romania	44
3	Latvia	21	3	Greece	23
	Lithuania	21	4	Poland	19
5	Poland	19	5	Croatia	17
6	Greece	18	6	Latvia	16
7	Croatia	16		Lithuania	16
8	Russia	15	8	Portugal	15
9	Ireland	13	9	Slovenia	12
10	Estonia	12	10	Russia	8
	Portugal	12			
	Slovenia	12			

Industry
% of workforce employed in industry, latest

Male			Female		
1	Czech Republic	50	1	Slovenia	30
2	Slovakia	49	2	Czech Republic	29
3	Slovenia	47	3	Slovakia	27
4	Germany	45	4	Hungary	26
	Portugal	45	5	Portugal	25
6	Austria	42	6	Estonia	24
	Estonia	42		Romania	24
8	Hungary	41	8	Russia	23
	Poland	41	9	Croatia	22
10	Spain	40		Italy	22
				Lithuania	22

Services
% of workforce employed in services, latest

Male			Female		
1	Netherlands	63	1	Belgium	87
2	Belgium	61		Norway	87
3	United Kingdom	60		Sweden	87
4	Norway	59	4	Netherlands	86
	Switzerland	59		United Kingdom	86
6	Belarus	58	6	Belarus	85
	Denmark	58	7	Denmark	83
	Sweden	58		Switzerland	83
9	Italy	55	9	Finland	81
10	Greece	54		Spain	81

% of workforce employed in agriculture, 1980

Male			Female		
1	Albania	54	1	Turkey	88
2	Moldova	46	2	Albania	62
3	Turkey	45	3	Macedonia	47
4	Serbia	34		Serbia	47
5	Georgia	31	5	Romania	45
6	Macedonia	30	6	Azerbaijan	42
7	Belarus	29	7	Moldova	41
8	Azerbaijan	28	8	Greece	39
	Poland	28	9	Bosnia	37
10	Ukraine	26	10	Georgia	34

% of workforce employed in industry, 1980

Male			Female		
1	Czech Republic	67	1	Czech Republic	44
2	Germany	54	2	Armenia	38
3	Austria	51		Hungary	38
4	Estonia	50	4	Slovenia	37
	Romania	50		Russia	37
	Russia	50	6	Estonia	36
7	Latvia	49	7	Latvia	35
	Slovenia	49	8	Slovakia	34
9	Armenia	48	9	Belarus	33
10	Hungary	47		Germany	33
	Lithuania	47		Ukraine	33
12	Poland	46	12	Lithuania	30
	Ukraine	46	13	Romania	29
14	Bosnia	45	14	Poland	28
	Sweden	45	15	Croatia	27

% of workforce employed in services, 1980

Male			Female		
1	Belgium	50	1	Norway	80
	Netherlands	50	2	Sweden	79
	Norway	50	3	Denmark	76
4	France	48	4	Netherlands	74
	Slovakia	48	5	United Kingdom	72
6	Sweden	46	6	France	71
7	Denmark	44	7	Belgium	68
	United Kingdom	44	8	Finland	64
9	Austria	41	9	Austria	62
10	Germany	40	10	Germany	59
	Greece	40	11	Spain	56
	Italy	40	12	Slovakia	54
13	Croatia	39	13	Estonia	52
14	Finland	38	14	Latvia	50
15	Georgia	37		Russia	50

Unemployment

The size of the problem

Total no. unemployed, '000, 1999

1	Russia	9,581		16	Croatia	322
2	Germany	3,771		17	Hungary	290
3	Ukraine	3,576		18	Macedonia	285
4	France	3,257		19	Finland	261
5	Italy	2,861		20	Sweden	241
6	Poland	2,350		21	Austria	222
7	Spain	1,655			Netherlands	222
8	Turkey	1,557		23	Portugal	212
9	United Kingdom	1,299		24	Denmark	155
10	Romania	1,130		25	Lithuania	142
11	Czech Republic	521		26	Slovenia	121
12	Belgium	508		27	Latvia	110
13	Slovakia	487		28	Switzerland	99
14	Bulgaria	424		29	Belarus	98
15	Greece	420			Ireland	98

The burden on the economy

Public expenditure on unemployment benefit as % of GDP, 1999

1	Netherlands	2.81		11	Switzerland[b]	1.07
2	Ireland[a]	2.29		12	United Kingdom[b]	0.82
3	Germany	2.11		13	Portugal	0.67
4	Belgium	1.95		14	Poland	0.56
5	Finland	1.87		15	Italy	0.55
6	Sweden	1.61		16	Greece	0.50
7	France	1.48		17	Hungary	0.47
8	Denmark	1.43			Norway	0.47
9	Spain	1.41		19	Luxembourg[c]	0.42
10	Austria	1.16		20	Czech Republic	0.31

The EU's record

Unemployed as % of labour force

a 1996
b 1998 c 1997

The problem in proportion
% of workforce unemployed, 1999

1	Macedonia	45.0		16	Greece	10.0
2	Croatia	21.7		17	Estonia	9.6
3	Slovakia	18.7		18	Germany	9.5
4	Spain	15.5		19	Latvia	9.1
5	Russia	14.6		20	Lithuania	7.4
6	Ukraine	13.7		21	Hungary	7.1
7	Slovenia	13.6		22	Austria	6.7
8	Poland	13.0		23	Turkey	6.1
9	France	12.6		24	Ireland	5.8
	Italy	12.6		25	Denmark	5.6
11	Belgium	11.7			Sweden	5.6
12	Romania	11.5		27	Malta	4.8
13	Bulgaria	11.1		28	United Kingdom	4.4
14	Czech Republic	10.2		29	Portugal	4.3
	Finland	10.2		30	Cyprus	3.7

Looking back

% of workforce unemployed, 1990				*% of workforce unemployed, 1985*		
1	Macedonia	23.6		1	Macedonia	21.6
2	Spain	15.9		2	Spain	19.5
3	Ireland	13.3		3	Ireland	17.4
4	Italy	10.3		4	Belgium	13.6
5	Denmark	9.7		5	Netherlands	12.9
6	Albania	9.5		6	United Kingdom	11.8
7	France	8.9		7	Turkey	11.2
8	Croatia	8.0		8	Italy	10.3
9	Netherlands	7.5		9	France	10.2
10	Turkey	7.4		10	Denmark	9.1
11	Belgium	7.2		11	Portugal	8.5
12	United Kingdom	6.9		12	Malta	8.1
13	Greece	6.4		13	Greece	7.8
14	San Marino	5.5		14	Albania	6.7
15	Austria	5.4		15	Croatia	6.5
16	Norway	5.2		16	Finland	5.0
17	Germany	4.8		17	Austria	4.8
18	Slovenia	4.7		18	Cyprus	3.3
19	Portugal	4.6		19	Sweden	2.8
20	Malta	3.9		20	Norway	2.5
21	Poland	3.5		21	Luxembourg	1.7
22	Finland	3.4		22	Slovenia	1.4
23	Cyprus	1.8		23	Switzerland	1.0
	Iceland	1.8		24	Iceland	0.9
	Sweden	1.8				
26	Bulgaria	1.7				
	Hungary	1.7				
28	Slovakia	1.5				
29	Luxembourg	1.3				

What people earn

Skilled industrial worker
1999, $ '000

	Gross income	Net income
Switzerland	45.3	32.7
Denmark	34.9	18.8
Norway	32.4	21.7
Belgium	30.7	17.2
Luxembourg	29.0	24.9
Austria	28.9	19.3
United Kingdom	28.9	21.9
Sweden	28.6	18.8
Netherlands	26.8	17.9
Germany	26.1	16.6
Finland	24.5	16.4
Ireland	23.4	18.8
France	18.2	14.0
Italy	16.3	11.2
Cyprus	15.6	13.4
Turkey	13.5	10.0
Greece	13.0	10.4
Spain	12.9	10.8
Portugal	10.6	8.8
Poland	5.1	3.2
Hungary	3.1	2.2
Russia	0.5	0.4

School teacher
1999, $ '000

	Gross income	Net income
Switzerland	60.1	42.6
Luxembourg	44.8	36.3
United Kingdom	35.8	26.5
Germany	34.3	20.4
Denmark	33.6	18.5
Norway	29.4	19.7
Ireland	28.4	22.4
Cyprus	26.7	21.1
Netherlands	26.3	17.6
Sweden	26.0	17.9
Austria	24.5	17.9
Finland	24.3	16.3
Belgium	24.0	14.1
France	20.1	15.2
Spain	18.8	14.9
Italy	18.5	12.6
Portugal	16.3	12.5
Greece	13.8	10.9
Turkey	5.5	4.3
Poland	3.7	2.3
Hungary	2.4	1.8
Russia	0.4	0.4

Department manager
1999, $ '000

	Gross income	Net income
Switzerland	85.2	58.1
Belgium	72.3	31.1
Luxembourg	72.2	53.4
Netherlands	65.2	37.1
Austria	58.1	34.3
Germany	57.5	29.0
France	57.3	37.8
Norway	56.4	35.0
Denmark	53.1	26.5
Sweden	52.3	29.3
Finland	48.1	27.4
United Kingdom	47.0	33.8
Ireland	44.9	31.0
Greece	34.8	23.7
Turkey	34.1	21.5
Cyprus	33.2	23.6
Spain	26.0	19.7
Italy	25.7	15.9
Portugal	24.5	17.6
Poland	9.9	5.0
Hungary	7.2	4.0
Russia	2.1	1.9

Secretary
1999, $ '000

	Gross income	Net income
Switzerland	38.9	27.4
Luxembourg	35.0	23.8
Denmark	33.2	18.3
United Kingdom	27.6	20.7
Germany	26.0	15.7
Norway	25.8	16.8
Belgium	25.6	14.3
Austria	23.5	16.2
Sweden	22.9	15.6
Ireland	21.1	15.6
Netherlands	20.9	14.2
France	20.4	14.7
Finland	18.4	12.7
Cyprus	14.5	12.0
Italy	14.5	9.6
Spain	14.4	11.7
Greece	11.2	8.7
Portugal	9.3	7.3
Turkey	6.7	5.2
Poland	4.4	2.7
Hungary	3.1	2.1
Russia	1.2	1.1

Taxing matters

The taxman's take

Marginal rates of personal income taxes, 2000

	Top/bottom rates, %		Top/bottom rates, %
Finland[a]	70[b]/7	Poland	40/19
Sweden[a]	61/23	Portugal	40/14
Netherlands	60/5	Ukraine	40/1[d]
Belgium	55/25	United Kingdom	40/20
France	54/11	Albania	40/1[d]
Germany[a]	53/26	Azerbaijan[c]	40/1[d]
Norway[a]	52/45	Belarus	40/12
Switzerland[a]	52/4	Cyprus[c]	40/20
Austria	50/21	Spain	38/15
Moldova[c]	50/1[d]	Russia	37/12
Denmark	49/34	Croatia	35/20
Italy	48/17	Macedonia[c]	35/15
Luxembourg	46/6	Armenia	30/15
Ireland	45/23	Estonia	28/26
Romania[c]	45/21	Latvia	25/25
Greece	43/5	Georgia[c]	20/12
Hungary	41/19	Serbia & Montenegro[c]	20/1[d]
Czech Republic	40/10		

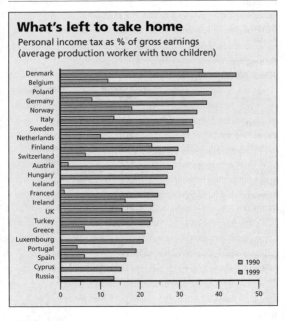

What's left to take home

Personal income tax as % of gross earnings
(average production worker with two children)

Denmark, Belgium, Poland, Germany, Norway, Italy, Sweden, Netherlands, Finland, Switzerland, Austria, Hungary, Iceland, France[d], Ireland, UK, Turkey, Greece, Luxembourg, Portugal, Spain, Cyprus, Russia

0   10   20   30   40   50

☐ 1990
☐ 1999

a Including local taxes.
b Level of ceiling limit on combined local and national income tax.
c 1998
d Theoretical low level.

Strikes

Time out
Working days not worked per 1,000 employees, all industries

1999			1988		
1	Greece	180.7	1	Spain	1,399
2	Malta[a]	114.0	2	Iceland	929
3	Spain	108.9	3	Greece	442
4	Romania	67.2	4	Turkey	264
5	Russia	56.1	5	Italy	226
6	Denmark[b]	31.7	6	Sweden	199
7	Sweden[b]	26.9	7	Ireland	177
8	Belgium[b]	19.8	8	United Kingdom	166
9	Turkey[b]	19.6	9	France	107
10	Portugal	11.6	10	Finland	88
11	Hungary	11.2	11	Portugal	67
12	United Kingdom	10.0	12	Belgium	66
13	Finland	9.5	13	Norway	45
	Italy	9.5	14	Denmark	41
15	Ireland	8.0	15	Austria	3
16	Netherlands[b]	5.8	16	Germany	2
17	France	5.6		Netherlands	2
18	Czech Republic	5.4	18	Luxembourg	0
19	Austria[b]	4.3		Switzerland	0
20	Poland	4.0			
21	Germany	2.5			
22	Switzerland	0.7			

Average working days lost
All industries per 1,000 employees

1993–99			1988–92		
1	Iceland	514	1	Spain	644
2	Spain	252	2	Greece	627
3	Denmark	228	3	Turkey	366
4	Finland	137	4	Iceland	341
5	Italy	123	5	Italy	248
6	Turkey	116	6	Finland	184
7	France	88	7	Ireland	165
8	Ireland	87	8	Sweden	102
9	Norway	75	9	United Kingdom	98
10	Greece	59	10	France	85
11	Russia	47	11	Norway	68
12	Sweden	42	12	Portugal	66
13	Romania	37	13	Belgium	46
14	Belgium	25	14	Denmark	33
15	Portugal	24	15	Germany	16
16	Netherlands	21	16	Netherlands	15
	United Kingdom	21	17	Austria	7
18	Poland	20	18	Luxembourg	0
19	Hungary	17		Switzerland	0
	EU average[c]	64		EU average	138

a 1996 b 1998 c Excluding Greece.

Work and play

Working hours
Average working hours, 1999

		Per week	Per year
1	Turkey	39.9	2,074
2	Hungary	38.2	1,988
3	Poland	36.0	1,870
4	Sweden	35.8	1,860
5	Switzerland	35.7	1,855
6	United Kingdom	35.3	1,833
7	Russia	35.1	1,824
8	Ireland	34.6	1,798
9	Luxembourg	34.4	1,790
10	Greece	34.2	1,780
11	Cyprus	33.8	1,760
12	Portugal	33.4	1,738
13	Italy	33.3	1,732
14	Norway	33.3	1,730
15	Spain	33.2	1,724
16	Finland	33.1	1,723
17	Belgium	32.9	1,712
18	Austria	32.7	1,699
19	Denmark	32.4	1,687
20	Netherlands	32.4	1,686
21	Germany	32.3	1,677
22	France	30.5	1,587

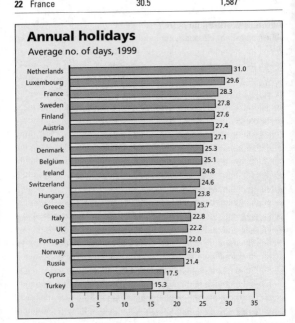

Annual holidays
Average no. of days, 1999

Netherlands	31.0
Luxembourg	29.6
France	28.3
Sweden	27.8
Finland	27.6
Austria	27.4
Poland	27.1
Denmark	25.3
Belgium	25.1
Ireland	24.8
Switzerland	24.6
Hungary	23.8
Greece	23.7
Italy	22.8
UK	22.2
Portugal	22.0
Norway	21.8
Russia	21.4
Cyprus	17.5
Turkey	15.3

Part VI

BUSINESS AND FINANCE

Agriculture: leading producers

Wheat

'000 tonnes
1999

1	France	37,050
2	Russia	30,995
3	Germany	19,615
4	Turkey	18,000
5	United Kingdom	14,870
6	Ukraine	13,585
7	Poland	9,051
8	Italy	7,743
9	Spain	5,084
10	Romania	4,658
11	Denmark	4,471
12	Czech Republic	4,028
13	Hungary	2,638
14	Bulgaria	2,637
15	Serbia & Montenegro	2,167
16	Greece	2,064
17	Sweden	1,659
18	Belgium & Lux	1,575
19	Austria	1,416
20	Slovakia	1,207

Coarse grains[a]

'000 tonnes
1999

1	France	27,663
2	Germany	24,845
3	Russia	22,406
4	Poland	16,699
5	Romania	12,372
6	Spain	12,054
7	Italy	11,896
8	Ukraine	10,304
9	Turkey	9,765
10	Hungary	8,761
11	United Kingdom	7,175
12	Serbia & Montenegro	6,567
13	Denmark	4,310
14	Austria	3,390
15	Sweden	3,272
16	Czech Republic	3,005
17	Belarus	2,693
18	Finland	2,625
19	Bulgaria	2,488
20	Greece	2,418

Oil crops[b]

'000 tonnes
1999

1	France	2,535
2	Russia	1,840
3	Germany	1,783
4	Italy	1,204
5	Ukraine	1,195
6	Spain	1,043
7	Turkey	737
	United Kingdom	737
9	Romania	613
10	Greece	558
11	Hungary	474
12	Czech Republic	473
13	Poland	438
14	Bulgaria	256
15	Serbia & Montenegro	174
16	Denmark	157
17	Slovakia	146
18	Portugal	133
19	Moldova	117
20	Austria	112

Sugar beets

'000 tonnes
1999

1	France	32,919
2	Germany	27,578
3	Turkey	20,000
4	Russia	15,227
5	Ukraine	13,890
6	Italy	13,326
7	Poland	12,564
8	United Kingdom	10,328
9	Spain	8,162
10	Belgium & Lux	7,112
11	Netherlands	5,505
12	Denmark	3,543
13	Austria	3,217
14	Hungary	2,934
15	Czech Republic	2,691
16	Greece	2,389
17	Serbia & Montenegro	2,318
18	Romania	1,415
19	Slovakia	1,405
20	Moldova	1,005

a Barley, maize, oats, rye, millet and sorghum.
b Sunflower seed, rapeseed, olives and soyabeans.

Fruit

'000 tonnes
1999

1	Italy	18,428
2	Spain	15,447
3	France	11,701
4	Turkey	10,389
5	Germany	5,344
6	Greece	4,303
7	Russia	2,413
8	Poland	2,386
9	Romania	2,059
10	Portugal	1,942
11	Hungary	1,404
12	Serbia & Montenegro	1,335
13	Austria	1,039
14	Ukraine	1,036
15	Belgium & Lux	809
16	Netherlands	715
17	Bulgaria	664
18	Switzerland	567
19	Croatia	565
20	Czech Republic	521

Vegetables

'000 tonnes
1999

1	Turkey	21,777
2	Italy	15,367
3	Russia	12,706
4	Spain	12,092
5	France	8,003
6	Ukraine	5,747
7	Poland	5,726
8	Greece	4,285
9	Romania	3,903
10	Netherlands	3,596
11	Germany	3,219
12	United Kingdom	2,983
13	Portugal	2,478
14	Hungary	2,007
15	Bulgaria	1,766
16	Belgium & Lux	1,719
17	Serbia & Montenegro	1,255
18	Albania	640
19	Austria	613
20	Bosnia	609

Meat

'000 tonnes
1999

1	France	6,608
2	Germany	6,398
3	Spain	4,962
4	Russia	4,291
5	Italy	4,156
6	United Kingdom	3,596
7	Poland	3,030
8	Netherlands	2,954
9	Denmark	2,006
10	Belgium & Lux	1,700
11	Ukraine	1,695
12	Turkey	1,243
13	Hungary	1,131
14	Romania	1,130
15	Ireland	1,089
16	Serbia & Montenegro	1,031
17	Czech Republic	829
18	Austria	818
19	Portugal	706
20	Belarus	653

Milk

'000 tonnes
1999

1	Russia	32,272
2	Germany	28,356
3	France	25,632
4	United Kingdom	15,017
5	Ukraine	13,362
6	Poland	12,273
7	Italy	12,236
8	Netherlands	10,895
9	Turkey	10,060
10	Spain	6,922
11	Ireland	5,121
12	Romania	4,795
13	Belarus	4,762
14	Denmark	4,530
15	Switzerland	3,837
16	Austria	3,373
17	Sweden	3,299
18	Belgium & Lux	3,294
19	Czech Republic	2,848
20	Finland	2,475

Industry: who makes what

Cars
Production, '000s, 1999

1	Germany	5,912	11	Netherlands	266
2	France	2,576	12	Portugal	255
3	Spain	2,305	13	Turkey	237
4	United Kingdom	1,822	14	Romania	105
5	Italy	1,474	15	Austria	89
6	Russia	956	16	Slovenia	81
7	Poland	622	17	Hungary	67
8	Sweden	362	18	Finland	32
9	Czech Republic	337		Slovakia	30
10	Belgium	272	20	Ukraine	30

Commercial vehicles
Production, '000s, 1999

1	Spain	648	10	Portugal	92
2	Germany	401	11	Poland	55
3	France	341	12	Croatia	40
4	Italy	276	13	Czech Republic	37
5	United Kingdom	217	14	Netherlands	30
6	Russia	200	15	Romania	28
7	Belgium	122	16	Belarus	13
	Sweden	122	17	Austria	10
9	Turkey	115	18	Ukraine	8

Steel
Production, m tonnes, 2000

1	Russia	57.6	11	Czech Republic	6.2
2	Germany	46.4	12	Netherlands	5.7
3	Ukraine	31.3	13	Austria	5.6
4	Italy	26.5	14	Sweden	5.2
5	France	21.0	15	Romania	4.7
6	Spain	16.0	16	Finland	4.1
7	United Kingdom	15.1	17	Slovakia	3.7
8	Turkey	14.3	18	Bulgaria	2.0
9	Belgium	11.6	19	Hungary	1.8
10	Poland	10.6	20	Belarus	1.5

Shipbuilding
Completions, gross tonnage '000, 2000

1	Germany	975	12	United Kingdom	104
2	Poland	626	13	Russia	67
3	Italy	537	14	Turkey	64
4	Spain	460	15	Portugal	47
5	Denmark	373	16	Sweden	33
6	Croatia	342	17	Bulgaria	21
7	Netherlands	296	18	Slovakia	15
8	Finland	223	19	Czech Republic	11
9	France	200	20	Lithuania	6
10	Romania	135	21	Malta	5
11	Norway	109		Ukraine	5

Inventiveness and investment

Patents granted
Average annual number, 1998

1	Germany	19,271	11	Finland	964
2	Russia	19,215	12	Italy	743
3	France	12,068	13	Belgium	732
4	United Kingdom	4,838	14	Norway	455
5	Netherlands	2,972	15	Ireland	395
6	Sweden	2,400	16	Czech Republic	291
7	Spain	1,684	17	Denmark	276
8	Austria	1,337	18	Hungary	263
9	Switzerland	1,313	19	Slovenia	210
10	Poland	1,174	20	Slovakia	130

Spending on research and development
As % of GDP, 1998

1	Sweden	3.67	11	Austria	1.80
2	Finland	3.09	12	Norway	1.69
3	Switzerland	2.73	13	Ireland	1.61
4	Germany	2.38	14	Slovenia	1.50
5	France	2.19	15	Czech Republic	1.29
6	Denmark	1.97	16	Russia	1.05
7	Netherlands	1.94	17	Italy	1.04
8	Iceland	1.88	18	Spain	0.89
9	Belgium	1.84	19	Poland	0.75
10	United Kingdom	1.83	20	Slovakia	0.68

Nobel prizes[a]
No. awarded in physics, chemistry, physiology or medicine and economics 1901–2000[b]

1	United Kingdom	67	6	Netherlands	10
2	Germany	46	7	Austria	9
3	France	21		Russia	9
4	Sweden	18	9	Denmark	8
5	Switzerland	15	10	Italy	7

Investment in telecommunications
As % of GDP, 1998

1	Czech Republic	1.83	12	Netherlands	0.55
2	Greece	1.30	13	Denmark	0.52
3	Hungary	1.15	14	Sweden	0.50
4	Poland	0.85	15	Finland	0.49
5	Portugal	0.83	16	Austria	0.44
6	Iceland	0.81	17	Spain	0.41
7	Slovenia	0.78	18	France	0.36
8	Ireland	0.71	19	Switzerland	0.34
9	Luxembourg	0.61	20	Italy	0.33
10	Norway	0.59	21	Turkey	0.30
11	United Kingdom	0.57	22	Russia	0.28

a Prizes by country of residence at time awarded. When prizes have been shared in the same field, one credit has been given to each country.
b Economics since 1969.

Service sectors

Working at it
% of labour force in service sector, 1999

#	Country	%	#	Country	%
1	Norway	73.4	19	Greece[a]	59.2
2	Netherlands[a]	72.8	20	Hungary	58.9
3	Sweden	72.2	21	Russia	58.8
	United Kingdom	72.2	22	Latvia	58.6
5	Denmark[a]	69.7	23	Czech Republic	54.9
6	Switzerland	69.5	24	Slovakia	54.2
7	France[b]	68.7	25	Lithuania	52.9
8	Luxembourg[a]	66.4	26	Croatia	52.8
9	Finland	66.1	27	Slovenia	51.2
10	Belgium[a]	65.8	28	Portugal[a]	50.8
11	Iceland[a]	65.6	29	Poland[a]	48.7
12	Germany	63.7	30	Ukraine[a]	46.9
13	Austria	63.4	31	Bulgaria	44.3
14	Cyprus[c]	63.0	32	Belarus[a]	40.0
15	Ireland	62.5	33	Moldova	37.5
16	Italy	62.1	34	Turkey	33.7
17	Spain	61.9	35	Romania	30.7
18	Estonia	59.4			

% of labour force in trade, restaurants and hotels, 1999

#	Country	%
1	Cyprus[c]	26.2
2	Switzerland	23.5
3	Greece[a]	23.1
4	Spain	22.5
5	Austria	21.4
6	Luxembourg[a]	21.2
7	Ireland	20.5
8	Netherlands[a]	20.1
9	United Kingdom	19.8
10	Italy	19.4
11	Portugal[a]	18.9
12	Croatia	18.2
	Norway	18.2

% of labour force in finance and business services, 1999

#	Country	%
1	United Kingdom	15.2
2	Switzerland	15.1
3	Netherlands[a]	14.8
4	Sweden	13.1
5	Ireland	12.3
6	Finland	11.5
7	Denmark[a]	11.4
8	Norway	11.2
9	Germany	11.1
10	France[b]	10.6
11	Austria	10.2
12	Iceland[a]	9.6
	Italy	9.6

% of labour force in transport and communication, 1999

#	Country	%
1	Russia	9.1
2	Estonia	8.9
3	Latvia	8.6
4	Hungary	8.1
5	Czech Republic	7.8
	Slovakia	7.8
7	Bulgaria	7.6
8	Norway	7.5
9	Finland	7.3
	Iceland[a]	7.3
	Ukraine[a]	7.3

% of labour force in social and personal services, 1999

#	Country	%
1	Sweden	37.0
2	Norway	36.5
3	Denmark[a]	35.3
4	France[b]	35.0
5	Belgium[a]	32.6
6	Russia	32.1
7	Finland	32.0
8	Netherlands[a]	31.9
9	Iceland[a]	31.8
10	Ukraine[a]	30.7
	United Kingdom	30.7

a 1998 b 1994 c 1995

Tourism receipts

$bn, 1999			*$ per head of population, 1999*	
1	Spain	32.9	1 Cyprus	2,942
2	France	31.7	2 Malta	1,776
3	Italy	28.4	3 Austria	1,386
4	United Kingdom	21.0	4 Switzerland	1,036
5	Germany	16.8	5 Ireland	894
6	Austria	11.1	6 Slovenia	838
7	Greece	8.8	7 Greece	835
8	Russia	7.8	Spain	835
9	Switzerland	7.4	9 Denmark	695
10	Netherlands	7.1	10 Croatia	556
11	Poland	6.1	11 France	521
12	Turkey	5.2	12 Portugal	517
13	Portugal	5.2	13 Norway	495
14	Sweden	3.9	14 Italy	466
15	Denmark	3.7	15 Netherlands	449
16	Hungary	3.4	16 Sweden	438
17	Ireland	3.3	17 Estonia	400
18	Czech Republic	3.0	18 United Kingdom	355
19	Croatia	2.5	19 Hungary	336
20	Norway	2.2	20 Czech Republic	298

Advertising expenditure
$ per head of population, 1999

1	Switzerland	357	11 Luxembourg	160
2	Norway	311	12 France	153
3	United Kingdom	254	13 Cyprus	150
4	Denmark	233	14 Ireland	149
5	Germany	231	15 Greece	136
6	Netherlands	229	16 Portugal	134
7	Sweden	210	17 Slovenia	129
8	Austria	199	18 Spain	120
9	Finland	197	19 Italy	118
10	Belgium	162	20 Hungary	71

Number of lawyers
Per 100,000 population, 1999

1	Gibraltar	362	13 Belgium	119
2	Spain	237	14 Italy	99
3	Greece	217	15 Bulgaria	90
4	United Kingdom	202	16 Switzerland	85
5	Liechtenstein[a]	177	17 Hungary	79
6	Portugal	172	Norway	79
7	Iceland	168	19 Denmark	77
8	Luxembourg	167	Monaco	77
9	Cyprus	156	21 Netherlands	66
10	Malta	145	22 France	60
11	Ireland	141	23 Czech Republic	58
12	Germany	125	24 Turkey	54

a 1996

Big business

Europe's biggest companies
By sales, 1999

	Company	Country	Sales, $bn	Profits/ losses, $bn
1	DaimlerChrysler	Germany	159.99	6.13
2	Royal Dutch/Shell Group	UK/Netherlands	105.37	8.58
3	AXA	France	87.65	2.16
4	BP Amoco	UK	83.57	5.01
5	Volkswagen	Germany	80.07	0.87
6	Siemens	Germany	75.34	1.77
7	Allianz	Germany	74.18	2.38
8	ING Group	Netherlands	62.49	5.25
9	Deutsche Bank	Germany	58.59	2.69
10	Assicurazioni Generali	Italy	53.72	0.87
11	E.ON	Germany	52.23	2.85
12	Fiat	Italy	51.33	0.38
13	Nestlé	Switzerland	49.69	3.14
14	Credit Suisse	Switzerland	49.36	3.48
15	Metro	Germany	46.66	0.30
16	Total Fina Elf	France	44.99	1.62
17	Vivendi	France	44.40	1.53
18	Unilever	UK/Netherlands	43.68	2.95
19	Fortis	Belgium	43.66	2.47
20	Prudential	Netherlands	42.22	0.88
21	CGNU	UK	41.97	0.83
22	Peugeot	France	40.33	0.78
23	Renault	France	40.10	0.57
24	BNP Paribas	France	40.10	1.58
25	Zurich Financial Services	Switzerland	39.96	3.26
26	Carrefour	France	39.86	0.81
27	HSBC Holdings	UK	39.35	5.41
28	ABN Amro Holding	Netherlands	38.82	2.74
29	Munich Re Group	Germany	38.40	1.21
30	RWE Group	Germany	38.36	1.30
31	Elf Aquitaine	France	37.92	2.21
32	Deutsche Telekom	Germany	37.84	1.34
33	BMW	Germany	36.70	-2.65
34	Koninklijke Ahold	Netherlands	35.80	0.80
35	Électricité De France	France	34.15	0.76
36	ENI	Italy	34.09	3.05
37	Suez Lyonnaise des Eaux	France	33.56	1.55
38	Royal Philips Electronics	Netherlands	33.56	1.92
39	Crédit Agricole	France	32.92	2.53
40	Thyssen Krupp	Germany	32.80	0.29

Note: The e-business readiness rankings opposite, compiled by the Economist Intelligence Unit, cover 60 countries. They consider a number of factors, primarily the general business environment (based on 70 indicators, including the strength of the economy, the outlook for political stability, the regulatory climate, taxation policies and openness to trade and investment); and connectivity (taking into account criteria such as the state of the telephone network, factors affecting Internet access, dial-up costs and literacy rates).

Europe's biggest employers
1999

	Company	Country	No. of employees, '000
1	DaimlerChrysler	Germany	466.9
2	Siemens	Germany	443.0
3	OAO Gazprom	Russia	386.9
4	Volkswagen	Germany	306.3
5	La Poste	France	306.0
6	Carrefour	France	297.3
7	Vivendi	France	275.0
8	Sodexho Alliance	France	270.0
9	Deutsche Post	Germany	264.4
10	Unilever	UK/Netherlands	255.0
11	Deutsche Bahn	Germany	241.6
12	Nestlé	Switzerland	230.9
13	Royal Philips Electronics	Netherlands	229.3
14	Suez Lyonnaise des Eaux	France	222.0
15	Fiat	Italy	221.0
16	SNCF	France	210.9
17	Koninklijke Ahold	Netherlands	209.0
18	British Post Office	United Kingdom	201.3
19	Deutsche Telekom	Germany	195.8
20	Robert Bosch	Germany	194.9

E-business readiness
Scores (out of 10), June 2000 (see note opposite)

		General business environment	Connectivity	E-business readiness
1	United Kingdom	8.76	9	8.10
2	Norway	8.06	9	8.07
3	Sweden	8.53	9	7.98
4	Finland	8.64	9	7.83
5	Denmark	8.41	9	7.70
6	Netherlands	8.79	9	7.69
7	Switzerland	8.67	8	7.67
8	Germany	8.50	8	7.51
9	Ireland	8.61	8	7.28
10	France	8.28	8	7.26
11	Austria	7.98	8	7.22
12	Belgium	8.29	8	7.10
13	Italy	7.89	8	6.74
14	Spain	8.04	8	6.43
15	Portugal	7.66	7	6.21
16	Greece	7.18	7	5.85
17	Czech Republic	7.03	6	5.71
18	Hungary	7.24	6	5.49
19	Poland	7.11	5	5.05
20	Slovakia	6.49	5	4.88
21	Turkey	6.02	5	4.51
22	Russia	5.47	5	3.84
23	Bulgaria	5.89	5	3.38

Banking

Europe's biggest banks[a]
By capital, $m, 1999

	Bank	Country	Capital
1	HSBC Holdings	United Kingdom	28,533
2	Crédit Agricole Groupe	France	23,335
3	BNP Paribas	France	19,939
4	UBS	Switzerland	18,460
5	ABN Amro Bank	Netherlands	17,817
6	Credit Suisse Group	Switzerland	17,668
7	Deutsche Bank	Germany	17,418
8	HypoVereinsbank	Germany	14,708
9	Banco Bilbao Vizcaya Argentaria	Spain	14,481
10	National Westminster Bank	United Kingdom	14,446
11	Barclays Bank	United Kingdom	14,055
12	ING Bank	Netherlands	13,964
13	Lloyds TSB Group	United Kingdom	13,674
14	Rabobank Nederland	Netherlands	13,067
15	Dresdner Bank	Germany	12,968
16	Banco Santander Central Hispano	Spain	12,514
17	Société Générale	France	12,256
18	Banca Intesa	Italy	12,249
19	Commerzbank	Germany	11,201
20	Fortis Bank	Belgium	11,057
21	Halifax	United Kingdom	10,002
22	Groupe Caisse d'Epargne	France	9,798
23	Crédit Mutual	France	9,690
24	Abbey National	United Kingdom	9,489
25	Westdeutsche Landesbank Girozentrale	Germany	8,790
26	MeritaNordbanken	Finland	8,246
27	UniCredito Italiano	Italy	7,752
28	Crédit Lyonnais	France	7,651
29	Royal Bank of Scotland	United Kingdom	7,583
30	SanPaolo IMI	Italy	7,540
31	Groupe Banques Populaires	France	7,228
32	KBC Bank	Belgium	6,959
33	Bayerische Landesbank	Germany	6,781
34	Dexia	European Union	6,074
35	Bank of Scotland	United Kingdom	5,654
36	Banca di Roma	Italy	5,352
37	DG Bank Deutsche Genossen	Germany	5,306
38	Standard Chartered	United Kingdom	4,891
39	Landesbank Baden-Württemberg	Germany	4,822
40	Bank Austria	Austria	4,569
41	C. de A. y Pen. de Barcelona	Spain	4,275
42	Bankgesellschaft Berlin	Germany	4,235
43	Den Danske Bank	Denmark	4,089
44	Skandinaviska Enskilda Banken	Sweden	4,034
45	Norddeutsche Landesbank Girozentrale	Germany	3,977
46	Nykredit Group	Denmark	3,858

a Does not allow for mergers since 1999.
Note: capital is essentially equity and reserves.

By assets, $m, 1999

	Bank	Country	Assets
1	Deutsche Bank	Germany	843,761
2	BNP Paribas	France	701,853
3	UBS	Switzerland	613,637
4	HSBC Holdings	United Kingdom	569,139
5	HypoVereinsbank	Germany	505,559
6	ABN Amro Bank	Netherlands	459,994
7	Credit Suisse Group	Switzerland	451,829
8	Crédit Agricole Groupe	France	441,524
9	Société Générale	France	408,420
10	Barclays Bank	United Kingdom	398,825
11	Dresdner Bank	Germany	398,687
12	Westdeutsche Landesbank Girozentrale	Germany	390,722
13	Commerzbank	Germany	373,766
14	ING Bank	Netherlands	351,211
15	Fortis Bank	Belgium	330,640
16	Banca Intesa	Italy	305,354
17	National Westminster Bank	United Kingdom	286,811
18	Rabobank Nederland	Netherlands	282,514
19	Bayerische Landesbank	Germany	273,487
20	Crédit Mutual	France	267,039

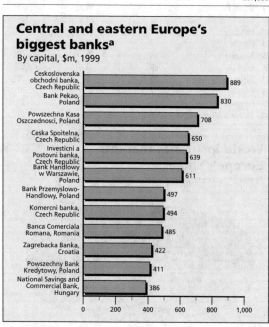

Central and eastern Europe's biggest banks[a]

By capital, $m, 1999

Bank	Capital
Ceskoslovenska obchodni banka, Czech Republic	889
Bank Pekao, Poland	830
Powszechna Kasa Oszczednosci, Poland	708
Ceska Spoitelna, Czech Republic	650
Investicni a Postovni banka, Czech Republic	639
Bank Handlowy w Warszawie, Poland	611
Bank Przemyslowo-Handlowy, Poland	497
Komercni banka, Czech Republic	494
Banca Comerciala Romana, Romania	485
Zagrebacka Banka, Croatia	422
Powszechny Bank Kredytowy, Poland	411
National Savings and Commercial Bank, Hungary	386

a Excluding Russia.

Insurance

Who buys most insurance?
Premiums per person, 1999, $

		Non-life	Life	Total
1	Switzerland	1,729	2,914	4,643
2	United Kingdom	742	2,503	3,244
3	Ireland	643	1,812	2,455
4	Netherlands	1,009	1,397	2,406
5	Finland	464	1,748	2,213
6	France	689	1,392	2,081
7	Denmark	789	1,282	2,071
8	Sweden	518	1,335	1,853
9	Belgium	672	1,045	1,717
10	Germany	914	762	1,676
11	Luxembourg	1,055	585	1,640
12	Norway	830	769	1,599
13	Austria	795	631	1,426
14	Italy	495	658	1,153
15	Cyprus	236	818	1,054
16	Spain	410	455	864
17	Iceland	743	46	789
18	Portugal	294	388	682
19	Slovenia	301	69	369
20	Greece	110	135	245
21	Czech Republic	120	56	175
22	Croatia	115	22	136
23	Hungary	74	50	124
24	Poland	79	38	117
25	Slovakia	68	38	106
26	Latvia	60	8	67
27	Turkey	29	6	35
28	Russia	17	10	27
29	Bulgaria	19	2	21
30	Serbia & Montenegro	19	0	19

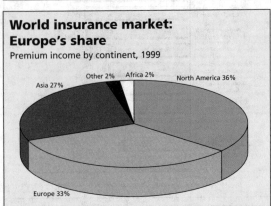

World insurance market: Europe's share
Premium income by continent, 1999

Other 2% Africa 2% North America 36%
Asia 27%
Europe 33%

More premium comparisons
Insurance premiums as % of GDP, 1999

		Non-life	Life	Total
1	United Kingdom	3.05	10.30	13.35
2	Switzerland	4.78	8.06	12.84
3	Ireland	2.57	7.26	9.83
4	Netherlands	4.05	5.60	9.65
5	Cyprus	2.00	6.92	8.92
6	Finland	1.86	7.02	8.88
7	France	2.82	5.70	8.52
8	Belgium	2.91	4.52	7.43
9	Sweden	1.92	4.96	6.88
10	Germany	3.55	2.96	6.51
11	Denmark	2.41	3.92	6.33
12	Portugal	2.71	3.58	6.29
13	Spain	2.71	3.01	5.72
14	Italy	2.44	3.24	5.68
15	Austria	3.09	2.45	5.54
16	Norway	2.41	2.23	4.64
17	Luxembourg	2.39	1.33	3.72
18	Slovenia	2.99	0.68	3.67
19	Czech Republic	2.32	1.08	3.40
20	Serbia & Montenegro	3.05	0.02	3.07
21	Croatia	2.54	0.48	3.02
22	Poland	1.97	0.96	2.93
23	Slovakia	1.86	1.05	2.91
24	Latvia	2.32	0.29	2.61
25	Hungary	1.55	1.05	2.60
26	Iceland	2.36	0.15	2.51
27	Russia	1.34	0.78	2.12
28	Greece	0.93	1.14	2.07
29	Bulgaria	1.24	0.12	1.36
30	Turkey	1.03	0.23	1.26

Europe's largest insurance companies[a]
Revenues, 1999, $bn

1	Axa	France	87.65
2	Allianz	Germany	74.18
3	ING Group	Netherlands	62.49
4	Assicurazioni Generali	Italy	53.72
5	Prudential	United Kingdom	42.22
6	CGU	United Kingdom	41.97
7	Zurich Financial Services	Switzerland	39.96
8	Munich Re	Germany	38.40
9	Royal & Sun Alliance	United Kingdom	26.02
10	CNP Assurances	France	26.80
11	Aegon	Netherlands	23.87
12	Norwich Union	United Kingdom	19.70
13	Swiss Reinsurance	Switzerland	19.64
14	Skandia Group	Sweden	19.29

a Takes no account of subsequent mergers.

Mergers and acquisitions

Activity in the EU

Mergers and acquisitions, 1998–99

Target	Targeter/Bidder, %		
	Own country	*EU15*	*Outside EU*
Austria	30.9	38.8	30.3
Belgium	32.3	46.1	21.6
Denmark	32.7	40.9	26.4
Finland	52.9	28.7	18.4
France	42.1	30.6	27.3
Germany	48.3	25.8	25.9
Greece	71.9	10.6	17.5
Ireland	27.9	42.6	29.5
Italy	44.7	31.5	23.8
Luxembourg	4.9	68.1	27.0
Netherlands	32.4	38.8	28.8
Portugal	48.5	31.6	19.9
Spain	58.7	21.6	19.7
Sweden	37.1	33.5	29.4
United Kingdom	59.1	14.7	26.2
EU15	55.8	14.8	29.4

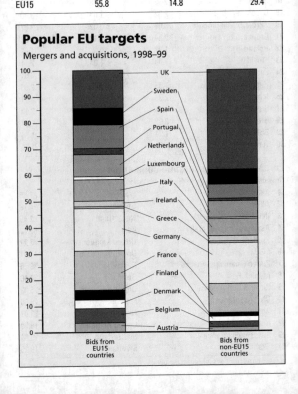

Popular EU targets

Mergers and acquisitions, 1998–99

UK
Sweden
Spain
Portugal
Netherlands
Luxembourg
Italy
Ireland
Greece
Germany
France
Finland
Denmark
Belgium
Austria

Bids from EU15 countries

Bids from non-EU15 countries

The big ones

Main EU mergers, demergers and acquisitions, 1995–May 2001

	Date	Target	Bidder	Amount, $m
1	Nov-99	Mannesmann	Vodafone AirTouch	202,785
2	Jan-00	SmithKline Beecham	Glaxo Wellcome	77,255
3	Jul-99	Elf Aquitaine	Total Fina	55,340
4	May-00	Orange (Mannesmann)	France Telecom	45,967
5	Nov-99	National Westminster Bank	Royal Bank of Scotland Grp	38,525
6	Oct-99	Orange	Mannesmann	35,320
7	Feb-99	Telecom Italia	Ing C Olivetti & Co	34,758
8	Dec-98	Astra	Zeneca Group	31,787
9	May-99	Hoechst	Rhone-Poulenc SA	28,526
10	Oct-99	Ente Nazionale per l'Energia	Investors	18,734
11	Mar-00	Seat Pagine Gialle	Tin.it	18,694
12	May-97	Guinness	Grand Metropolitan	18,290
13	Dec-00	Granada Compass-Hospitality	Shareholders	17,915
14	Sep-99	VIAG	VEBA	16,275
15	Aug-99	Promodès	Carrefour	15,837
16	Oct-95	Lloyds Bank	TSB Group	15,316
17	Jul-00	Airtel	Vodafone AirTouch	14,365
18	Jun-00	Canal Plus	Vivendi	14,112
19	Aug-00	Viag Interkom	British Telecommunications	13,813
20	Jul-99	One 2 One	Deutsche Telekom	13,629
21	Jan-95	Wellcome	Glaxo Holdings	13,408
22	Mar-99	Paribas	BNP	13,201
23	Jan-99	Marconi Electronic Systems	British Aerospace	12,863
24	May-99	Banca Commerciale Italiana	Banca Intesa	12,791
25	May-98	Generale de Banque	Fortis	12,299

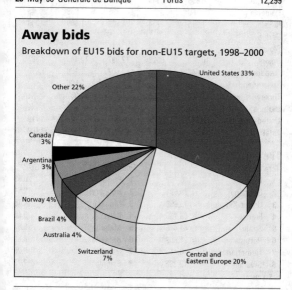

Away bids

Breakdown of EU15 bids for non-EU15 targets, 1998–2000

- United States 33%
- Other 22%
- Canada 3%
- Argentina 3%
- Norway 4%
- Brazil 4%
- Australia 4%
- Switzerland 7%
- Central and Eastern Europe 20%

Privatisation

How much has been sold

Privatisation proceeds (public offers and private sales), $m

	1988–95	1996	1997	1998	1999
Armenia	...	...	80	30	...
Austria	3,188	948	1,710	2,940	301
Belgium	4,120	680	985	2,271	9
Bulgaria	102	26	386	128	252
Croatia	13	140	...	222	850
Czech Republic	2,231	...	72	216	1,175
Denmark	4,263	185	3,200	...	...
Estonia	0	22	80	25	252
Finland	1,825	1,105	743	2,060	3,685
France	27,739	4,989	7,454	16,768	9,805
Germany	39,662	14,796	6,418	2,611	16,204
Greece	1,216	530	1,359	2,401	3,638
Hungary	4,995	1,004	2,116	315	638
Iceland	...	...	...	102	137
Ireland	1,264	290	...	...	4,183
Italy	20,277	8,189	32,396	16,490	31,410
Latvia	160	16	235	...	...
Lithuania	29	...	9	519	79
Macedonia	...	...	...	...	58
Malta	...	...	...	91	250
Monaco	...	...	...	...	118
Netherlands	11,264	1,040	6	...	6,105
Norway	719	651	...	...	906
Poland	2,253	1,061	2,319	2,334	3,280
Portugal	6,898	2,945	4,944	4,351	2,814
Romania	60	...	396	969	43
Russia	1,215	734	4,102	1,409	200
Serbia	0	...	15	...	...
Slovakia	113	16	11	...	...
Spain	10,099	2,523	12,997	12,440	3,387
Sweden	8,840	1,338	907	180	1,970
Switzerland	...	...	...	5,500	...
Turkey	1,584	255	293	1,967	...
Ukraine	25	...	...	...	...
United Kingdom	63,347	9,534	234	64	719
Total	**217,501**	**53,017**	**83,467**	**76,403**	**92,468**

The biggest privatisers

Total 1988–99, $m

1	Italy	108,762
2	Germany	79,691
3	United Kingdom	73,898
4	France	66,755
5	Spain	41,446
6	Portugal	21,952
7	Netherlands	18,415
8	Sweden	13,235

Total 1988–99, as % of 1998 GDP

1	Portugal	20.63
2	Hungary	19.84
3	Monaco[a]	14.75
4	Italy	9.40
5	Malta	8.97
6	Bulgaria	8.85
7	Ireland	8.28
8	Estonia	7.73

a Estimate.

Big ones
Biggest European privatisations, $bn, 1988–2000

1	Italy	Enel	17.46
2	Italy	Telecom Italia	14.90
3	Germany	Deutsche Telekom 1	13.30
4	Germany	Deutsche Telekom 2	11.80
5	France	France Telecom	10.20
6	United Kingdom	BritishTelecom (BT2)	9.99
7	United Kingdom	BritishTelecom (BT3)	8.06
8	Italy	ENI 3	7.80
9	Spain	Endesa	7.60
10	Italy	ENI 4	7.30
11	France	France Telecom	7.10
12	Sweden	Telia	7.00
13	France	Elf Aquitaine	6.82
14	Germany	Vereinigte Energiewerke	5.70
15	Italy	Finmeccanica	5.50
	Switzerland	Swisscom	5.50
17	Italy	ENI 2	5.06
18	Italy	Cariplo bank	5.00
19	France	Banque Nationale de Paris	4.81
20	Spain	Endesa	4.56
21	United Kingdom	British Steel	4.50
22	Italy	Autostrade	4.42
23	Spain	Telefonica	4.36
24	Portugal	Gescartao	4.32
25	Poland	Telekomunikacja Polska	4.30
26	Ireland	Telecom Eireann	4.18
27	Italy	ENI 1	3.97
28	Sweden	Procordia	3.82
29	Netherlands	Koninklijke PTT Nederland (KPN1)	3.75
30	France	Credit Lyonnais	3.70

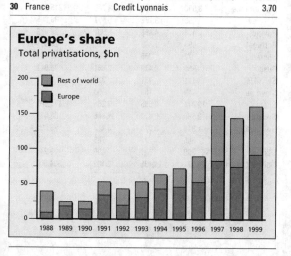

Europe's share
Total privatisations, $bn

Foreign direct investment

Inward

	Inflows, $m			Stock, $bn[a]
	1988–93 av.	*1996*	*1999*	*1999*
Albania	39	90	41	425
Armenia	7	18	130	441
Austria	768	4,426	2,813	23,363
Azerbaijan	...	627	691	3,808
Belarus	12	73	225	697
Belgium & Lux	8,613	14,064	15,862	181,184
Bosnia	...	-2[b]	10[b]	...
Bulgaria	35	109	770	2,258
Croatia	120	506	1,382	4,028
Cyprus	78	50	65	1,717
Czech Republic	502	1,428	5,108	16,246
Denmark	1,168	742	7,454	37,830
Estonia	114	151	306	2,441
Finland	472	1,109	3,023	16,540
France	13,976	21,960	39,101	181,974
Georgia	...	45	96[b]	306
Germany	3,052	6,572	26,822	225,595
Greece	987	1,058	900[b]	22,948
Hungary	1,033	2,275	1,944	19,095
Iceland	11	84	66	529
Ireland	787	2,618	18,322	43,969
Italy	4,105	3,546	4,901	107,995
Latvia	36	382	366	1,885
Lithuania	20	152	486	2,063
Macedonia	...	12	22	200
Malta	52	325	811	2,547
Moldova	16	24	34	335
Netherlands	8,058	15,052	33,785	215,234
Norway	455	3,172	6,577	30,885
Poland	478	4,498	7,500[b]	29,979
Portugal	1,854	1,368	570	20,513
Romania	72	265	961	5,441
Russia	956	2,479	2,861	16,541
Slovakia	111	251	322	2,044
Slovenia	49	185	90	2,997
Spain	10,814	6,585	9,355	112,582
Sweden	2,586	5,070	59,968	68,035
Switzerland	1,948	3,078	3,413	73,099
Turkey	665	722	783	8,353
Ukraine	200	521	496	3,248
United Kingdom	21,271	24,435	82,182	394,560

Outward

	Outflows, $m			Stock, $bn[a]
	1988–93 av.	1996	1999	1999
Albania	14	10[b]	…	69
Armenia	…	…	13	25
Austria	1,177	1,934	2,797	17,522
Azerbaijan	…	36[b]	336	473
Belarus	-8	4[b]	–	5
Belgium & Lux	6,528	8,026	24,928	159,461
Bosnia	…	29[b]	0[b]	41
Bulgaria	8	-29	5	8
Croatia	19	24	34	1,024
Cyprus	12	48	158	457
Czech Republic	56	153	197	908
Denmark	1,622	1,970	8,214	42,035
Estonia	4	40	74	272
Finland	1,469	3,595	4,192	31,803
France	24,246	30,419	107,952	298,012
Georgia	…	…	…	…
Germany	18,383	50,804	50,596	420,908
Greece	12	-18[b]	-21[b]	783
Hungary	13	-3	249	1,553
Iceland	9	63	85	420
Ireland	400	727	5,418	15,096
Italy	5,545	8,697	2,958	168,370
Latvia	-1	3	–	281
Lithuania	…	–	9	26
Macedonia	…	–	1[b]	4
Malta	…	6	30	73
Moldova	…	–	–	20
Netherlands	12,886	31,224	45,858	306,396
Norway	1,031	5,900	5,420	38,423
Poland	8	53	200[b]	1,365
Portugal	271	776	2,679	9,605
Romania	9	2	12	133
Russia	142	771	2,144	8,586
Slovakia	12	52	-372	296
Slovenia	9	8	44	607
Spain	2,675	5,397	35,414	97,553
Sweden	6,925	4,667	19,549	104,985
Switzerland	7,379	16,152	17,916	199,452
Turkey	23	110	645	1,641
Ukraine	…	-5	7	105
United Kingdom	25,083	34,047	199,289	664,103

a Current value of outstanding FDI. Stock figures in some countries based on
  accumulated flows for available years.
b Estimate.

Stockmarkets

Largest by market capitalisation
End 1999, $bn

1	United Kingdom	2,933.28	16	Norway	63.70
2	France	1,475.46	17	Ireland	42.46
3	Germany	1,432.19	18	Luxembourg	35.94
4	Italy	728.27	19	Austria	33.03
5	Netherlands	695.21	20	Poland	29.58
6	Switzerland	693.13	21	Hungary	16.32
7	Spain	431.67	22	Czech Republic	11.80
8	Sweden	373.28	23	Serbia & Montenegro	10.82
9	Finland	349.41	24	Cyprus	8.08
10	Greece	204.21	25	Iceland	4.81
11	Belgium	184.94	26	Croatia	2.58
12	Turkey	112.72	27	Slovenia	2.18
13	Denmark	105.29	28	Estonia	1.79
14	Russia	72.21		United States	16,635.11
15	Portugal	66.49		Japan	4,546.94

Largest by annual value traded
1999, $m

1	United Kingdom	1,377,859	16	Portugal	40,796
2	Germany	1,357,841	17	Hungary	14,395
3	Netherlands	941,804	18	Austria	12,705
4	France	769,951	19	Poland	11,149
5	Spain	744,315	20	Czech Republic	9,038
6	Switzerland	538,955	21	Russia	2,839
7	Italy	536,475	22	Cyprus	2,095
8	Sweden	238,237	23	Luxembourg	1,041
9	Greece	188,722	24	Slovenia	733
10	Finland	111,585	25	Slovakia	474
11	Turkey	81,277	26	Romania	317
12	Denmark	61,297	27	Lithuania	290
13	Belgium	59,129	28	Estonia	285
14	Norway	54,135		United States	18,574,100
15	Ireland	50,531		Japan	1,849,228

Largest by number of companies listed
End 1999

1	United Kingdom	1,945	14	Denmark	233
2	France	968	15	Poland	221
3	Germany	933	16	Russia	207
4	Bulgaria	860	17	Norway	195
5	Slovakia	845	18	Belgium	172
6	Spain	718	19	Czech Republic	164
7	Romania	582	20	Finland	147
8	Netherlands	344	21	Portugal	125
9	Turkey	285		Ukraine	125
10	Greece	281	23	Austria	97
11	Sweden	277	24	Armenia	95
12	Italy	241		United States	7,651
13	Switzerland	239		Japan	2,470

1990, $bn

1	United Kingdom	848.87
2	Germany[b]	355.07
3	France	314.38
4	Switzerland	160.04
5	Italy	148.77
6	Netherlands	119.83
7	Spain	111.40
8	Sweden	92.10
9	Belgium	65.45
10	Denmark	39.06
11	Norway	26.13
12	Finland	22.72
13	Turkey	19.07
14	Greece	15.23
15	Austria	11.48

1980, $bn

1	United Kingdom	205.20
2	Germany[b]	71.70
3	France	54.60
4	Switzerland	37.60
5	Netherlands	29.30
6	Italy	25.30
7	Spain	16.60
8	Sweden	12.90
9	Belgium	10.00
10	Denmark	5.40
11	Greece	3.02
12	Austria	2.00
13	Turkey	0.48

1990, $m

1	Germany[b]	501,805
2	United Kingdom	278,740
3	France	116,893
4	Italy	42,566
5	Spain	40,967
6	Netherlands	40,199
7	Austria	18,609
8	Sweden	15,718
9	Norway	13,996
10	Denmark	11,105
11	Belgium	6,425
12	Turkey	5,841
13	Finland	3,933
14	Portugal	1,687

1980, $m

1	Switzerland	96,262
2	United Kingdom	35,791
3	Germany[b]	15,248
4	France	10,118
5	Italy	8,574
6	Netherlands	5,099
7	Sweden	1,796
8	Spain	981
9	Belgium	838
10	Austria	105
11	Greece	86
12	Denmark	58

1990

1	United Kingdom	1,701
2	France	578
3	Spain	427
4	Germany[b]	413
5	Netherlands	260
6	Denmark	258
7	Italy	220
8	Switzerland	182
	Belgium	182
10	Portugal	181

1980

1	United Kingdom	2,655
2	France	586
3	Spain	496
4	Germany[b]	459
5	Belgium	225
6	Denmark	218
7	Netherlands	214
8	Italy	134
9	Greece	116
10	Sweden	103

a 1996
b Western Germany.

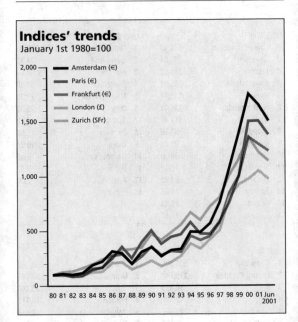

Indices' trends
January 1st 1980=100

- Amsterdam (€)
- Paris (€)
- Frankfurt (€)
- London (£)
- Zurich (SFr)

80 81 82 83 84 85 86 87 88 89 90 91 92 93 94 95 96 97 98 99 00 01 Jun 2001

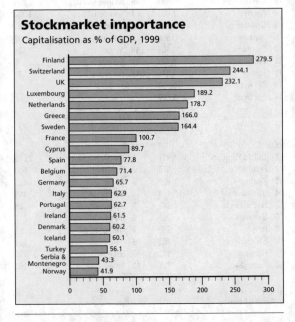

Stockmarket importance
Capitalisation as % of GDP, 1999

Finland	279.5
Switzerland	244.1
UK	232.1
Luxembourg	189.2
Netherlands	178.7
Greece	166.0
Sweden	164.4
France	100.7
Cyprus	89.7
Spain	77.8
Belgium	71.4
Germany	65.7
Italy	62.9
Portugal	62.7
Ireland	61.5
Denmark	60.2
Iceland	60.1
Turkey	56.1
Serbia & Montenegro	43.3
Norway	41.9

0   50   100   150   200   250   300

Part VII

TOURISM AND TRANSPORT

Tourism

Most popular destinations
Tourist arrivals, '000s

	1999			% increase on year earlier	
1	France	73,042	1	Albania	39.3
2	Spain	51,772	2	Armenia	28.1
3	Italy	36,097	3	Georgia	21.1
4	United Kingdom	25,740	4	Ukraine	20.8
5	Russia	18,496	5	Russia	17.0
6	Poland	17,950	6	Kirgizstan	16.9
7	Austria	17,467	7	Macedonia	15.3
8	Germany	17,116	8	Estonia	15.2
9	Czech Republic	16,031	9	Iceland	13.4
10	Hungary	12,930	10	Greece	9.9
11	Greece	12,000	11	Cyprus	9.5
12	Portugal	11,600	12	Spain	9.2
13	Switzerland	10,800	13	Slovakia	8.8
14	Netherlands	9,881	14	Romania	8.2
15	Ukraine	7,500	15	Ireland	7.4
16	Turkey	6,893	16	Netherlands	6.0
17	Ireland	6,511	17	France	4.3
18	Belgium	6,369	18	Germany	3.7
19	Norway	4,481	19	Italy	3.3
20	Croatia	3,443	20	Belgium	3.1
21	Romania	3,209	21	Malta	2.7
22	Finland	2,700		Portugal	2.7
23	Sweden	2,595	23	Finland	2.1
24	Bulgaria	2,472	24	Liechtenstein	1.7
25	Cyprus	2,434	25	Sweden	0.9
26	Denmark	2,023	26	Austria	0.7
27	Lithuania	1,422	27	Lithuania	0.4
28	Malta	1,214	28	Monaco	0.0
29	Slovakia	975		United Kingdom	0.0
30	Estonia	950	30	Switzerland	-0.9

Biggest spenders
Spending on tourism, $m, 1999

1	Germany	48,158	16	Ireland	2,413
2	United Kingdom	33,516	17	Ukraine	2,390
3	Spain	23,968	18	Portugal	2,291
4	France	17,732	19	Czech Republic	2,092
5	Italy	16,913	20	Finland	1,944
6	Austria	13,349	21	Turkey	1,471
7	Netherlands	11,366	22	Hungary	1,191
8	Belgium	8,424	23	Slovenia	595
9	Switzerland	6,963	24	Croatia	490
10	Sweden	5,544	25	Slovakia	463
11	Norway	4,751	26	Romania	395
12	Denmark	4,415	27	Iceland	365
13	Russia	4,199	28	Lithuania	311
14	Greece	3,989	29	Latvia	265
15	Poland	3,600	30	Bulgaria	237

Biggest earners

Earnings from tourism, $m

	1999			*% change on year earlier*	
1	Spain	32,913	1	Armenia	170.0
2	France	31,699	2	Greece	41.6
3	Italy	28,357	3	Lithuania	19.6
4	United Kingdom	20,972	4	Russia	19.4
5	Germany	16,828	5	Denmark	14.7
6	Austria	11,088	6	Cyprus	13.3
7	Greece	8,765	7	Spain	10.7
8	Russia	7,771	8	France	5.9
9	Switzerland	7,355	9	Estonia	4.9
10	Netherlands	7,092	10	Netherlands	4.5
11	Poland	6,100	11	Germany	2.4
12	Turkey	5,203	12	Malta	2.1
13	Portugal	5,169	13	Ireland	1.7
14	Sweden	3,894	14	Norway	0.8
15	Denmark	3,682	15	United Kingdom	0.0
16	Hungary	3,394	16	Austria	-0.9
17	Ireland	3,306	17	Portugal	-2.9
18	Czech Republic	3,035	18	Hungary	-3.4
19	Croatia	2,502	19	Bulgaria	-3.7
20	Norway	2,229	20	Italy	-5.1
21	Cyprus	1,894	21	Georgia	-5.4
22	Finland	1,460	22	Slovakia	-5.7
23	Slovenia	1,005	23	Switzerland	-5.9
24	Bulgaria	930	24	Sweden	-7.0
25	Malta	675	25	Croatia	-8.5
26	Estonia	560	26	Slovenia	-10.0
27	Lithuania	550	27	Finland	-10.5
28	Slovakia	461	28	Czech Republic	-18.4
29	Georgia	400	29	Poland	-23.2
30	Armenia	27	30	Turkey	-33.4

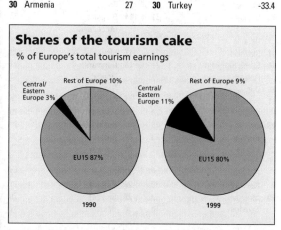

Shares of the tourism cake

% of Europe's total tourism earnings

Central/Eastern Europe 3%
Rest of Europe 10%
EU15 87%
1990

Central/Eastern Europe 11%
Rest of Europe 9%
EU15 80%
1999

Road transport

Longest road networks

Km

1	Russia	948,000	16	Greece	117,000
2	France	893,500	17	Netherlands	116,500
3	Spain	663,795	18	Ireland	92,500
4	Germany	656,140	19	Norway	90,880
5	Italy	654,676	20	Finland	77,900
6	Turkey	385,960	21	Lithuania	73,650
7	Poland	381,046	22	Latvia	73,227
8	United Kingdom	371,913	23	Denmark	71,462
9	Sweden	210,907	24	Switzerland	71,115
10	Austria	200,000	25	Portugal	68,732
11	Romania	198,589	26	Belarus	65,994
12	Hungary	188,203	27	Serbia & Montenegro	49,525
13	Ukraine	168,674	28	Slovakia	42,713
14	Belgium	145,850	29	Bulgaria	37,284
15	Czech Republic	127,854	30	Croatia	28,009

Car congestion

Private cars per km of road

1	Monaco	422
2	Malta	99
3	Germany	65
4	United Kingdom	61
5	Netherlands	52
6	Bulgaria	51
7	Luxembourg	49
	Switzerland	49
9	Italy	48
10	Portugal	47
11	Slovenia	41
12	Croatia	38
13	Macedonia	32
14	Belgium	31
	France	31
	Ukraine	31
17	Slovakia	29
18	Czech Republic	27
	Finland	27
20	Denmark	26
21	Poland	24
	Spain	24
23	Cyprus	23
	Greece	23
25	Russia	21
26	Austria	20
	Belarus	20
	Norway	20
29	Moldova	18
	Sweden	18

Vehicle congestion

All vehicles per km of road

1	Monaco	480
2	Malta	126
3	Germany	66
4	Portugal	63
5	United Kingdom	62
6	Bulgaria	58
	Netherlands	58
8	Luxembourg	55
9	Switzerland	53
10	Italy	52
11	Slovenia	45
12	Croatia	42
13	France	37
14	Belgium	35
	Macedonia	35
16	Cyprus	34
17	Slovakia	33
18	Denmark	31
	Finland	31
	Greece	31
21	Czech Republic	29
	Poland	29
	Spain	29
24	Russia	26
25	Norway	25
26	Moldova	24
27	Austria	22
28	Belarus	21
29	Sweden	20
30	Romania	17

Road accidents
No. of accidents

1	Germany	395,689	16	Netherlands	19,176
2	United Kingdom	235,000	17	Hungary	18,719
3	Italy	190,131	18	Sweden	15,514
4	Russia	156,515	19	Croatia	12,958
5	France	124,500	20	Bosnia	12,865
6	Spain	97,811	21	Slovakia	8,578
7	Turkey	66,763	22	Norway	8,248
8	Poland	55,106	23	Romania	7,846
9	Belgium	51,167	24	Denmark	7,604
10	Portugal	49,938	25	Bulgaria	7,586
11	Austria	42,348	26	Finland	6,997
12	Ukraine	34,554	27	Slovenia	6,929
13	Czech Republic	26,918	28	Belarus	6,709
14	Greece	24,836	29	Lithuania	6,356
15	Switzerland	22,434	30	Latvia	4,442

Injuries in road accidents
No. of injuries

1	Germany	521,127	16	Hungary	23,267
2	United Kingdom	317,000	17	Sweden	21,356
3	Italy	270,962	18	Croatia	18,103
4	Russia	205,589	19	Ireland	12,528
5	France	167,600	20	Netherlands	11,733
6	Spain	148,632	21	Slovakia	11,466
7	Turkey	113,656	22	Norway	11,313
8	Belgium	72,260	23	Denmark	9,393
9	Poland	68,449	24	Bulgaria	9,098
10	Portugal	67,432	25	Finland	9,052
11	Austria	56,046	26	Slovenia	8,980
12	Ukraine	38,277	27	Lithuania	7,696
13	Czech Republic	34,710	28	Belarus	6,690
14	Greece	33,417	29	Romania	6,601
15	Switzerland	29,527	30	Latvia	5,244

Deaths in road accidents
No. of deaths

1	Russia	27,665	16	Belgium	1,373
2	France	8,029	17	Austria	1,079
3	Germany	7,772	18	Netherlands	1,066
4	Poland	6,730	19	Bulgaria	1,047
5	Italy	6,226	20	Lithuania	748
6	Spain	5,738	21	Slovakia	671
7	Ukraine	5,269	22	Croatia	662
8	Turkey	4,606	23	Latvia	604
9	United Kingdom	3,423	24	Switzerland	583
10	Romania	2,505	25	Azerbaijan	554
11	Greece	2,226	26	Georgia	539
12	Portugal	1,799	27	Sweden	529
13	Belarus	1,764	28	Denmark	513
14	Czech Republic	1,455	29	Ireland	472
15	Hungary	1,399	30	Finland	431

Rail transport

Railway networks
'000 km

1	Russia	86.0	21	Belgium	3.5
2	Germany	37.5	22	Switzerland	3.1
3	France	31.6	23	Netherlands	2.8
4	Poland	23.0	24	Portugal	2.8
5	Ukraine	22.5	25	Croatia	2.7
6	United Kingdom	17.8	26	Latvia	2.4
7	Italy	16.1	27	Denmark	2.3
8	Spain	14.1		Greece	2.3
9	Romania	11.4	29	Azerbaijan	2.1
10	Sweden	10.8	30	Ireland	1.9
11	Czech Republic	9.3		Lithuania	1.9
12	Turkey	8.7	32	Georgia	1.6
13	Hungary	7.8	33	Slovenia	1.2
14	Finland	5.8	34	Moldova	1.1
15	Austria	5.7	35	Estonia	1.0
16	Belarus	5.5	36	Armenia	0.8
17	Bulgaria	4.3	37	Macedonia	0.7
	Serbia & Montenegro	4.3	38	Bosnia	0.6
19	Norway	4.2	39	Albania	0.4
20	Slovakia	3.7	40	Luxembourg	0.3

Passenger travel
m km

1	Russia	141,042	21	Bulgaria	3,819
2	Germany	72,542	22	Finland	3,415
3	France	66,495	23	Slovakia	2,968
4	Ukraine	47,600	24	Norway	2,456
5	Italy	40,971	25	Greece	1,583
6	United Kingdom	38,875	26	Ireland	1,421
7	Poland	21,158	27	Latvia	984
8	Spain	19,245	28	Croatia	943
9	Belarus	16,874	29	Lithuania	745
10	Netherlands	14,330	30	Slovenia	623
11	Switzerland	13,128	31	Azerbaijan	422
12	Romania	12,304	32	Georgia	355
13	Austria	8,109	33	Moldova	343
14	Sweden	7,434	34	Luxembourg	310
15	Belgium	7,354	35	Estonia	238
16	Czech Republic	6,929	36	Macedonia	150
17	Hungary	6,835	37	Albania	121
18	Turkey	6,146	38	Armenia	52
19	Denmark	5,369	39	Bosnia	10
20	Portugal	4,329			

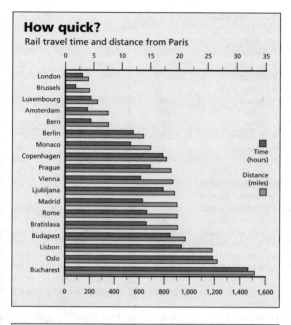

How quick?
Rail travel time and distance from Paris

- Time (hours)
- Distance (miles)

London
Brussels
Luxembourg
Amsterdam
Bern
Berlin
Monaco
Copenhagen
Prague
Vienna
Ljubljana
Madrid
Rome
Bratislava
Budapest
Lisbon
Oslo
Bucharest

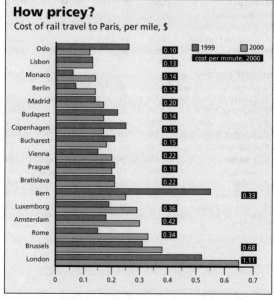

How pricey?
Cost of rail travel to Paris, per mile, $

- 1999
- 2000
- cost per minute, 2000

Oslo	0.10
Lisbon	0.13
Monaco	0.14
Berlin	0.12
Madrid	0.20
Budapest	0.14
Copenhagen	0.15
Bucharest	0.15
Vienna	0.22
Prague	0.19
Bratislava	0.22
Bern	0.33
Luxemborg	0.36
Amsterdam	0.42
Rome	0.34
Brussels	0.68
London	1.11

Air transport

Who flies most[a]

Total travel '000, 1999		Domestic travel '000, 1999	
1 United Kingdom	160,362	1 France	34,689
2 Germany	105,221	2 Russia	29,001
3 France	102,152	3 Spain	15,158
4 Netherlands	71,282	4 Italy	9,673
5 Russia	45,863	5 Germany	8,208
6 Spain	44,217	6 United Kingdom	7,311
7 Italy	40,143	7 Turkey	3,348
8 Switzerland	33,562	8 Austria	548
9 Belgium	17,692	9 Ireland	362
10 Turkey	13,350	10 Switzerland	283

Busiest airports[a]

Passengers, '000s, 1999

1 Heathrow, London	64,607	16 Arlanda, Stockholm	18,446
2 Rhiem, Frankfurt	49,361	17 Copenhagen	18,294
3 Charles de Gaulle, Paris	48,240	18 Dusseldorf	16,028
4 Schiphol, Amsterdam	39,605	19 Ataturk, Istanbul	15,831
5 Barajas, Madrid	32,766	20 Fornebu, Oslo	14,215
6 Gatwick, London	32,057	21 Dublin	13,844
7 Fiumicino, Rome	25,922	22 Vienna International	11,940
8 Orly, Paris	25,399	23 Stansted, London	11,875
9 Munich	23,126	24 Sheremetyevo, Moscow	10,828
10 Zurich	22,650	25 Tegel, Berlin	10,344
11 Brussels	21,604	26 Vantaa, Helsinki	10,015
12 Linate, Milan	20,717	27 Fühlsbuttel, Hamburg	9,949
13 Barcelona	19,797	28 Malaga	9,438
14 Palma de Mallorca	19,402	29 Lisbon	9,396
15 Manchester	18,804	30 Nice International	9,392

Busiest airports

Average daily aircraft movements, take-offs and landings

1 Charles de Gaulle, Paris	1,418	11 Arlanda, Stockholm	765
2 Heathrow, London	1,279	12 Gatwick, London	715
3 Rhiem, Frankfurt	1,257	13 Barcelona	704
4 Schiphol, Amsterdam	1,185	14 Linate, Milan	682
5 Barajas, Madrid	982	15 Orly, Paris	667
6 Brussels	893	16 Nice International	596
7 Zurich	892	17 Vienna International	567
8 Munich	874	18 Fornebu, Oslo	560
9 Copenhagen	832	19 Dusseldorf	532
10 Fiumicino, Rome	769	20 Manchester	530

a Passengers arriving and departing from airports participating in ACI survey.

Sea transport

Largest merchant fleets
No. of vessels over 100 GRT[a]

1	Russia	4,723	19	Iceland	315
2	Norway	2,325	20	Azerbaijan	287
3	Cyprus	1,602	21	Finland	284
4	Spain	1,570	22	Estonia	239
5	Greece	1,545	23	Lithuania	206
6	United Kingdom	1,421	24	Latvia	186
7	Malta	1,416	25	Belgium	183
8	Italy	1,329	26	Bulgaria	181
9	Netherlands	1,214	27	Ireland	150
10	Germany	1,158	28	Georgia	95
11	Turkey	1,135	29	Luxembourg	45
12	Denmark	1,056	30	Albania	32
13	Ukraine	966	31	Austria	22
14	France	808	32	Switzerland	17
15	Sweden	562	33	Slovenia	10
16	Poland	447	34	Slovakia	3
17	Romania	389	35	Hungary	2
18	Portugal	323	36	Czech Republic	1

Largest ports
Total cargo, '000 tonnes

1	Greece	25,225	20	Poland	1,424
2	Malta	24,075	21	Bulgaria	1,091
3	Cyprus	23,302	22	Luxembourg	932
4	Norway	23,136	23	Azerbaijan	651
5	United States	11,852	24	Estonia	522
6	Russia	11,090	25	Lithuania	481
7	Germany	8,084	26	Switzerland	383
8	Italy	6,819	27	Portugal	290
9	Turkey	6,251	28	Iceland	198
10	Denmark	5,790	29	Ireland	184
11	France	4,849	30	Belgium	127
12	Bermuda	4,811	31	Georgia	118
13	Netherlands	4,263		Latvia	118
14	United Kingdom	4,085	33	Austria	68
15	Sweden	2,552	34	Albania	29
16	Romania	2,088	35	Hungary	15
17	Ukraine	2,033		Slovakia	15
18	Spain	1,838	37	Slovenia	2
19	Finland	1,629			

a GRT = gross tonnage, which is the total volume within the hull and above deck.
1 GRT = 100 cubic feet.

Freight

Road importance
% inland freight carried by road, 1998 or latest

1	Greece	98.27	17	Sweden	54.60
2	Turkey	94.70	18	Norway	49.66
3	Ireland	92.19	19	Lithuania	49.64
4	Italy	90.68	20	Austria	47.49
5	Spain	86.84	21	Moldova	44.42
6	Portugal	85.85	22	Slovakia	42.38
7	Denmark	85.12	23	Romania	40.90
8	France	80.30	24	Estonia	35.88
9	Belgium	73.81	25	Luxembourg	30.77
10	Netherlands	72.05	26	Azerbaijan	23.25
11	United Kingdom	67.85	27	Belarus	23.16
12	Czech Republic	67.55	28	Russia	10.28
13	Finland	67.26	29	Ukraine	10.11
14	Switzerland	64.07	30	Slovenia	8.83
15	Germany	62.89			
16	Poland	55.52		**EU15**	**74.29**

Rail importance
% inland freight carried by rail, 1997 or latest

1	Bulgaria	96.37	17	Czech Republic	30.77
2	Ukraine	86.77	18	Latvia	30.76
3	Russia	84.28	19	Finland	24.87
4	Belarus	76.58	20	Germany	19.77
5	Estonia	64.10	21	France	17.67
6	Moldova	55.57	22	Denmark	14.88
7	Lithuania	50.34	23	Portugal	14.15
8	Slovakia	49.30	24	Belgium	13.29
9	Romania	48.40	25	Spain	13.16
10	Luxembourg	46.15	26	Italy	9.28
11	Austria	45.72	27	Netherlands	8.32
12	Poland	43.71	28	United Kingdom	8.28
13	Azerbaijan	39.58	29	Ireland	7.81
14	Switzerland	35.35	30	Slovenia	7.48
15	Georgia	34.80			
16	Sweden	31.51		**EU15**	**15.81**

Water importance
% inland freight carried by water, 1997 or latest

1	Croatia	97.98	12	Belgium	12.91
2	Slovenia	83.69	13	Romania	10.70
3	Latvia	61.86	14	Slovakia	8.32
4	Georgia	60.54	15	Finland	7.87
5	Norway	43.29	16	Austria	6.78
6	Azerbaijan	37.17	17	Russia	5.44
7	United Kingdom	23.86	18	Ukraine	3.12
8	Luxembourg	23.08	19	France	2.03
9	Netherlands	19.63	20	Czech Republic	1.68
10	Germany	17.34			
11	Sweden	13.89		**EU15**	**9.90**

HEALTH
AND
EDUCATION

Life and death

Life expectancy

At birth, years

2000–05			2020–25		
1	Sweden	80.1	1	Sweden	82.1
2	Iceland	79.4	2	Malta	81.6
3	Switzerland	79.1	3	France	81.5
4	France	79.0	4	Belgium	81.4
5	Norway	78.9	5	Austria	81.2
6	Belgium	78.8		Norway	81.2
	Spain	78.8	7	Iceland	81.1
8	Italy	78.7		United Kingdom	81.1
9	Austria	78.5	9	Finland	81.0
	Greece	78.5		Germany	81.0
	Malta	78.5	11	Switzerland	80.9
12	Cyprus	78.3	12	Luxembourg	80.8
	Netherlands	78.3	13	EU15	80.6
14	EU15	78.2		Euro-11	80.6
	Germany	78.2		Italy	80.6
	United Kingdom	78.2		Spain	80.6
17	Euro-11	78.1	17	Greece	80.4
18	Finland	78.0	18	Cyprus	80.2
19	Luxembourg	77.9		Netherlands	80.2
20	Ireland	77.0	20	Slovenia	79.7
21	Denmark	76.6	21	Czech Republic	79.3
22	Portugal	76.2		Ireland	79.3
23	Slovenia	76.1	23	Denmark	79.2
24	Czech Republic	75.4	24	Portugal	78.8
25	Croatia	74.2	25	Poland	77.4
26	Bosnia	74.0	26	Albania	76.9
27	Poland	73.9	27	Croatia	76.6
28	Albania	73.7	28	Bosnia	76.5
	Slovakia	73.7		Lithuania	76.5
30	Georgia	73.6		Slovakia	76.5
	Macedonia	73.6	31	Macedonia	76.4
32	Armenia	73.4	32	Georgia	76.3
33	Serbia & Montenegro	73.2	33	Armenia	76.1
34	Lithuania	72.7		Hungary	76.1

Infant mortality

Rates per 1,000 live births, 2000–05

1	Turkey	38.5	12	Latvia	13.6
2	Azerbaijan	29.3	13	Bosnia	13.5
3	Albania	25.0	14	Serbia & Montenegro	13.0
4	Romania	22.1	15	Belarus	12.5
5	Moldova	20.5	16	Estonia	9.7
6	Georgia	17.6	17	Poland	9.1
7	Russia	16.8	18	Lithuania	8.9
8	Macedonia	16.0	19	Hungary	8.7
9	Armenia	15.4	20	Croatia	8.1
10	Ukraine	15.3	21	Slovakia	8.0
11	Bulgaria	15.2	22	Cyprus	7.7

Death rate
Crude death rates per 1,000 population

2000–05			2020–25		
1	Ukraine	15.4	**1**	Bulgaria	15.4
2	Russia	15.3	**2**	Latvia	14.9
3	Bulgaria	15.1	**3**	Ukraine	14.8
4	Belarus	14.1	**4**	Russia	14.6
5	Hungary	13.5	**5**	Estonia	14.3
6	Latvia	13.4	**6**	Hungary	13.9
7	Estonia	13.3	**7**	Italy	13.7
8	Romania	12.8	**8**	Belarus	13.5
9	Moldova	12.3	**9**	Romania	13.2
10	Croatia	11.3	**10**	Croatia	13.1
	Denmark	11.3		Greece	13.1
12	Lithuania	11.2	**12**	Switzerland	12.9
13	Italy	10.9	**13**	Lithuania	12.7
14	Czech Republic	10.8	**14**	Germany	12.6
	Germany	10.8	**15**	Serbia & Montenegro	12.4
	Portugal	10.8		Slovenia	12.4
17	Serbia & Montenegro	10.7	**17**	Denmark	12.3
18	Sweden	10.6	**18**	Czech Republic	12.2
19	United Kingdom	10.5		Spain	12.2
20	Greece	10.4	**20**	Portugal	12.1
21	Belgium	10.0	**21**	Sweden	12.0
	EU15	10.0	**22**	Bosnia	11.9
	Norway	10.0		Georgia	11.9
24	Austria	9.9	**24**	Austria	11.8
	Georgia	9.9	**25**	Finland	11.7
	Poland	9.9	**26**	Belgium	11.5
	Slovenia	9.9		EU15	11.5
28	Euro-11	9.8		Slovakia	11.5
	Finland	9.8	**29**	Poland	11.4
	Slovakia	9.8	**30**	Euro-11	11.3
	Spain	9.8	**31**	Moldova	11.1
	Switzerland	9.8	**32**	United Kingdom	11.0
33	France	9.4	**33**	Macedonia	10.8
34	Luxembourg	9.1		Netherlands	10.8

2000–05			2020–25		
23	Malta	7.0	**35**	Denmark	5.0
24	Greece	6.3		France	5.0
25	Portugal	6.1	**37**	Switzerland	4.8
26	Ireland	6.0	**38**	Austria	4.7
27	Luxembourg	5.6	**39**	Germany	4.6
	Slovenia	5.6	**40**	Iceland	4.5
29	Czech Republic	5.4		Netherlands	4.5
	Italy	5.4		Norway	4.5
	United Kingdom	5.4	**43**	Belgium	4.2
32	Euro-11	5.3	**44**	Finland	4.0
	Spain	5.3	**45**	Sweden	3.4
34	EU15	5.2			

Causes of death

Heart disease
Deaths per 100,000 population

1	Moldova	576.2	14	Ireland[a]	205.0
2	Ukraine	483.5	15	Czech Republic	199.0
3	Belarus	455.5	16	Croatia	193.2
4	Azerbaijan	413.2	17	Finland[a]	192.9
5	Russia	364.0	18	Malta	187.0
6	Estonia	337.6	19	United Kingdom[b]	158.4
7	Armenia	328.5	20	Iceland[a]	149.4
8	Latvia	326.7	21	Sweden[a]	149.0
9	Lithuania	307.1	22	Austria	142.4
10	Slovakia	275.6	23	Denmark[a]	142.0
11	Hungary	254.1	24	Germany[b]	141.0
12	Romania	249.7	25	Norway[c]	134.7
13	Bulgaria	206.9	26	Slovenia	114.0

Cancer
Deaths per 100,000 population

1	Hungary	284.6	14	Lithuania	195.1
2	Croatia	240.0	15	Luxembourg[c]	193.0
3	Czech Republic	237.1	16	Estonia	192.4
4	Slovakia	229.9	17	Germany[b]	189.1
5	Denmark[a]	226.5	18	France[c]	187.8
6	Poland[a]	213.8	19	Belarus	185.5
7	Slovenia	210.0	20	Italy[c]	185.0
8	Ireland[a]	208.1	21	Norway[c]	184.3
9	Iceland[a]	204.7	22	Malta	178.4
10	Netherlands[c]	204.6	23	Austria	176.6
11	Latvia	198.0	24	Spain[c]	175.9
12	United Kingdom[b]	197.2	25	Ukraine	174.4
13	Russia	196.0	26	Portugal[b]	172.2

Injuries and poisons
Deaths per 100,000 population

1	Russia	203.4	14	Croatia	63.9
2	Belarus	170.9	15	Czech Republic	61.5
3	Latvia	156.6	16	France[c]	59.9
4	Estonia	151.4	17	Slovakia	58.0
5	Lithuania	142.6	18	Denmark[a]	52.3
6	Ukraine	141.2	19	Bulgaria	52.2
7	Moldova	104.5	20	Luxembourg[c]	48.8
8	Hungary	92.3	21	Portugal[b]	48.2
9	Slovenia	77.1	22	Austria	47.4
10	Finland[a]	73.5	23	Norway[c]	42.5
11	Poland[a]	72.4	24	Ireland[a]	39.8
12	Albania[b]	66.2	25	Greece[b]	39.1
13	Romania	64.6	26	Sweden[a]	38.6

a 1996 b 1998 c 1997

Infectious and parasitic diseases
Deaths per 100,000 population

1	Azerbaijan	27.6	14	Switzerland[c]	9.3
2	Russia	25.1	15	Spain[c]	8.3
3	Ukraine	23.8	16	Denmark[a]	8.2
4	Moldova	19.9	17	France[c]	8.1
5	Latvia	16.4	18	Bulgaria	8.0
6	Romania	15.0	19	Netherlands[c]	7.7
7	Lithuania	13.1	20	Germany[b]	7.0
8	Estonia	12.4	21	Finland[a]	6.8
9	Belarus	11.8		Norway[c]	6.8
10	Portugal[b]	11.3	23	Malta	6.7
11	Macedonia[c]	10.9	24	Hungary	6.6
12	Armenia	10.3	25	Poland[a]	6.5
13	Croatia	10.1	26	Sweden[a]	5.2

Motor vehicle traffic accidents
Deaths per 100,000 population

1	Latvia	26.0	14	Hungary	13.3
2	Lithuania	21.0	15	Czech Republic	12.7
3	Greece[b]	20.1	16	France[c]	12.3
4	Russia[b]	19.7	17	Italy[c]	12.1
5	Portugal[b]	17.8	18	Moldova	12.0
6	Poland[a]	17.2	19	Romania	11.5
7	Belarus	17.0	20	Ireland[a]	11.4
8	Estonia	16.8	21	Austria	11.2
9	Slovenia	15.0	22	Ukraine	10.4
10	Croatia	14.1	23	Bulgaria	10.2
11	Luxembourg[c]	13.5	24	Denmark[a]	9.1
	Spain[c]	13.5	25	Germany[b]	8.7
	Slovakia	13.5	26	Albania[b]	7.5

AIDS

Cumulative cases to June 2000

1	Spain	58,091
2	France	51,799
3	Italy	46,559
4	Germany	18,700
5	United Kingdom	17,209
6	Portugal	7,191
7	Switzerland	6,899
8	Romania	6,301
9	Netherlands	5,242
10	Belgium	2,699
11	Denmark	2,279
12	Greece	2,107
13	Austria	2,008
14	Sweden	1,725
15	Ukraine	1,277
16	Poland	873
17	Serbia & Montenegro	860

Cumulative deaths to June 2000

1	Spain	31,364
2	Italy	31,333
3	France	31,054
4	United Kingdom	11,871
5	Germany	11,790
6	Switzerland	4,951
7	Portugal	4,052
8	Romania	2,372
9	Denmark	1,795
10	Belgium	1,563
11	Austria	1,228
12	Greece	1,223
13	Sweden	1,173
14	Serbia & Montenegro	621
15	Norway	518
16	Poland	489
17	Ireland	360

Drinking and smoking

Alcoholic drinks
Spending per head, $, 1999

1	Finland	449.3
2	Denmark	414.8
3	Belgium	386.9
4	France	360.7
5	United Kingdom	341.5
6	Sweden	307.8
7	Ireland	259.6
8	Austria	207.7
9	Netherlands	185.7
10	Germany	154.9
11	Portugal	126.4
12	Italy	96.2
13	Norway	86.9
14	Spain	84.0
15	Slovenia	66.5
16	Singapore	54.3
17	Switzerland	38.0
18	Greece	32.6
19	Latvia	27.0
20	Estonia	20.5
21	Hungary	14.3
22	Slovakia	7.6
23	Lithuania	6.8
24	Bulgaria	4.8
25	Czech Republic	4.5
26	Poland	3.6
27	Azerbaijan	2.8
28	Belarus	2.6
29	Romania	1.1
30	Russia	0.4

Spirits
Sales per head, litres, 1999

1	Russia	15.9
2	Hungary	6.5
3	Poland	5.9
4	Slovakia	5.3
5	Germany	5.2
6	Czech Republic	4.4
7	Ireland	4.2
	Romania	4.2
9	Finland	4.1
10	Bulgaria	3.7
11	Portugal	3.6
	Netherlands	3.6
13	France	3.4
14	Spain	2.8
15	Greece	2.7
	United Kingdom	2.7
17	Sweden	2.6
18	Belgium	2.3
19	Austria	1.9
	Denmark	1.9
21	Norway	1.8
22	Switzerland	1.1

Wine
Sales per head, litres, 1999

1	France	44.7	12	Belgium	15.0
2	Hungary	30.8	13	Slovakia	13.4
3	Switzerland	28.5	14	Sweden	11.9
4	Denmark	26.0	15	Czech Republic	10.9
5	Germany	21.3	16	United Kingdom	10.2
6	Greece	20.0	17	Norway	9.7
7	Romania	19.5	18	Ireland	6.7
8	Portugal	17.9	19	Finland	6.6
9	Spain	17.8		Poland	6.6
10	Austria	16.9	21	Russia	4.5
11	Netherlands	16.0	22	Bulgaria	4.1

Beer

Sales per head, litres, 1999

1	Czech Republic	85.5	12	Bulgaria	40.1
2	Germany	76.3	13	Poland	39.9
3	Austria	66.2	14	Belgium	38.8
4	Netherlands	57.9	15	Romania	31.6
5	Norway	57.9	16	Switzerland	28.4
6	Finland	55.2	17	France	26.4
7	Denmark	53.6	18	Spain	23.6
8	Sweden	52.5	19	Ireland	23.0
9	Slovakia	51.7	20	Portugal	22.6
10	United Kingdom	46.2	21	Russia	18.0
11	Hungary	45.5	22	Greece	11.1

Heaviest smokers

Cigarettes smoked per head per day, 1999

1	Greece	7.8		Ireland	4.6
2	Poland	7.3	16	Italy	4.4
3	Hungary	7.1	17	Portugal	4.3
4	Switzerland	6.6		Ukraine	4.3
5	Czech Republic	5.9	19	Finland	3.9
6	Bulgaria	5.8	20	Turkey	3.7
	Serbia & Montenegro	5.8	21	Denmark	3.6
	Spain	5.8		Russia	3.6
9	Austria	5.1	23	Sweden	3.4
10	Belarus	5.0	24	Netherlands	3.2
	Germany	5.0	25	Romania	2.1
12	Slovakia	4.9	26	Norway	1.9
13	Belgium	4.6		United Kingdom	1.9
	France	4.6			

Cutting back

% change in number of cigarettes smoked, 1990–99

1	Sweden	-38.2	15	Serbia & Montenegro	-1.9
	United Kingdom	-38.2	16	Denmark	1.5
3	Finland	-34.8	17	Greece	3.1
4	Belarus	-16.3	18	Italy	3.7
5	France	-16.2	19	Portugal	4.0
6	Switzerland	-15.3	20	Spain	4.6
7	Norway	-12.5	21	Austria	5.3
8	Poland	-11.9	22	Slovakia	9.4
9	Netherlands	-9.2	23	Belgium	10.2
10	Hungary	-6.4	24	Bulgaria	19.0
11	Ukraine	-5.9	25	Turkey	30.3
12	Ireland	-4.5	26	Russia	61.3
13	Czech Republic	-4.1	27	Romania	81.8
14	Germany	-3.8			

Health matters

Population per doctor

1	Monaco	100		Portugal	316
2	Italy	171	18	Sweden	317
3	Hungary	218	19	Austria	319
4	Ukraine	221	20	Finland	330
5	Spain	225	21	Czech Republic	335
6	Greece	229	22	Denmark	344
7	Russia	232	23	Latvia	364
8	Lithuania	242	24	Netherlands	404
9	Belarus	247	25	Norway	426
10	Slovakia	257	26	Poland	430
11	Slovenia	269	27	Ireland	438
12	Belgium	281	28	Switzerland	524
13	Germany	282	29	Croatia	532
14	France	286	30	Romania	562
15	Bulgaria	293	31	United Kingdom	569
16	Estonia	316	32	Cyprus	632

Population per nurse

1	Monaco	19	16	Russia	155
2	Ireland	59	17	Estonia	158
3	Finland	70	18	France	178
4	Switzerland	76	19	Poland	182
5	Slovenia	91	20	United Kingdom	184
	Ukraine	91	21	Bulgaria	186
7	Sweden	95	22	Italy	191
8	Germany	105	23	Hungary	197
9	Austria	110	24	Latvia	235
	Croatia	110	25	Portugal	254
	Norway	110	26	Greece	278
12	Czech Republic	122	27	Cyprus	344
13	Lithuania	129	28	Malta	345
14	Belarus	136	29	Iceland	398
15	Denmark	137	30	Turkey	913

Population per hospital bed

1	Norway	70	16	Bulgaria	132
2	Moldova	80	17	Slovakia	138
3	Belarus	82	18	Romania	139
4	Russia	83	19	Belgium	146
5	Netherlands	88	20	Germany	147
6	Georgia	95	21	Switzerland	151
7	Lithuania	97	22	Croatia	167
8	Estonia	108	23	Italy	177
9	Latvia	109	24	Macedonia	182
	Slovenia	109	25	Poland	192
11	Austria	111	26	Greece	202
12	Czech Republic	113	27	Denmark	220
13	Hungary	122	28	United Kingdom	242
14	France	123	29	Portugal	250
15	Finland	130	30	Albania	254

Fighting measles
% of one-year-olds fully immunised against measles

1	Hungary	100		Portugal	96
	Iceland	100		Slovenia	96
	Monaco	100		Sweden	96
	San Marino	100	**22**	Georgia	95
5	Moldova	99	**23**	Norway	93
	Slovakia	99		Spain	93
	Ukraine	99	**25**	Croatia	92
8	Belarus	98		Estonia	92
	Finland	98	**27**	Armenia	91
	Macedonia	98		Luxembourg	91
	Romania	98		United Kingdom	91
	Russia	98	**30**	Andorra	90
13	Czech Republic	97		Austria	90
	Latvia	97		Cyprus	90
	Lithuania	97	**33**	Greece	88
	Poland	97	**34**	Azerbaijan	87
17	Bulgaria	96	**35**	Albania	85
	Netherlands	96			

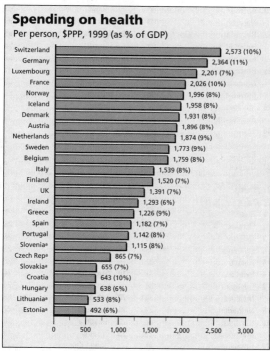

Spending on health
Per person, $PPP, 1999 (as % of GDP)

- Switzerland 2,573 (10%)
- Germany 2,364 (11%)
- Luxembourg 2,201 (7%)
- France 2,026 (10%)
- Norway 1,996 (8%)
- Iceland 1,958 (8%)
- Denmark 1,931 (8%)
- Austria 1,896 (8%)
- Netherlands 1,874 (9%)
- Sweden 1,773 (9%)
- Belgium 1,759 (8%)
- Italy 1,539 (8%)
- Finland 1,520 (7%)
- UK 1,391 (7%)
- Ireland 1,293 (6%)
- Greece 1,226 (9%)
- Spain 1,182 (7%)
- Portugal 1,142 (8%)
- Slovenia[a] 1,115 (8%)
- Czech Rep[a] 865 (7%)
- Slovakia[a] 655 (7%)
- Croatia 643 (10%)
- Hungary 638 (6%)
- Lithuania[a] 533 (8%)
- Estonia[a] 492 (6%)

a 1998

Education enrolment ratios

Primary

% of age group, 1997

1	Portugal	128		1	Portugal	123
2	United Kingdom	116		2	Azerbaijan	115
3	Netherlands	108		3	Albania	113
4	Albania	107		4	France	111
	Russia	107		5	Spain	109
	Spain	107		6	Belarus	104
	Sweden	107			Belgium	104
	Turkey	107			Romania	104
9	Azerbaijan	106		9	Estonia	103
10	France	105			Greece	103
	Ireland	105			United Kingdom	103
12	Czech Republic	104		12	Latvia	102
	Germany	104			Russia	102
	Romania	104			Ukraine	102
15	Belgium	103		15	Ireland	100
	Hungary	103			Italy	100
17	Denmark	102			Macedonia	100
	Slovakia	102			Netherlands	100
19	Italy	101			Norway	100
20	Austria	100			Poland	100
	Norway	100		21	Austria	99
22	Bulgaria	99		22	Bulgaria	98
	Finland	99			Slovenia	98
	Macedonia	99		24	Sweden	97
25	Belarus	98		25	Czech Republic	96
	Lithuania	98			Denmark	96
	Slovenia	98			Finland	96
28	Moldova	97			Hungary	96
	Switzerland	97			Turkey	96
30	Latvia	96		30	Georgia	93
	Poland	96		31	Switzerland	84
32	Estonia	94		32	Moldova	83
33	Greece	93		33	Lithuania	79

1980 (heading for right-hand column)

Tertiary

% of age group, 1997

1	Russia	46			Italy	27
2	Ukraine	42		14	Belgium	26
3	Belarus	39			Norway	26
4	Lithuania	35		16	Estonia	25
5	Finland	32			France	25
6	Sweden	31		18	Azerbaijan	24
7	Georgia	30			Latvia	24
	Moldova	30		20	Spain	23
9	Netherlands	29		21	Austria	22
10	Denmark	28		22	Slovenia	20
	Macedonia	28		23	Croatia	19
12	Germany	27			United Kingdom	19

Secondary

% of age group, 1997

1	Belgium	146
2	Sweden	140
3	Netherlands	132
4	United Kingdom	129
5	Denmark	121
6	Spain	120
7	Norway	119
8	Finland	118
	Ireland	118
10	France	111
	Portugal	111
12	Estonia	104
	Germany	104
14	Austria	103
15	Switzerland	100
16	Czech Republic	99
17	Hungary	98
	Poland	98
19	Greece	95
	Italy	95
21	Slovakia	94
22	Belarus	93
23	Slovenia	92
24	Armenia	90
25	Lithuania	86
26	Latvia	84
27	Croatia	82
28	Moldova	81
29	Romania	78
30	Azerbaijan	77
	Bulgaria	77
	Georgia	77
33	Macedonia	63

1980

1	Estonia	127
2	Lithuania	114
3	Georgia	109
4	Denmark	105
5	Finland	100
6	Czech Republic	99
	Latvia	99
8	Belarus	98
9	Russia	96
10	Azerbaijan	95
11	Norway	94
	Romania	94
	Switzerland	94
	Ukraine	94
15	Austria	93
	Netherlands	93
17	Belgium	91
18	Ireland	90
19	Sweden	88
20	Spain	87
21	Bulgaria	85
	France	85
23	United Kingdom	84
24	Greece	81
25	Moldova	78
26	Croatia	77
	Poland	77
28	Italy	72
29	Hungary	70
30	Albania	67
31	Macedonia	61
32	Portugal	37
33	Turkey	35

1980

1	Finland	74
2	Norway	62
3	Belgium	57
4	Spain	53
5	United Kingdom	52
6	France	51
7	Sweden	50
8	Austria	48
9	Germany	47
	Greece	47
	Italy	47
	Netherlands	47
13	Denmark	45
	Estonia	45
15	Belarus	44
16	Ukraine	42
17	Bulgaria	41
	Georgia	41
	Ireland	41
	Russia	41
21	Portugal	38
22	Slovenia	36
23	Switzerland	34
24	Latvia	33

Education spending

Spending on education

As % GDP, 1996			As % of general govt. exp., 1995–96		
1	Moldova	10.9	1	Moldova	28.1
2	Sweden	8.3	2	Lithuania	22.8
3	Denmark	8.2	3	Estonia	22.3
4	Poland	7.5	4	Macedonia	20.0
5	Finland	7.5	5	Belarus	17.8
	Norway	7.5	6	Norway	16.7
7	Ukraine[a]	7.3	7	Poland[a]	15.7
8	Estonia[b]	7.2		Ukraine[a]	15.7
9	Latvia	6.3	8	Luxembourg	15.1
10	France	6.0	10	Switzerland	14.7
	Ireland	6.0	11	Latvia	14.1
12	Belarus	5.9	12	Czech Republic	13.6
13	Portugal	5.8	12	Ireland	13.5
14	Slovenia[a]	5.7	14	Denmark	13.1
15	Austria	5.5	15	Spain	12.8
16	Lithuania	5.5	16	Slovenia	12.6
17	Iceland	5.4	17	Iceland	12.3
	Switzerland	5.4	18	Finland	12.2
19	United Kingdom[a]	5.3	19	Sweden	11.6
20	Croatia	5.3	20	Malta	11.4
21	Czech Republic	5.1		United Kingdom[b]	11.4
	Malta	5.1	21	France	11.1
	Macedonia	5.1	23	Austria	10.6
	Netherlands	5.1	24	Romania	10.5
25	Spain	5.0	25	Russia[b]	9.6

Spending per student

EU15 countries[c], $PPP, 1996

Primary

1	Denmark	6,318	6	Netherlands	3,392
2	Austria	5,678	7	France	3,361
3	Sweden	5,206	8	Germany	3,200
4	Italy	4,664	9	Luxembourg	3,192
5	Finland	4,247	10	United Kingdom	3,167

Secondary

1	Luxembourg	9,570	6	Sweden	5,396
2	Austria	7,589	7	Netherlands	5,198
3	Denmark	6,360	8	Finland	4,695
4	France	6,314	9	United Kingdom	4,661
5	Italy	5,701	10	Germany	4,106

Tertiary

1	Sweden	12,156	6	Ireland	7,738
2	Austria	9,969	7	Denmark	7,494
3	Netherlands	8,907	8	Finland	7,024
4	Germany	8,887	9	France	6,246
5	United Kingdom	7,851	10	Portugal	5,878

a 1995   b 1997   c Belgium unavailable.

Current spending
% of total spending on education allocated to current spending

Primary, 1996

1	Belarus	72.5
2	Germany[a]	72.2
3	Albania[b]	57.2
4	Ukraine[a]	54.7
5	Macedonia	54.4
6	Bulgaria	52.4
7	Luxembourg[a]	51.9
8	Turkey[a]	43.0
9	Poland	42.8
10	Romania[c]	36.5
11	Greece	35.3
12	Portugal	35.2
13	Malta[b]	32.0
14	Sweden	31.1
15	San Marino	30.9
16	Iceland	30.8
17	Slovakia	30.6
18	Norway	30.5
19	United Kingdom[a]	29.7
20	Switzerland[a]	26.8
21	Finland[a]	24.5
	Ireland	24.5
23	Spain	24.1
24	Italy[a]	23.4
25	Netherlands[a]	23.2
26	Denmark[a]	21.5
	Hungary	21.5
28	Austria	21.1
	Belgium[b]	21.1
30	France[a]	19.8
31	Czech Republic	19.7
32	Slovenia[a]	19.3

Secondary, 1996

1	Latvia	58.9
2	Moldova	52.9
3	Lithuania	50.9
4	Estonia	50.7
	Spain	50.7
6	France[a]	50.0
7	Czech Republic	49.7
8	Slovenia[a]	48.4
9	Austria	47.7
10	Italy[a]	47.5
	Switzerland[a]	47.5
12	Belgium[b]	46.9
13	Hungary	46.3
14	Monaco	44.9
15	United Kingdom[a]	44.0
16	Luxembourg[a]	43.3
17	Portugal	42.7
18	Iceland	41.9
19	Ireland	41.5
20	Denmark[a]	39.7
	Netherlands[a]	39.7
22	Greece	38.0
23	Finland[a]	36.1
24	Sweden	35.9
25	San Marino	32.5
26	Slovakia	28.0
27	Malta[b]	24.0
28	Romania[c]	23.8
29	Macedonia	23.6
30	Norway	23.0
31	Turkey[a]	22.0
32	Albania[b]	20.6

Tertiary, 1996

1	Turkey[a]	34.7
2	Netherlands[a]	29.9
3	Finland[a]	28.8
4	Norway	27.9
5	Sweden	25.5
6	Greece	25.0
7	Ireland	23.8
8	United Kingdom[a]	23.7
9	Denmark[a]	22.8
10	Germany[a]	22.6
11	Macedonia	22.0
12	Austria	21.6
13	Belgium[b]	20.3
14	Switzerland[a]	19.7
15	Lithuania	18.3
16	Bulgaria	18.0
17	Estonia	17.9
18	Iceland	17.7
19	France[a]	17.0
20	Slovenia[a]	16.9
21	Portugal	16.4
22	Romania[c]	15.9
23	Hungary	15.6
24	Czech Republic	15.1

a 1995 b 1994 c 1993

School time

Pupil:teacher ratio

Primary, 1996 or latest

1	Turkey	28
2	Liechtenstein	25
3	Moldova	23
4	Bosnia	22
	Ireland	22
6	Azerbaijan	20
	Belarus	20
	Romania	20
	Russia	20
	Ukraine	20
11	Armenia	19
	Croatia	19
	Czech Republic	19
	France	19
	Macedonia	19
	Malta	19
	Monaco	19
	Netherlands	19
	Slovakia	19
	United Kingdom	19

Secondary, 1996 or latest

1	Turkey	22
2	Netherlands	21
3	Poland	21
4	Macedonia	16
5	Germany	15
6	Ireland	14
	United Kingdom	14
8	Romania	13
9	Cyprus	12
	France	12
	Greece	12
12	Bulgaria	11
	Malta	11
	Sweden	11

Usual expectations

Number of years of formal education

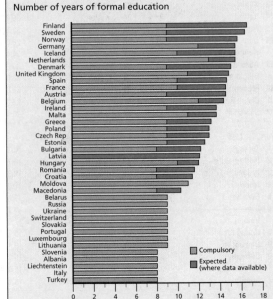

Compulsory

Expected (where data available)

Part IX

SOCIETY

Family matters

Tying the knot
Marriages per 1,000 population

1	Cyprus	11.0		Switzerland	5.2
2	United Kingdom	10.7	21	Lithuania	5.1
3	Denmark	9.1	22	Finland	5.0
4	Turkey	8.0		Slovakia	5.0
5	Macedonia	7.0	24	France	4.9
6	Belarus	6.9	25	Austria	4.8
7	Albania	6.8	26	Hungary	4.7
8	Portugal	6.7		Italy	4.7
9	Malta	6.1		Sweden	4.7
	Ukraine	6.1	29	Luxembourg	4.6
11	Moldova	6.0	30	Czech Republic	4.5
	Romania	6.0	31	Bulgaria	4.1
13	Croatia	5.7	32	Belgium	3.8
14	Iceland	5.6	33	Poland	3.7
15	Greece	5.5		Slovenia	3.7
16	Germany	5.4	35	Estonia	3.6
	Netherlands	5.4		Georgia	3.6
18	Norway	5.3	37	Latvia	3.3
19	Spain	5.2	38	Ireland	2.2

Breaking up
Divorces per 1,000 population

1	Belarus	4.7	22	Iceland	1.8
2	Ukraine	3.6		Luxembourg	1.8
3	Lithuania	3.4	24	Portugal	1.6
	United Kingdom	3.4		Slovakia	1.6
5	Estonia	3.3	26	Bulgaria	1.4
6	Russia	3.2		Cyprus	1.4
7	Czech Republic	3.1		Georgia	1.4
8	Moldova	3.0	29	Liechtenstein	1.2
9	Belgium	2.7		Poland	1.2
10	Finland	2.6	31	Slovenia	1.1
	Hungary	2.6	32	Croatia	0.9
	Latvia	2.6		Greece	0.9
	Switzerland	2.6	34	Albania	0.8
14	Denmark	2.5		Azerbaijan	0.8
15	Germany	2.4		Spain	0.8
	Norway	2.4	37	Italy	0.7
17	Sweden	2.3	38	Armenia	0.6
18	Austria	2.1	39	Turkey	0.5
19	France	2.0	40	Bosnia	0.4
	Netherlands	2.0	41	Macedonia	0.3
21	Romania	1.9			

Births outside marriage
Per 100 births, 1996

1	Iceland	60.1	22	Belgium[c]	15.9
2	Sweden	53.9	23	Luxembourg	15.0
3	Norway	48.3	24	Moldova	14.6
4	Estonia	48.1	24	Slovakia	14.0
5	Denmark[a]	46.5	26	Ukraine[b]	12.8
6	France[b]	36.1	27	Lithuania[a]	12.6
7	Finland	35.4	28	Belarus[b]	12.1
8	United Kingdom[a]	33.6	29	Spain[b]	10.8
9	Latvia	33.1	30	Poland	10.2
10	Slovenia	31.8	31	Armenia[a]	9.3
11	Bulgaria	28.2	32	Macedonia[a]	8.1
12	Austria	28.0	33	Italy[a]	7.7
13	Ireland[a]	22.7	34	Croatia[b]	7.6
14	Hungary	22.6	35	Bosnia[d]	7.4
15	Georgia[c]	21.8	36	Switzerland	7.3
16	Russia[a]	21.1	37	Liechtenstein[d]	6.9
17	Romania	20.7	38	Azerbaijan[c]	4.4
18	Portugal	18.3		Turkey[d]	4.4
19	Czech Republic	16.9	40	Malta	3.2
	Netherlands	16.9	41	Greece	3.0
21	Germany[a]	16.1	42	Cyprus	1.5

Abortion
No. per 1,000 women of child-bearing age, 1996

1	Romania	78.0	19	Slovakia	19.7
2	Russia[a]	68.4	20	Sweden	18.7
3	Belarus	67.5	21	Denmark[a]	16.1
4	Ukraine	57.2	22	Azerbaijan	16.0
5	Estonia	53.8	23	England and Wales	15.6
6	Bulgaria	51.3	24	Norway	15.6
7	Latvia	44.1	25	Croatia	12.9
8	Moldova	38.8	26	France[a]	12.4
9	Liechtenstein[b]	37.0	27	Italy	11.4
10	Armenia	35.4	28	Scotland	11.2
11	Hungary	34.7	29	Finland	10.0
12	Lithuania	34.4	30	Switzerland	8.4
13	Macedonia	28.5	31	Germany	7.6
14	Albania	27.2	32	Belgium	6.8
15	Turkey[e]	25.0	33	Netherlands	6.5
16	Slovenia	23.2	34	Ireland	5.9
17	Georgia	21.9	35	Spain	5.7
18	Czech Republic	20.7			

a 1995
b 1994
c 1992
d 1990
e 1993

Age factors

Legal sex
Age of consent

	Heterosexuals	Lesbians	Gay men
Albania	14	14	14
Andorra	16	16	16
Austria	14	14	14/18
Belgium	16/18	16/18	16/18
Bulgaria	14	14	14
Croatia	14	18	18
Cyprus	16	16	18
Czech Republic	15	15	15
Denmark	15/18	15/18	15/18
Estonia	14	14	16
Finland	16	18	18
France	15/18	15/18	15/18
Germany	14/16	14/16	14/16
Greece	15	15	17
Hungary	14	18	18
Iceland	14	14	14
Ireland[a]	17	15	17
Italy	14/16	14/16	14/16
Liechtenstein	14	14	14/18
Luxembourg	16	16	16
Malta	12/18	12/18	12/18
Netherlands	12/16	12/16	12/16
Norway	16	16	16
Poland	15	15	15
Portugal	14/16	14/16	14/16
Romania	14	banned	banned
Russia	14/16	14/16	14/16
San Marino	14/16	14/16	14/16
Serbia	14	14	18
Slovakia	15	15	15
Slovenia	14	14	14
Spain	13/16	13/16	13/16
Sweden	15	15	15
Switzerland	16	16	16
Turkey[b]	16/18	16/18	16/18
United Kingdom[c]	16	16	16

a Ireland: the age of consent shown is the age for intercourse, including anal intercourse, which is 17, except in the case of heterosexual couples who marry at 16 with their parents' consent. The age of consent for other sexual acts is 15 for heterosexuals and lesbians, and 17 for gay men.

b Turkey: the age of consent is 18 for vaginal intercourse and for anal intercourse, and 16 for all other sexual acts.

c United Kingdom: the age of consent for heterosexual sex is 17 in Northern Ireland, except in the case of couples who marry at 16 with their parents' consent.

Notes
Male homosexuality is banned in Armenia, Azerbaijan, Bosnia, Georgia, Macedonia and Romania. Female homosexuality is also banned in Romania.

When two ages are shown this is either because a higher age applies where the older person is in a position of authority or influence over the younger, or because sexual activity is legal at the lower age unless the younger person subsequently complains.

Voting age

Monaco	21	Lithuania	18
Liechtenstein	20	Luxembourg	18
Albania	18	Macedonia	18
Andorra	18	Malta	18
Armenia	18	Moldova	18
Austria	18	Netherlands	18
Azerbaijan	18	Norway	18
Belarus	18	Poland	18
Belgium	18	Portugal	18
Bulgaria	18	Romania	18
Cyprus	18	Russia	18
Czech Republic	18	San Marino	18
Denmark	18	Slovakia	18
Estonia	18	Spain	18
Finland	18	Sweden	18
France	18	Switzerland	18
Georgia	18	Turkey	18
Germany	18	Ukraine	18
Greece	18	United Kingdom	18
Hungary	18	Bosnia[b]	16
Iceland	18	Croatia[b]	16
Ireland	18	Serbia[b]	16
Italy[a]	18	Slovenia[b]	16
Latvia	18		

Retirement age
EU15

	Men	Women
Austria	65	60
Belgium	65	61
Denmark	67	67
Finland	65	65
France	60	60
Germany	65	65
Greece	65	65
Ireland	65	65
Italy	64	59
Luxembourg	65	65
Netherlands	65	65
Portugal	65	63
Spain	65	65
Sweden	65	65
United Kingdom	65	60

a Senatorial elections, minimun age 25.
b If employed, otherwise 18.

Religion

Who belongs to which faith
% of total population

Albania

Muslim 70	Orthodox 20	Other 10

Andorra

Roman Catholic 99	Other 1

Armenia

Orthodox 94	Other 6

Austria

Roman Catholic 85	Protestant 6	Other 9

Azerbaijan

Muslim 93	Orthodox 5	Other 2

Belarus

Orthodox 80	Other 20

Belgium

Roman Catholic 75	Protestant 20	Other 5

Bosnia

Muslim 40	Orthodox 31	Other 29

Bulgaria

Orthodox 85	Muslim 13	Other 2

Croatia

Roman Catholic 77	Orthodox 11	Other 12

Cyprus

Orthodox 78	Muslim 18	Other 4

Czech Republic

Atheist 40	Roman Catholic 39	Other 21

Denmark

Evangelical Lutheran 91	Protestant 2	Other 7

Estonia

Lutheran 78	Orthodox 19	Other 3

Finland

Evangelical Lutheran 89	Orthodox 1	Other 10

France

Roman Catholic 90	Protestant 2	Other 8

Georgia

Orthodox 65	Muslim 11	Other 24

Germany

Protestant 38	Roman Catholic 34	Other 28

Greece

Orthodox 98	Muslim 1	Other 1

Hungary

Roman Catholic 68	Calvinist 20	Other 12

Iceland

Evangelical Lutheran 96	Roman Catholic 1	Other 3

Ireland

Roman Catholic 93	Anglican 3	Other 4

Italy

Roman Catholic 98	Other 2

Latvia

Evangelical Lutheran 70	Orthodox 28	Other 2

Liechtenstein

Roman Catholic 80	Protestant 7	Other 13

Lithuania

Roman Catholic 70	Orthodox 4	Other 26

Luxembourg

Roman Catholic 97		Other 3

Macedonia

Orthodox 67	Muslim 30	Other 3

Malta

Roman Catholic 98		Other 2

Moldova

Orthodox 98	Jewish 2	

Monaco

Roman Catholic 95		Other 5

Netherlands

Roman Catholic 34	Protestant 25	Other 41

Norway

Evangelical Lutheran 88		Other 12

Poland

Roman Catholic 95	Orthodox 2	Other 3

Portugal

Roman Catholic 97	Protestant 1	Other 2

Romania

Orthodox 70	Roman Catholic 6	Other 24

Russia

Orthodox 56	Muslim 23	Other 21

Serbia and Montenegro

Orthodox 65	Muslim 19	Other 16

Slovakia

Roman Catholic 60	Protestant 8	Other 32

Slovenia

Roman Catholic 71	Lutheran 1	Other 28

Spain

Roman Catholic 99		Other 1

Sweden

Evangelical Lutheran 94	Roman Catholic 2	Other 4

Switzerland

Roman Catholic 47	Protestant 40	Other 13

Turkey

Muslim 99		Other 1

Ukraine

Orthodox 76	Roman Catholic 14	Other 10

United Kingdom

Anglican 47	Roman Catholic 16	Other 37

Vatican

Roman Catholic 100		

Income and savings

Poor shares[a]
% of income

Lowest 20% share		Lowest 10% share	
Georgia[c]	4.4	Georgia[c]	1.5
Russia[bd]	4.4	Russia[bd]	1.7
Armenia[bc]	5.5	Moldova[e]	2.2
Moldova[e]	5.6	Armenia[bc]	2.3
Turkey[bf]	5.8	Turkey[bf]	2.3
United Kingdom[g]	6.6	Ireland[h]	2.5
Ireland[h]	6.7	Switzerland[i]	2.6
Azerbaijan[i]	6.9	United Kingdom[g]	2.6
Switzerland[i]	6.9	Azerbaijan[i]	2.8
Estonia[d]	7.0	France[i]	2.8
France[i]	7.2	Netherlands[f]	2.8
Netherlands[f]	7.3	Spain[l]	2.8
Portugal[i]	7.3	Latvia[d]	2.9
Greece[k]	7.5	Estonia[d]	3.0
Spain[l]	7.5	Greece[k]	3.0
Latvia[d]	7.6	Lithuania[bc]	3.1
Lithuania[bc]	7.8	Portugal[i]	3.1
Poland[bd]	7.8	Poland[bd]	3.2
Germany[f]	8.2	Germany[f]	3.3
Italy[i]	8.7	Italy[i]	3.5
Croatia[d]	8.8	Denmark[j]	3.6
Ukraine[b]	8.8	Belgium[j]	3.7
Romania[f]	8.9	Croatia[d]	3.7
Slovenia[d]	9.1	Romania[f]	3.7
Luxembourg[f]	9.4	Sweden[j]	3.7
Belgium[j]	9.5	Ukraine[b]	3.7
Denmark[j]	9.6	Slovenia[d]	3.9
Sweden[j]	9.6	Luxembourg[f]	4.0
Norway[i]	9.7	Norway[i]	4.1

Rich shares[a]
% of income, highest 10% share

Russia[bd]	38.7	Spain[l]	25.2
Armenia[bc]	35.2	Switzerland[i]	25.2
Turkey[bf]	32.3	France[i]	25.1
Moldova[e]	30.7	Netherlands[f]	25.1
Estonia[d]	29.8	Poland[bd]	24.7
Portugal[i]	28.4	Germany[f]	23.7
Georgia[c]	27.9	Croatia[d]	23.3
Azerbaijan[i]	27.8	Ukraine[b]	23.2
Ireland[h]	27.4	Slovenia[d]	23.0
United Kingdom[g]	27.3	Bulgaria[e]	22.8
Latvia[d]	25.9	Romania[f]	22.7
Lithuania[bc]	25.6	Czech Republic[c]	22.4
Greece[k]	25.3	Luxembourg[f]	22.0

a Income shares by percentiles of population and ranked by income per person.
b Spending shares by percentiles of population and ranked by spending per person.
c 1996   d 1998   e 1997   f 1994   g 1991   h 1987   i 1995   j 1992   k 1993   l 1990

Distribution of income[a]

Gini index[m]

Russia[bd]	48.7	Spain[l]	32.5
Armenia[bc]	44.4	Latvia[d]	32.4
Turkey[bf]	41.5	Lithuania[c]	32.4
Moldova[e]	40.6	Germany[f]	30.0
Estonia[d]	37.6	Croatia[d]	29.0
Georgia[c]	37.1	Ukraine[b]	29.0
United Kingdom[g]	36.1	Slovenia[d]	28.4
Azerbaijan[i]	36.0	Romania[f]	28.2
Ireland[h]	35.9	Italy[i]	27.3
Portugal[i]	35.6	Luxembourg[f]	26.9
Switzerland[j]	33.1	Bulgaria[e]	26.4
France[i]	32.7	Norway[i]	25.8
Greece[k]	32.7	Finland[g]	25.6
Netherlands[f]	32.6	Czech Republic[c]	25.4
Poland[bd]	32.6	Belgium[i]	25.0

Household savings rates

% of disposable income

1980			1990		
1	Portugal	24.3	1	Italy[n]	18.4
2	Italy[n]	23.4	2	Portugal	16.4
3	Belgium[n]	19.3	3	Germany[n]	16.1
4	France[n]	17.6	4	Belgium[n]	13.9
5	Ireland	15.8	5	France[n]	12.6
6	United Kingdom[n]	13.4	6	Austria[n]	12.2
7	Germany[n]	12.8	7	Netherlands[o]	11.9
8	Austria[n]	11.5	8	Spain[n]	11.8
9	Spain[n]	11.3	9	Denmark	11.4
10	Sweden	6.7	10	Switzerland	10.3
11	Finland	5.4	11	Ireland	9.8
12	Norway	2.7	12	United Kingdom[n]	7.7

1995			1999		
1	Italy[n]	16.6	1	Hungary	17.5
2	France[n]	15.9	2	France[n]	15.7
3	Belgium[n]	15.1	3	Belgium[n]	12.9
4	Spain[n]	13.4	4	Italy[n]	12.7
5	United Kingdom[n]	10.5	5	Ireland	11.3
6	Germany[n]	10.3	6	Czech Republic	10.3
	Portugal	10.3	7	Spain[n]	10.2
8	Austria[n]	10.2	8	Portugal	9.5
9	Ireland	9.9	9	Germany[n]	8.6
10	Switzerland	9.5	10	Switzerland	8.1
11	Denmark	7.1	11	Norway	6.7
12	Sweden	6.9	12	United Kingdom[n]	6.2

m The Gini index is a measure of income inequality. 0 means all households have the same income, 100 means one household has all the income.
n Gross savings.
o Excludes mandatory savings through occupational pension schemes.

Consumer spending

Who spends how much

	Household consumption expenditure, $bn, 1999			Household expenditure per head $, 1999	
1	Germany	1,220	1	Switzerland	22,006
2	United Kingdom	950	2	Norway	16,780
3	France	785	3	Denmark	16,686
4	Italy	697	4	United Kingdom	16,191
5	Spain	354	5	Germany	14,848
6	Russia	211	6	Austria	14,409
7	Netherlands	197	7	Sweden	13,593
8	Switzerland	161	8	France	13,373
9	Belgium	133	9	Belgium	13,130
10	Turkey	125	10	Finland	12,665
11	Sweden	121	11	Netherlands	12,586
12	Austria	117	12	Ireland	12,444
13	Poland	100	13	Italy	12,154
14	Denmark	88	14	Spain	8,941
15	Greece	87	15	Greece	8,176
16	Norway	74	16	Portugal	7,229
17	Portugal	71	17	Slovenia	5,566
18	Finland	65	18	Hungary	3,029
19	Ireland	46	19	Czech Republic	2,757
20	Hungary	31	20	Croatia	2,614
21	Czech Republic	28	21	Poland	2,590
22	Romania	24	22	Estonia	2,119
23	Ukraine	22	23	Slovakia	1,980
24	Belarus	16	24	Turkey	1,945
25	Croatia	12	25	Lithuania	1,869
26	Slovakia	11	26	Latvia	1,693
	Slovenia	11	27	Belarus	1,516
28	Bulgaria	9	28	Russia	1,431
29	Lithuania	7	29	Macedonia	1,275
30	Latvia	4	30	Bulgaria	1,113
31	Albania	3	31	Albania	1,064
	Azerbaijan	3	32	Romania	1,054
	Estonia	3	33	Armenia	498
	Macedonia	3	34	Georgia	486
35	Armenia	2	35	Ukraine	436
	Georgia	2	36	Azerbaijan	342
37	Moldova	1	37	Moldova	195

Growth in consumer spending
Average annual growth, volume, %
1990–98

#	Country	Value	#	Country	Value
1	Moldova	7.1	16	Finland	1.7
2	Poland	5.2	17	Macedonia	1.6
3	Ireland	5.1	18	Russia	1.5
4	Albania	4.4	19	Belgium	1.4
5	Slovenia	3.9	20	Germany	1.3
6	Turkey	3.7	21	Italy	1.2
7	Norway	3.3	22	France	1.1
8	Portugal	2.9	23	Sweden	0.7
9	Denmark	2.7		Switzerland	0.7
	Netherlands	2.7	25	Romania	0.4
11	United Kingdom	2.6	26	Slovakia	0.3
12	Czech Republic	2.5	27	Estonia	-0.4
13	Austria	2.0	28	Azerbaijan	-0.7
14	Greece	1.8	29	Hungary	-0.8
	Spain	1.8	30	Bulgaria	-1.5

Working time to buy

All manufacturing industries
1 kilo bread, minutes

#	Country	Value
1	Slovenia	27
2	Lithuania	24
3	Croatia	19
4	Bulgaria	18
	Hungary	18
	Russia[a]	18
	Slovakia	18
8	France	16
9	Italy	15
10	Austria	13
	Ireland	13
12	Greece	12
	Poland	12
14	Czech Republic	11
	Finland	11
	Romania	11
17	Norway	9
	Spain	9
19	Cyprus	8
	Turkey	8
21	Germany	7
	Sweden[a]	7
	Switzerland	7
24	Malta	6
25	Netherlands	5
	United Kingdom	5
27	Denmark	4

All manufacturing industries
Colour TV, hours

#	Country	Value
1	Romania	334.9
2	Croatia	266.8
3	Slovakia	241.4
4	Slovenia	212.2
5	Bulgaria	190.8
6	Hungary	179.2
7	Lithuania	162.3
8	Russia[a]	151.7
9	Turkey	135.9
10	Portugal	122.4
11	Poland	97.5
12	Czech Republic	96.1
13	Austria	95.4
14	Malta	95.3
15	Cyprus[a]	85.9
16	Greece	76.7
17	Germany	36.8
18	Spain[a]	34.4
19	Ireland	32.1
20	Sweden	28.2
21	Italy	26.6
22	Netherlands	25.6
23	Norway	24.5
24	Switzerland[a]	22.0
25	France[a]	21.4
26	United Kingdom[a]	20.6
27	Finland	20.0

a Estimate.

Wired world

Televisions
Colour TVs, % of households, 1999

1	Ireland	99.1	15	South Korea	92.5
2	Belgium	98.5	16	Denmark	92.0
3	United Kingdom	98.3	17	Greece	90.8
4	Netherlands	98.2	18	Slovenia	90.5
5	Spain	98.1	19	Czech Republic	87.1
6	Austria	97.2	20	Croatia	86.8
	Portugal	97.2	21	Kuwait	86.7
8	Sweden	97.1	22	Slovakia	85.7
9	Finland	97.0	23	Hungary	85.2
	Switzerland	97.0	24	Poland	81.9
11	Germany	96.9	25	Russia	79.5
12	France	95.8	26	Estonia	77.6
13	Italy	95.4	27	Belarus	76.5
14	Norway	92.8	28	Ukraine	71.4

Video cassette recorders
% of households, 1999

1	United Kingdom	85.3	15	Portugal	47.1
2	Denmark	82.1	16	Hungary	47.0
3	Ireland	78.6	17	Slovenia	45.1
4	Sweden	76.9	18	Czech Republic	43.0
5	Netherlands	76.1		Greece	43.0
6	Poland	74.4	20	Slovakia	40.1
7	Belgium	73.5	21	Germany	35.8
8	Switzerland	72.9	22	Croatia	32.7
9	Finland	67.3	23	Bulgaria	29.1
10	Italy	65.0	24	Latvia	21.1
11	Spain	64.9	25	Estonia	20.5
12	France	59.8	26	Belarus	17.1
13	Austria	56.9		Lithuania	17.1
14	Norway	55.4	28	Russia	12.1

Internet
Hosts by country, 2001

1	United Kingdom	2,291,369	16	Portugal	177,828
2	Germany	2,163,326	17	Hungary	158,732
3	Italy	1,630,526	18	Czech Republic	153,902
4	Netherlands	1,309,911	19	Greece	148,552
5	France	1,229,763	20	Turkey	113,603
6	Finland	771,725	21	Ireland	88,406
7	Sweden	764,011	22	Iceland	44,040
8	Spain	663,553	23	Romania	41,326
9	Norway	525,030	24	Estonia	40,094
10	Austria	504,144	25	Ukraine	39,655
11	Switzerland	461,456	26	Croatia	23,814
12	Denmark	435,556	27	Slovenia	23,594
13	Belgium	417,130	28	Latvia	19,059
14	Poland	371,943	29	Lithuania	18,320
15	Russia	320,217	30	Bulgaria	17,166

Cable
% of TV-owning households
1999

1	Belgium	92.7	15	Poland	33.7
2	Netherlands	87.7	16	Russia	30.5
3	Switzerland	84.6	17	Iceland	30.3
4	Ireland	82.7	18	Portugal	25.1
5	Romania	63.4	19	Lithuania	19.5
6	Slovenia	57.5	20	United Kingdom	14.2
7	Slovakia	57.4	21	France	13.8
8	Denmark	55.4	22	Bulgaria	8.8
9	Sweden	52.9	23	Turkey	7.6
10	Germany	50.5	24	Croatia	5.5
11	Finland	45.1	25	Estonia	4.3
12	Norway	39.6	26	Spain	3.6
13	Hungary	38.4	27	Italy	1.1
14	Austria	34.3	28	Greece	0.8

Satellite dishes
% of TV-owning households
1999

1	Poland	73.4	14	Ireland	14.7
2	France	60.9	15	Switzerland	14.0
3	Denmark	51.6	16	Portugal	11.5
4	Croatia	42.5	17	Spain	10.6
5	Slovenia	42.4	18	Estonia	10.4
6	Austria	36.7	19	Lithuania	9.1
7	Germany	34.0	20	Bulgaria	8.0
8	Slovakia	29.7	21	Romania	5.7
9	Norway	23.8	22	Italy	4.8
10	United Kingdom	23.0	23	Netherlands	4.1
11	Sweden	20.3	24	Belgium	3.9
12	Hungary	19.4	25	Turkey	3.8
13	Finland	15.1			

Cellular mobile subscribers
Per 100 inhabitants, 2000

1	Luxembourg	87.2	13	Germany	57.9
2	Austria	78.6	14	Greece	55.9
3	Italy	73.7	15	Belgium	54.9
4	Finland	72.6	16	France	49.4
5	Norway	70.3	17	Ireland	44.7
6	Netherlands	67.1	18	Slovenia	30.9
7	United Kingdom	67.0	19	Spain	30.6
8	Portugal	66.5	20	Estonia	26.8
9	Switzerland	63.6	21	Cyprus	22.5
10	Iceland	61.9	22	Czech Republic	19.0
11	Denmark	61.4	23	Slovakia	17.0
12	Sweden	58.3	24	Hungary	16.2

Books, news, movies, museums

Books

Sales per head, $, 1999

1	Norway	127.2
2	Germany	119.6
3	Finland	97.5
4	Belgium	95.6
5	Switzerland	89.8
6	United Kingdom	78.0
7	Sweden	75.2
8	Denmark	70.4
9	Netherlands	62.2
10	Spain	61.2
11	Ireland	56.1
12	Austria	47.8
13	France	46.7
14	Italy	46.1
15	Portugal	35.0
16	Greece	22.0
17	Czech Republic	15.4
18	Hungary	13.5
19	Poland	12.8
20	Slovakia	3.6
21	Bulgaria	2.5
22	Russia	0.8
23	Turkey	0.5

Libraries

Books per head, latest

1	Bulgaria	11.6
2	Lithuania	9.0
3	Belarus	7.6
	Estonia	7.6
5	Finland	7.2
6	Russia	7.1
7	Iceland	6.8
	Ukraine	6.8
9	Georgia	6.2
10	Denmark	5.9
	Latvia	5.9
12	Sweden	5.0
13	Norway	4.7
14	Hungary	4.5
15	Moldova	4.3
16	Czech Republic	4.1
17	Ireland	3.9
18	Slovenia	3.8
	Switzerland	3.8
20	Slovakia	3.6
21	Poland	3.5
22	Belgium	2.9
	Netherlands	2.9

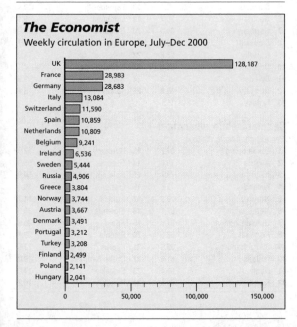

The Economist

Weekly circulation in Europe, July–Dec 2000

UK	128,187
France	28,983
Germany	28,683
Italy	13,084
Switzerland	11,590
Spain	10,859
Netherlands	10,809
Belgium	9,241
Ireland	6,536
Sweden	5,444
Russia	4,906
Greece	3,804
Norway	3,744
Austria	3,667
Denmark	3,491
Portugal	3,212
Turkey	3,208
Finland	2,499
Poland	2,141
Hungary	2,041

0   50,000   100,000   150,000

Daily newspapers
Circulation per 1,000 population, latest

1	Liechtenstein	606		Estonia		173
2	Iceland	535	23	France		147
3	Norway	494		Ireland		147
4	Sweden	464	25	Bosnia		146
5	Finland	453	26	Malta		130
6	Switzerland	344	27	Croatia		114
7	Luxembourg	327	28	Cyprus		111
8	Romania	324		Turkey		111
9	United Kingdom	315	30	Serbia & Montenegro		110
10	Germany	309	31	Russia		105
11	Denmark	303	32	Spain		99
12	Netherlands	287	33	Greece		95
13	Czech Republic	256	34	Lithuania		92
14	Bulgaria	253	35	San Marino		72
15	Monaco	250	36	Portugal		68
16	Latvia	246	37	Moldova		59
17	Slovenia	206	38	Andorra		58
18	Austria	205		Slovakia		58
19	Hungary	196	40	Ukraine		54
20	Belarus	174	41	Italy		39
21	Belgium	173	42	Poland		32

Cinemas
Attendance per person, latest year

1	Iceland	7.1
2	Spain	3.3
3	Ireland	3.2
4	France	2.5
5	Norway	2.4
	United Kingdom	2.4
7	Belgium	2.3
	Luxembourg	2.3
9	Denmark	2.1
	Switzerland	2.1
11	Austria	1.9
12	Germany	1.8
	Italy	1.8
	Sweden	1.8
15	Slovenia	1.7
16	Hungary	1.6
17	Portugal	1.5
18	Cyprus	1.3
19	Finland	1.2
	Greece	1.2
	Netherlands	1.2
22	Czech Republic	1.0
23	Belarus	0.9

Museums
Visits per person, latest year

1	Switzerland	4.4
2	Iceland	3.6
3	Austria	2.9
4	Malta	2.6
5	Sweden	2.1
6	Norway	2.0
7	Denmark	1.9
8	Slovenia	1.7
9	Cyprus	1.3
	Netherlands	1.3
11	Germany	1.1
12	Finland	1.0
	Hungary	1.0
14	Czech Republic	0.7
	Estonia	0.7
	Spain	0.7
17	Slovakia	0.6
18	France	0.5
	Lithuania	0.5
	Poland	0.5
	Portugal	0.5
	Romania	0.5

Crime and punishment

Offensive records
Total criminal offences per 100,000 population, 1999

1	Iceland	31,332	18	Slovenia	3,138
2	Russia	20,514	19	Poland	2,901
3	Finland	14,350	20	Andorra	2,617
4	Sweden[a]	13,455	21	Romania	2,206
5	Norway	9,769	22	Latvia	2,097
6	Denmark	9,301	23	Lithuania	2,029
7	Germany	7,682	24	Bulgaria	1,771
8	Switzerland	7,030	25	Ireland	1,696
9	Luxembourg	6,281	26	Belarus	1,282
10	France	6,097	27	Croatia	1,216
11	Austria	6,095	28	Ukraine	1,115
12	Hungary	5,011	29	Cyprus[a]	667
13	Spain	4,449	30	Portugal	661
14	Czech Republic	4,142	31	Turkey	547
15	Greece	3,641	32	Armenia	264
16	Estonia	3,565	33	Azerbaijan	176
17	Monaco	3,430	34	Albania	169

Juvenile crime
% of total crime committed by people under age 21 yrs, 1999

1	Norway	38.0	16	Belarus	11.9
2	France	21.3	17	Russia	10.7
3	Monaco	20.6	18	Latvia	10.1
4	Finland	20.4	19	Croatia	10.0
5	Slovenia	19.8	20	Ireland	9.0
6	Switzerland	19.5	21	Cyprus[a]	8.8
7	Andorra	18.2		Hungary	8.8
8	Ukraine	16.7	23	Bulgaria	8.5
9	Estonia	16.3	24	Luxembourg	8.4
10	Austria	15.3	25	Czech Republic	7.5
11	Poland	14.5	26	Greece	6.6
12	Bosnia	14.3	27	Armenia	6.0
13	Lithuania	13.3	28	Azerbaijan	4.5
14	Germany	13.1	29	Turkey	4.1
15	Albania	12.0	30	Spain	3.8

Murder most foul
Murder per 100,000 population, 1999

1	Albania	26.2	12	Croatia	6.1
2	Russia	21.3	13	Azerbaijan	4.2
3	Luxembourg	17.2	14	Armenia	4.1
4	Estonia	13.8		Denmark	4.1
5	Belarus	11.6		Hungary	4.1
6	Sweden[a]	10.4	17	Turkey	3.9
7	Ukraine	10.0	18	Slovenia	3.6
8	Latvia	9.3	19	Germany	3.5
9	Lithuania	9.0	20	France	3.4
10	Bulgaria	7.3	21	Cyprus[a]	3.1
11	Romania	7.1		Portugal	3.1

a 1998 Note: comparable data not available for some countries.

Prisoners en masse
Total prison population, 2000

1	Russia	923,765	14	Hungary	15,588
2	Ukraine	219,955	15	Netherlands	13,847
3	Germany	79,493	16	Portugal[b]	13,093
4	Turkey	71,860	17	Moldova	9,837
5	Poland	70,544	18	Bulgaria	9,424
6	England and Wales	64,631	19	Lithuania	8,960
7	Belarus[a]	58,879	20	Georgia	8,779
8	Italy	53,481	21	Belgium	8,671
9	Romania	49,682	22	Latvia	8,603
10	France	48,835	23	Greece	8,038
11	Spain	45,633	24	Armenia[c]	7,608
12	Azerbaijan[a]	24,851	25	Slovakia	7,128
13	Czech Republic	21,538	26	Austria	6,896

Prisoners in proportion
Prisoners per 100,000 population, 2000

1	Russia	635	15	Slovakia	132
2	Belarus[a]	577	16	Portugal[b]	131
3	Ukraine	436	17	England and Wales	122
4	Latvia	357	18	Spain	116
5	Estonia	330	19	Bulgaria	115
6	Azerbaijan[a]	323	20	Turkey	108
7	Moldova	266	21	Germany	97
8	Lithuania	242	22	Italy	93
9	Romania	221	23	Luxembourg	90
10	Czech Republic	210	24	Switzerland	89
11	Armenia[c]	200	25	Albania[c]	87
12	Poland	183		Netherlands	87
13	Georgia	176	27	Austria	85
14	Hungary	156		Belgium	85

How crowded prisons are
Prison population per 100 places, 2000

1	Bulgaria[c]	197	15	Poland	104
2	Greece	167	16	Ireland	103
3	Albania[c]	165	17	Armenia[c]	102
4	Hungary	152	18	England and Wales	101
5	Romania	149		Sweden	101
6	Italy	126	20	France	100
7	Belgium	117	21	Turkey	99
	Portugal[b]	117	22	Russia	96
9	Belarus[a]	113	23	Cyprus[c]	94
10	Ukraine	110		Switzerland	94
11	Slovenia	108	25	Luxembourg	91
	Spain	108	26	Denmark	90
13	Czech Republic	106		Netherlands	90
14	Germany	105		Norway	90

a 1997   b 1999   c 1998

Music

Album sales
Sales of LPs, CDs and music cassettes per head, 2000

1	United Kingdom	3.7	15	Portugal	1.5
2	Denmark	3.6	16	Cyprus	1.3
3	Switzerland	3.5	17	Poland	0.9
4	Norway	3.3		Slovenia	0.9
5	Sweden	3.0	19	Greece	0.8
6	Iceland	2.9		Italy	0.8
7	Germany	2.8		Russia	0.8
8	Belgium	2.6	22	Czech Republic	0.7
9	Austria	2.4		Hungary	0.7
	Ireland	2.4		Romania	0.7
11	Finland	2.2	25	Estonia	0.6
	Netherlands	2.2	26	Latvia	0.3
13	France	2.0		Lithuania	0.3
14	Spain	1.8		Slovakia	0.3

CD popularity
Penetration of CDs as % of total album sales of LPs, CDs and music cassettes, 2000

1	Iceland	100.0	17	Portugal	81.3
2	Azerbaijan	99.3	18	Italy	79.8
	Norway	99.3	19	Czech Republic	69.6
4	Netherlands	99.1	20	Slovenia	64.7
5	Denmark	98.9	21	Slovakia	62.5
6	Sweden	98.7	22	Poland	58.7
7	Austria	96.8	23	Lithuania	58.3
8	Greece	94.8	24	Hungary	54.7
9	Finland	94.6	25	Croatia	54.5
10	United Kingdom	93.2	26	Estonia	50.0
11	France	92.2	27	Latvia	37.5
12	Ireland	90.6	28	Ukraine	16.7
13	Germany	90.4	29	Bulgaria	15.8
14	Cyprus	90.0	30	Russia	9.1
15	Switzerland	88.6	31	Romania	1.3
16	Spain	87.3			

CD players per 100 households, 1999

1	Netherlands	86.5	14	Hungary	28.1
2	Denmark	85.1	15	France	23.6
3	Norway	82.1	16	Greece	18.3
4	Sweden	78.1	17	Slovenia	14.1
5	Germany	75.3	18	Poland	13.3
6	United Kingdom	75.1	19	Croatia	13.1
7	Austria	63.6	20	Italy	12.6
8	Belgium	62.6	21	Czech Republic	12.1
9	Finland	59.1	22	Russia	8.0
10	Switzerland	50.7	23	Estonia	7.1
11	Ireland	39.2		Slovakia	7.1
12	Spain	33.0	25	Turkey	6.4
13	Portugal	30.3	26	Ukraine	6.1

Recorded music sales

		$, 2000			*$ per head, 2000*
1	United Kingdom	2,829	1	Iceland	54.9
2	Germany	2,421	2	Norway	52.2
3	France	1,695	3	United Kingdom	47.9
4	Spain	563	4	Denmark	43.9
5	Italy	532	5	Ireland	38.2
6	Netherlands	455	6	Switzerland	37.1
7	Sweden	323	7	Sweden	36.5
8	Austria	289	8	Austria	35.8
9	Belgium	267	9	Germany	29.5
10	Switzerland	264	10	Netherlands	28.8
11	Denmark	233	11	France	27.9
12	Norway	232	12	Belgium	26.1
13	Russia	197	13	Finland	22.4
14	Poland	157	14	Cyprus	22.1
15	Ireland	142	15	Spain	14.3
	Portugal	142	16	Portugal	14.2
17	Turkey	121	17	Italy	9.2
18	Finland	116	18	Slovenia	9.1
19	Greece	90	19	Greece	8.6
20	Hungary	57	20	Hungary	5.7
21	Czech Republic	41	21	Estonia	4.6
22	Romania	30	22	Poland	4.0
23	Slovenia	18	23	Czech Republic	3.9
24	Cyprus	17	24	Latvia	2.6
25	Iceland	15	25	Croatia	2.3
26	Ukraine	13	26	Turkey	1.9
27	Croatia	10	27	Slovakia	1.8
	Slovakia	10	28	Romania	1.3
29	Estonia	7		Russia	1.3

Pirates

Piracy level as % of units, 1999

<10%	10–25%	25–50%	50%>
Austria	Finland	Cyprus	Bulgaria
Belgium	Hungary	Greece	Estonia
Czech Republic	Italy	Poland	Latvia
Denmark		Slovenia	Lithuania
France			Romania
Germany			Russia
Iceland			Ukraine
Ireland			
Netherlands			
Norway			
Portugal			
Slovakia			
Spain			
Sweden			
Switzerland			
United Kingdom			

Pets

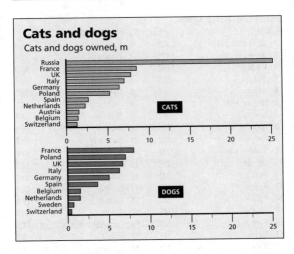

Cats and dogs
Cats and dogs owned, m

CATS

DOGS

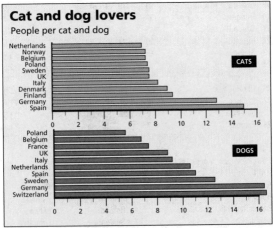

Cat and dog lovers
People per cat and dog

CATS

DOGS

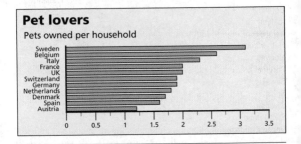

Pet lovers
Pets owned per household

GOVERNMENT AND DEFENCE

Europe's national governments

Albania

Parliamentary republic with a constitution adopted in 1998. Legislative power is vested in the People's Assembly, a single chamber of at least 155 deputies with elections held every four years. Forty deputies are elected by proportional representation. The People's Assembly elects a president of the republic as head of state whose term of office is five years. Executive power is the responsibility of a council of ministers, led by a prime minister who is the head of government. The president appoints a prime minister who appoints a Council of Ministers subject to the approval of the People's Assembly.

Andorra

Parliamentary monarchy with a constitution adopted in 1993. Andorra is uniquely a co-principality. Its joint heads of state are the bishop of Urgel and the president of France, though since 1993 the positions have been almost entirely honorary. The legislature is the General Council (*Conseil General*) whose 28 councillors are elected for four-year terms. Executive authority resides with a head of government (*Cap du Govern*) elected by a majority of the General Council. Government ministers are nominated by the head of government.

Armenia

Parliamentary republic with a constitution adopted in 1995. Legislative authority resides with the National Assembly, made up of 131 deputies, elected for terms of four years. A president, directly elected for five years, is head of state and exercises executive power. In addition the president appoints a prime minister and, subject to the prime minister's recommendation, members of the government.

Austria

Federal parliamentary republic with a constitution adopted in 1920. The bicameral legislature, the Federal Assembly, consists of the National Council (*Nationalrat*) and the Federal Council (*Bundesrat*). The former has 183 members, elected for four-year terms by a system of proportional representation. The latter has 64 members, allocated according to the strengths of the parties in the provincial assemblies, with terms corresponding to those of the provincial government represented. A president is elected directly every six years as head of state and appoints a chancellor as head of the federal executive branch, and other ministers on the chancellor's advice.

The provincial assemblies (*landtage*) of the nine states elect state governments of a provincial governor and councillors.

Azerbaijan

Presidential republic with a constitution adopted in 1995. The national assembly (*Milli Majlis*) is the supreme legislative body and has 125 members elected directly for terms of five years, one-fifth by proportional representation from a party list and the remainder in single-member constituencies. Executive power is held by the head of state, a president, who is also elected for five years. The president appoints and exercises executive power through a cabinet of ministers headed by a prime minister. The president retains the right to call legislative elections.

Belarus

Presidential republic with a constitution adopted in 1994 and amended in 1996. The bicameral national assembly exercises legislative power. It comprises the 110-member House of Representatives elected directly and the House of the Republic with 64 members, 56 members elected by local councils (eight per region) and eight appointed by the president. The terms for all members of the National Assembly are four years.

The president, elected directly every five years, is head of state. Executive power resides with a cabinet of ministers under a chairman appointed by the president, subject to ratification by the House of Representatives.

Belgium

Parliamentary monarchy with a constitution adopted in 1831 but subsequently considerably revised. Legislative power is exercised by a bicameral parliament and the monarch who is head of state. Parliament comprises the Chamber of Representatives with 150 members, elected by proportional representation, and a Senate with 71 members, of whom 40 are elected directly by proportional representation and 10 are appointed by the elected senators, 21 appointed by the assemblies of the three linguistic communities. Children of the monarch are also entitled to honorary membership of the Senate. Members of both houses are elected for terms of up to four years. Supreme executive power is nominally held by the monarch but is exercised by a cabinet headed by a prime minister. Considerable autonomy is exercised by assemblies representing the three regions of Flanders, Wallonia and Brussels, and the three linguistic communities.

Bosnia

Presidential republic with a constitution adopted in 1994 and amended to incorporate the terms of the Dayton peace agreement and the division of the country into a Serb republic and a Croat-Muslim federation. A president is head of state and is one of three members of a rotating presidency representing Croats, Muslims and Serbs, elected directly for terms of four years. A bicameral parliament comprises the 42-member, directly elected Chamber of Representatives (made up one-third of Serbs and two-thirds of Croats and Muslims) and the 15-member Chamber of Peoples, comprises five members representing each community, elected by sub-national self-governing ethnic assemblies. Both houses are elected for two-year terms by a system of proportional representation. The central government is responsible for defence, commerce and foreign affairs.

At sub-national level the Croat-Muslim federation has a president (alternately Croat and Muslim) and a bicameral legislative assembly, comprising the 140-member House of Representatives and the 74-member House of Peoples, both elected for terms of two years by a system of proportional representation. The Serb Republic has a unicameral 83-member legislature and a president elected for two-year terms by a system of proportional representation.

Bulgaria

Parliamentary republic with a constitution adopted in 1991. The single chamber National Assembly holds legislative power. It has 240 members elected for four-year terms. Executive power is exercised by a Council of Ministers headed by a chairman who is also prime minister. A president, who is directly elected as head of state for five years, appoints the prime minister, usually from one of the two largest parties.

Croatia

Presidential republic with a constitution adopted in 1990. The assembly (*Sabor*) exercises legislative power through the Chamber of Representatives (*Zastupnicki dom*) and the Chamber of Counties (*Zupanijski dom*), both of which are directly elected for four-year terms. The former comprises up to 151 members; the latter has 68 members, five appointed by the president. The president, prime minister and ministers have executive authority. The prime minister and members of the government are appointed by the president and are responsible both to the president and the Chamber of Representatives. The president is elected directly for five-year terms and is head of state.

Cyprus

The island of Cyprus is divided between two administrations. The southern (Greek-Cypriot) presidential republic has an executive president who exercises power through a council of ministers. The legislative House of Representatives nominally contains 80 members according to the 1960 power-sharing constitution but in 1963 the 24 members elected by the Turkish-Cypriot minority stopped attending. Members are elected for five-year terms by proportional representation.

The Turkish Republic of Northern Cyprus, which is not recognised internationally, has a 50-seat Legislative Assembly and an executive president as head of state who exercises power through a council of ministers.

Czech Republic

Parliamentary republic with a constitution adopted in 1992. A bicameral legislature consists of the 200-member Chamber of Deputies, elected for four-year terms, and an 81-member Senate directly elected for six-year terms. The president is head of state and is elected by a joint session of both chambers for five years. Executive power is vested in a council of ministers under a prime minister appointed by the president.

Denmark

Parliamentary monarchy with a constitution adopted in 1849 and last revised in 1953. A unicameral parliament (*Folketing*) holds legislative power jointly with the monarch though the latter's powers are nominal. Parliament's 179 members, including 2 each for Greenland and the Faroe Islands, are elected by proportional representation for terms of four years. The monarch is head of state. A prime minister is head of government and exercises executive power through a cabinet.

Estonia

Parliamentary republic with a constitution adopted in 1992. The 101-member state assembly (*Riigikogu*) has legislative power and is elected every four years by proportional representation. It elects a president, who is head of state, for a five-year term. The president nominates a prime minister for approval by the State Assembly.

Finland

Parliamentary republic with a constitution adopted in 1919. Legislative power is the responsibility of the unicameral 200-member parliament (*Eduskunta*), elected for four-year terms by proportional representation. The president, elected directly for six years, is head of state and holds supreme executive power. The president appoints a council of state, which includes a prime minister and other ministers.

France

Presidential republic with a constitution adopted in 1958. The 577-member national assembly is directly elected for five-year terms. The Senate has 321 members elected for nine-year terms, one third every three years, by an electoral college in each Department. The president, directly elected for seven years, holds executive power and is head of state. A council of ministers headed by a prime minister is appointed by the president and is responsible to parliament.

Georgia

Presidential republic with a constitution adopted in 1995. Legislative power is vested in a unicameral parliament elected for four years. Of its 235 members, 150 are elected by proportional representation and 85 by simple majority. A bicameral legislature is planned. The head of state and holder of supreme executive power is the president, who is directly elected for five years. Ministers are appointed by the president with the approval of parliament.

Germany

Federal parliamentary republic with a constitution adopted in 1949. A bicameral legislature comprises the federal assembly (*Bundestag*) and the federal council (*Bundesrat*). The former contains 669 members elected for terms of four years by a system combining simple majority and proportional representation. The latter contains 69 members appointed by the 16 state (*Land*) governments, each having between three and six seats in proportion to state population. The head of state is the federal president, who is elected for five years by a special federal convention. The federal government exercises executive authority and is headed by the federal chancellor, elected by the federal assembly. The chancellor proposes federal ministers who are appointed by the federal president.

Greece

Parliamentary republic with a constitution adopted in 1975. Legislative authority resides with a unicameral parliament of 300 members elected for terms of four years by proportional representation. Executive power is vested in a prime minister and cabinet. The president is head of state and is elected by parliament for five years.

Hungary

Parliamentary republic with a constitution adopted in 1949 but greatly revised in 1989. The single chamber national assembly (*Orszaggyules*) contains 386 members who are elected for terms of four years. 176 are elected by simple majority, 120 by proportional representation with a further 90 from a national list. Executive power is held by a council of ministers, which is responsible to the national assembly. The head of state is a president, who is elected by the national assembly for five years.

Iceland

Parliamentary republic with a constitution adopted in 1944. Legislative authority is vested jointly in the president and parliament (*Althing*). The president is elected directly for four-year terms and is head of state. Parliament comprises 63 members and is elected every four years by a system of proportional representation. Executive authority is held by a Cabinet appointed by the president. The Cabinet and prime minister are responsible to parliament. The president has supreme executive authority under the constitution but in practice waives it in favour of the Cabinet.

Ireland

Parliamentary republic with a constitution adopted in 1937. A bicameral parliament consisting of the senate (*Seanad*) and the house of representatives (*Dail*) holds legislative power. The senate has 60 members of which 11 are nominated by the prime minister, 6 elected by the universities and the remainder elected from vocationally-based panels by other branches of the Irish polity. The house of representatives has 166 members elected for five-year terms by the single transferable vote system of proportional representation. The president, directly elected for seven years, is head of state, and a prime minister (*taoiseach*) is head of government.

Italy

Parliamentary republic with a constitution adopted in 1948. A bicameral parliament holds legislative authority. The senate has 315 members of whom 10 are life members. The chamber of deputies has 630 members. Elected members of both houses – 75% of whom are elected by simple majority and the remainder by proportional representation – serve five-year terms. Executive power is vested in a council of ministers headed by a prime minister who is appointed by the president. The president is head of state and is elected by a specially convened electoral college comprising both houses of parliament and 58 regional representatives.

Latvia

Parliamentary republic with a constitution first adopted in 1922 and restored in 1993. Legislative authority resides with a single-chamber parliament (*Saiema*). It comprises 100 members elected for terms of three years under a system of proportional representation. Executive power is held by a cabinet and prime minister. The prime minister is appointed by a president who is head of state and is appointed by parliament for a term of three years and and must command the support of an absolute majority.

Liechtenstein

Parliamentary monarchy with a constitution adopted in 1921. Legislative authority is the joint reponsibility of a prince and a 25-member parliament (*Landtag*). Members of parliament are elected by a system of proportional representation for four-year terms. In addition, legislation can be proposed by citizen's groupings and referendums can be applied to parliamentary legislation. The prince is head of state and appoints an executive, comprising a prime minister and four councillors, for four-year terms, subject to the approval of parliament.

Lithuania

Parliamentary republic with a constitution adopted in 1992. A unicameral parliament (*Seimas*) has legislative power. Of its 141 members, 71 are elected by simple majority and the remainder by a party-list system of proportional representation for four-year terms. A council of ministers headed by a prime minister holds executive authority. The prime minister, with parliament's approval, is appointed by the president, who is head of state and is elected directly for a five-year term.

Luxembourg

Parliamentary monarchy with a constitution adopted in 1868 but subsequently considerably revised. A unicameral parliament (*Chambre des Députés*) exercises legislative authority, its 60 members are elected for five-year terms by a system of proportional representation. The Grand Duke is head of state and is nominally the constitutional executive head. However a council of ministers under a prime minister has assumed executive responsibility.

Macedonia (Former Yugoslav Republic of)

Parliamentary republic with a constitution adopted in 1991. Legislative power is exercised by an assembly (*Sobranje*) of 120 members directly elected for four-year terms, 85 by simple majority and the rest by a system of proportional representation. Executive authority resides with a prime minister appointed by a president and assisted by other ministers appointed by the assembly. The president, elected directly for five years, is head of state.

Malta

Parliamentary republic with a constitution adopted in 1974. Legislative authority resides with the 65-member House of Representatives elected for five-year terms by a system of proportional representation. The executive comprises a prime minister appointed by a president and a cabinet appointed by the president on the prime minister's advice. The president is head of state and is appointed for five years by the House of Representatives.

Moldova

Presidential republic with a constitution adopted in 1994. A 104-member unicameral legislature is directly elected for terms of four years. Executive authority lies jointly with a president and a council of ministers headed by a prime minister. A president, elected directly for four years, is head of state.

Monaco

Parliamentary monarchy with a constitution adopted in 1962. Legislative authority is held by the reigning prince in conjunction with an 18-member legislature (*Conseil National*) elected by a system of proportional representation for terms of five years. Executive authority is exercised by a four-member Council of Government under the authority of the monarch. The Council of Government is headed by a minister of state, a French civil servant selected by the monarch from a short list of three nominated by the French government. The monarch is head of state. Under agreements established in 1918 and 1919, if a reigning prince dies without leaving a male heir Monaco will be incorporated into France.

Netherlands
Parliamentary monarchy with a constitution adopted in 1814 and most recently revised in 1983. A bicameral national assembly (*Staten-Generaal*) is the legislative authority. The first chamber has 75 members elected for four-year terms by the provincial councils. The second chamber has 150 members and is elected directly for four-year terms by a system of proportional representation. The first chamber can only approve or reject bills. Executive authority resides with a council of ministers lead by a prime minister appointed by the monarch. The monarch is head of state.

Norway
Parliamentary monarchy with a constitution adopted in 1814. Legislative authority resides with a unicameral parliament (*Storting*) of 165 members elected for four-year terms by a system of proportional representation. A quarter of the members are elected by parliament to form an upper house (*Lagting*). The remainder make up the lower house (*Odelsting*). Legislation is decided by both houses or in the event of deadlock by the entire parliament. Constitutional questions are decided by parliament as a unified body. Executive power is exercised by a state council headed by a prime minister. The monarch is head of state.

Poland
Presidential republic with a constitution adopted in 1997. Legislative authority is vested in a bicameral national assembly comprising a 100-member upper chamber (*Senat*) and a 460-member lower chamber (*Sejm*).Both are elected for terms of four years, the latter by a system of proportional representation. A president is head of state and is elected directly for terms of five years.

Portugal
Parliamentary republic with a constitution adopted in 1976 and revised fundamentally in 1982. Legislative authority is vested in a unicameral assembly comprising 230 members elected for four-year terms by a system of proportional representation. Executive authority resides with a prime minister appointed by a president, and a council of ministers appointed by the president on the recommendation of the prime minister. The president, who is elected directly for five years, is head of state.

Romania
Presidential republic with a constitution adopted in 1991. Legislative authority is the responsibility of a bicameral parliament comprising the 343-member Chamber of Deputies and the 143-member Senate. Members

of both houses are elected for terms of four years by a system of proportional representation. A president has executive authority and is directly elected for four-year terms. As head of state the president appoints a prime minister who in turn appoints a council of ministers.

Russia

Presidential republic with a constitution adopted in 1993. A bicameral federal assembly is the supreme legislative body comprising a 178-member upper chamber, the Federation Council, and a 450-member lower chamber (*Duma*). The Federation Council is appointed by regional assemblies: two members from each territorial unit. The lower chamber is elected directly for terms of four years. A president, directly elected for four-year terms, is head of state and holds executive authority in tandem with a prime minister and ministers. The prime minister and ministers have competence in budgetary matters and law and order. The president appoints the prime minister with the approval of the lower chamber.

San Marino

Parliamentary republic with a constitution which has evolved since the 12th century. Legislative authority is vested in the Great and General Council, comprising 60 members, elected for five-year terms by a system of proportional representation. Two Captains-Regent are elected by the council every six months to serve as joint heads of state. The council also elects a ten-member Congress of State with concurrent terms which has executive authority.

Serbia & Montenegro

Federal republic with a constitution adopted in 1992 to cover Serbia and Montenegro – the rump of the Federal Republic of Yugoslavia. Legislative authority resides with a bicameral federal assembly. The Chamber of Citizens contains 138 members directly elected for terms of four years; the Chamber of the Republics has 40 members, 20 each from Serbia and Montenegro. A federal president is head of state and is elected for a four-year term by a joint session of the federal assembly. The president is responsible for appointing a federal prime minister. Legislative authority is shared with the directly elected assemblies of Serbia and Montenegro. The republics also have their own elected executive presidents.

The province of Kosovo is under "interim administration" by the UN pending probable independence.

Slovakia

Parliamentary republic with a constitution adopted in 1992. The National Council for the Slovak Republic has supreme legislative authority, comprising a single chamber of 150 members elected directly for terms of four years. Executive power is vested in a prime minister and ministers responsible to the National Council. A president is elected by the National Council for five years and is head of state.

Slovenia

Parliamentary republic with a constitution adopted in 1991. Legislative authority resides with a unicameral national assembly (*Drzavni Zbor*) comprising 90 members serving terms of four years. Of these 88 are elected by simple majority. The remaining two represent the minority ethnic Italian and Hungarian communities. Some legislative powers are shared with a national council (*Drzavni Svet*) comprising 18 members appointed by an electoral college representing social, economic and local interest-groups and 22 members directly elected for five-year terms. Executive authority is vested in a prime minister, elected by a majority vote of the national assembly, and ministers appointed by the national assembly on the prime minister's recommendation. The head of state is a president who is directly elected for five years but whose powers are nominal.

Spain

Parliamentary monarchy with a constitution adopted in 1978. A bicameral parliament (*Cortes Generales*) is the legislative authority with both chambers elected for four-year terms. The senate contains 259 members, 208 directly elected, the remainder elected by the regional assemblies. The Congress of Deputies has 350 members elected by proportional representation. Executive power is in the hands of a prime minister and a council of ministers appointed by the monarch, who is head of state.

Sweden

Parliamentary monarchy with a constitution adopted in 1975 formalising and revising former basic laws which previously served as a constitution. A unicameral parliament (*Riksdag*) holds legislative power, comprising 349 members elected for four-year terms by a system of proportional representation. Executive authority rests with a cabinet (*Regeringen*) headed by a prime minister nominated by the speaker and subject to the approval of parliament. The monarch is head of state but has only a limited ceremonial role.

Switzerland

Federal republic with a constitution adopted in 1874. The legislature, a bicameral federal assembly, comprises the Council of States and the National Council. The former contains 46 members elected for three- to four-year terms, two members from each of the 23 Cantons (three cantons are divided, so each half Canton sends one member). The latter contains 200 members elected for terms of four years by proportional representation. Executive authority resides with a federal council of 7 members elected for four years by the federal assembly. One member of the federal council is then elected president of the confederation by the federal assembly for a one-year term and is head of state. Each Canton has its own legislature and executive power is devolved further by the relative ease with which referendums can be called to propose or mandate legislation.

Turkey

Presidential republic with a constitution adopted in 1982. The unicameral Turkish Grand National Assembly holds legislative authority; its 550 members are directly elected for five-year terms. A president, who holds executive power and is head of state, is elected for a seven-year term by the assembly.

Ukraine

Presidential republic with a constitution adopted in 1996. Legislative authority is vested in the 450-member Supreme Council elected directly for four-year terms. Executive authority is jointly held by a prime minister and a president, who is directly elected for five years and appoints the prime minister and cabinet. The president is head of state.

United Kingdom

Parliamentary monarchy without a formal written constitution. The system of government is defined by convention, the common law, acts of parliament and tradition. Legislative authority is vested in a bicameral parliament. The pre-eminent chamber, the House of Commons, contains 659 members elected directly for five years, though elections can be held more frequently. The upper chamber, the House of Lords (part hereditary, episcopal and appointed), has power to delay or modify legislation. Executive power is vested in a prime minister, usually the leader of the largest party in the House of Commons, who appoints a cabinet. The monarch is head of state. Scotland and Wales now have their own elected parliaments. Scotland's has 129 members with some legislative and tax-raising autonomy, Wales's 60-member assembly has not and the extent of its powers remains unclear. An assembly was re-established for Northern Ireland in 1999.

Vatican City

The Vatican city state was established in 1929 by the Lateran Treaty. The Pope, who is head of state and head of the Roman Catholic church, is appointed for life by a college of cardinals appointed by his predecessors. Cardinals appointed to the Vatican (*in curia*) administer the church while a pontifical commission under a president administers the state itself.

Defence

Spending on defence

	$bn (1999 prices)		% of GDP	
	1985	1999	1985	1999
NATO Europe				
Belgium	6.1	3.5	3.0	1.5
Czech Republic[ab]	...	1.2	...	2.3
Denmark	3.1	2.7	2.2	1.6
France	48.4	37.9	4.0	2.7
Germany	52.2	31.1	3.2	1.6
Greece	3.5	5.2	7.0	5.0
Hungary[a]	3.5	0.7	7.2	1.6
Iceland	...	...	...	...
Italy	25.5	22.0	2.3	2.0
Luxembourg	0.1	0.1	0.9	0.8
Netherlands	8.8	6.9	3.1	1.8
Norway	3.1	3.1	3.1	2.2
Poland[a]	8.5	3.2	8.1	2.1
Portugal	1.8	2.3	3.1	2.2
Spain	11.2	7.3	2.4	1.3
Turkey	3.4	10.2	4.5	5.5
United Kingdom	47.2	36.9	5.2	2.6
Total	**214.4[e]**	**174.3**	**4.0[e]**	**2.3**
Non-NATO Europe				
Albania	0.3	0.1	5.3	3.6
Armenia[c]	...	0.2	...	8.6
Austria	1.9	1.7	1.2	0.8
Azerbaijan[c]	...	0.2	...	4.4
Belarus[c]	...	0.5	...	5.0
Bosnia[d]	...	0.4	...	8.4
Bulgaria	2.4	0.4	14.0	3.3
Croatia[d]	...	0.8	...	4.1
Cyprus	0.1	0.5	3.6	6.1
Czechoslovakia	3.5	...	8.2	...
Estonia[c]	...	0.1	...	1.5
Finland	2.2	1.7	2.8	1.4
Georgia[c]	...	0.1	...	2.4
Ireland	0.5	0.7	1.8	0.9
Latvia[c]	...	0.1	...	1.0
Lithuania[c]	...	0.1	...	1.0
Macedonia[d]	...	0.1	...	2.0
Malta	0.0	0.0	1.4	0.8
Moldova[c]	...	0.0	...	0.5
Romania	2.1	0.6	4.5	1.8
Russia[c]	...	56.8	...	5.1
Serbia & Montenegro[d]	...	1.7	...	12.4
Slovakia[b]	...	0.3	...	1.9
Slovenia[d]	...	0.3	...	1.8
Soviet Union	364.7	...	16.1	...
Sweden	4.7	5.2	3.3	2.3
Switzerland	2.9	3.1	2.1	1.3
Ukraine[c]	...	1.4	...	2.9
Yugoslavia	5.0	...	3.8	...

Armed forces
'000s

	1985	1999		1985	1999
NATO Europe					
Belgium	91.6	41.8	Luxembourg	0.7	0.8
Czech Republic[ab]	...	58.2	Netherlands	105.5	56.4
Denmark	29.6	24.3	Norway	37.0	30.7
France	464.3	317.3	Poland[a]	319.0	240.7
Germany	478.0	332.8	Portugal	73.0	49.7
Greece	201.5	165.6	Spain	320.0	186.5
Hungary[a]	106.0	43.4	Turkey	630.0	639.0
Iceland	...	...	United Kingdom	327.1	212.4
Italy	385.1	265.5	**Total**	3143.4[e]	**2,665.0**

	1985	1999		1985	1999
Non-NATO Europe					
Albania	40.4	54.0	Lithuania[c]	...	12.1
Armenia[c]	...	53.4	Macedonia[d]	...	16.0
Austria	54.7	40.5	Malta	0.8	1.9
Azerbaijan[c]	...	69.9	Moldova[c]	...	10.7
Belarus[c]	...	80.9	Romania	189.5	207.0
Bosnia[d]	...	40.0	Russia[c]	...	1,004.1
Bulgaria	148.5	80.8	Serbia & Mont[d]	...	108.7
Croatia[d]	...	61.0	Slovakia[b]	...	44.9
Cyprus	10.0	10.0	Slovenia[d]	...	9.6
Czechoslovakia	203.3	...	Soviet Union	5,300.0	...
Estonia[c]	...	4.8	Sweden	65.7	53.1
Finland	36.5	31.7	Switzerland	20.0	27.7
Georgia[c]	...	26.3	Ukraine[c]	...	311.4
Ireland	13.7	11.5	Yugoslavia	241.0	...
Latvia[c]	...	5.7			

Conscripts
1999

1	Turkey	528,000	16	Finland	23,100
2	Russia	330,000	17	Hungary	22,900
3	Germany	128,400	18	Croatia	21,320
4	Poland	111,950	19	Austria	17,500
5	Italy	111,800	20	Norway	15,200
6	Romania	108,600	21	Slovakia	13,600
7	Greece	98,321	22	Cyprus	8,700
8	France	58,710	23	Macedonia	8,000
9	Spain	51,700	24	Portugal	5,860
10	Bulgaria	49,000	25	Moldova	5,200
11	Ukraine	45,000	26	Denmark	5,025
12	Serbia & Montenegro	43,000	27	Slovenia	4,500
13	Belarus	40,000	28	Lithuania	4,000
14	Sweden	32,800	29	Estonia	2,870
15	Czech Republic	25,000	30	Latvia	1,690

a Joined NATO in 1999. b Still part of Czechoslovakia in 1985.
c Still part of the Soviet Union in 1985. d Still part of Yugoslavia in 1985.
e Total excludes countries not in NATO in 1985.

Military equipment

1999	Tanks	Combat aircraft
Armenia	102	6
Austria	283	52
Azerbaijan	220	48
Belarus	1,724	224
Belgium	140	135
Bosnia	500	–
Bulgaria	1,475	232
Croatia	305	41
Cyprus	145	3
Czech Republic	792	110
Denmark	228	68
Estonia	–	3
Finland	230	64
France	1,234	588
Georgia	79	7
Germany	2,728	517
Greece	1,735	525
Hungary	806	107
Ireland	–	7
Italy	1,301	533
Latvia	3	19
Macedonia	98	14
Malta	–	6
Netherlands	348	161
Norway	170	73
Poland	1,674	271
Portugal	187	101
Romania	1,373	323
Russia	5,375	2,733
Serbia & Montenegro	1,035	183
Slovakia	275	82
Slovenia	100	19
Spain	681	209
Sweden	658	250
Switzerland	556	154
Turkey	2,464	359
Ukraine	3,939	911
United Kingdom	584	520

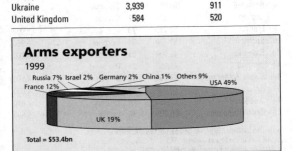

Arms exporters

1999

Russia 7% Israel 2% Germany 2% China 1% Others 9%
France 12%
USA 49%
UK 19%

Total = $53.4bn

THE EUROPEAN UNION

Members and votes

Who joined what when

ECSC 1951	EEC Treaty of Rome 1957	EC 1973
Belgium	Belgium	Denmark
W. Germany	W. Germany	Ireland
France	France	United Kingdom
Italy	Italy	
Luxembourg	Luxembourg	
Netherlands	Netherlands	

EC 1981	EC 1986	EC 1990	EU 1995
Greece	Spain	E. Germany	Austria
	Portugal		Finland
			Sweden

Other applicants: Morocco and Turkey* (1987), Malta* and Cyprus* (1990), Norway (1961, 1967, 1992), Switzerland (1992), Hungary* and Poland* (1994), Bulgaria*, Estonia*, Latvia*, Lithuania*, Romania* and Slovakia* (1995), Czech Republic* and Slovenia* (1996). (*Enlargement applicant countries.)

Presidency of the Council
Held for 6 months

	Jan–Jun	Jul–Dec
2001	Sweden	Belgium
2002	Spain	Denmark
2003	Greece	Italy
2004	Ireland	Netherlands
2005	Luxembourg	United Kingdom

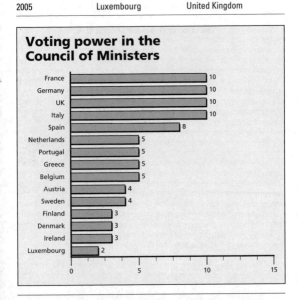

Voting power in the Council of Ministers

France	10
Germany	10
UK	10
Italy	10
Spain	8
Netherlands	5
Portugal	5
Greece	5
Belgium	5
Austria	4
Sweden	4
Finland	3
Denmark	3
Ireland	3
Luxembourg	2

A question of identity

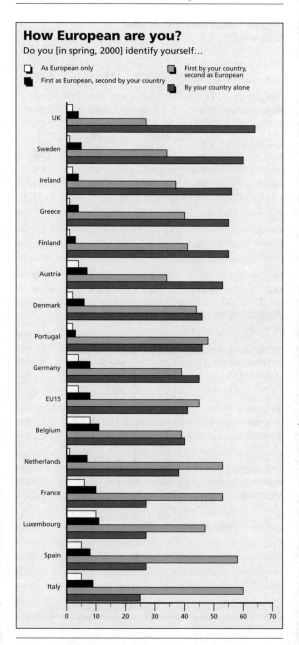

How European are you?

Do you [in spring, 2000] identify yourself...

☐ As European only
■ First as European, second by your country
▨ First by your country, second as European
▦ By your country alone

UK
Sweden
Ireland
Greece
Finland
Austria
Denmark
Portugal
Germany
EU15
Belgium
Netherlands
France
Luxembourg
Spain
Italy

0 10 20 30 40 50 60 70

Budget contributions

Who pays what and receives what

Ecus/euros, m

	1980		1985	
	Contributions to Brussels	Receipts from Brussels	Contributions to Brussels	Receipts from Brussels
Germany	4,610	2,940	7,504	4,185
United Kingdom	3,168	1,803	5,090	3,107
France	2,992	3,372	5,319	5,416
Italy	1,929	2,611	3,630	4,480
Netherlands	1,273	1,667	1,889	2,232
Belgium	951	677	1,293	1,070
Denmark	346	680	620	913
Ireland	139	827	296	1,549
Luxembourg	20	15	51	9
Greece	...	...	388	1,703
Spain	...	...	...	...
Portugal	...	...	...	...
Sweden	...	...	...	...
Austria	...	...	...	...
Finland	...	...	...	...
Miscellaneous	...	12	...	40
Total	**15,428**	**14,604**	**26,080**	**24,704**

Accounting budgetary balances, 1999

Net contributions

		Ecus, m			% of GDP
1	Germany	11,359	1	Netherlands	0.87
2	United Kingdom	5,290	2	Luxembourg	0.65
3	Netherlands	3,358	3	Germany	0.55
4	Italy	1,752	4	Sweden	0.54
5	Belgium	1,275	5	Belgium	0.52
6	Sweden	1,227	6	Austria	0.40
7	France	1,164	7	United Kingdom	0.39
8	Austria	836	8	Finland	0.25
9	Finland	310	9	Italy	0.15
10	Denmark	144	10	Denmark	0.08
11	Luxembourg	114		France	0.08
12	Ireland	-1,822	12	Spain	-1.18
13	Portugal	-2,677	13	Ireland	-2.15
14	Greece	-3,641	14	Portugal	-2.49
15	Spain	-6,656	15	Greece	-2.94

Note: Presentational changes in the EU budget mean that different years are not strictly comparable. On top of contributions there are other revenue sources and carried-over annual surpluses.

1990		1999	
Contributions to Brussels	Receipts from Brussels	Contributions to Brussels	Receipts from Brussels
10,358	4,807	21,069	9,710
6,534	3,147	11,083	5,793
8,090	6,285	13,994	12,830
6,098	5,681	10,766	9,014
2,615	2,984	5,092	1,734
1,764	990	3,196	1,921
775	1,198	1,656	1,512
368	2,261	1,060	2,882
75	14	194	80
564	3,034	1,351	4,992
3,671	5,383	6,231	12,887
502	1,103	1,228	3,905
…	…	2,349	1,122
…	…	2,054	1,218
…	…	1,211	901
…	391		5,303
41,413	**37,278**	**82,533**	**75,803**

% shares of

		Financing			GDP
1	Germany	25.5	1	Germany	25.1
2	France	17.0	2	France	17.0
3	United Kingdom	13.4	3	United Kingdom	16.6
4	Italy	13.0	4	Italy	13.9
5	Spain	7.5	5	Spain	6.8
6	Netherlands	6.2	6	Netherlands	4.6
7	Belgium	3.9	7	Belgium	3.0
8	Sweden	2.8	8	Sweden	2.7
9	Austria	2.5	9	Austria	2.5
10	Denmark	2.0	10	Denmark	2.1
11	Greece	1.6	11	Finland	1.5
12	Finland	1.5		Greece	1.5
	Portugal	1.5	13	Portugal	1.3
14	Ireland	1.3	14	Ireland	1.0
15	Luxembourg	0.2	15	Luxembourg	0.2

Budget breakdown

Payments to member states by sector

	euros, m	% of total
1999		
Common agricultural policy	39,574	41.6
Structural operations	38,881	40.9
Administration	4,347	4.6
External actions	6,319	6.6
Internal policies	5,701	6.0
Repayment, guarantees, reserves	300	0.3
Total	**95,122**	**100.0**
1990		
EAGGF-Guarantee	24,980	57.7
Structural operations	10,368	23.9
Repayment, guarantees, reserves	2,381	5.5
Administration	2,298	5.3
Research and technological development	1,429	3.3
Co-operation	1,225	2.8
Training, youth and social operations	334	0.8
Energy, environment, internal market	309	0.7
Total	**43,325**	**100.0**
1985		
EAGGF-Guarantee	19,726	70.2
Regional policy and transport	1,726	6.2
Social policy	1,491	5.3
Administration	1,296	4.6
Repayments	1,248	4.4
Co-operation with developing countries	1,085	3.9
Agricultural structures, fisheries	820	2.9
Research, energy etc	708	2.5
Total	**28,099**	**100.0**
1980		
EAGGF-Guarantee	11,283	69.3
Regional policy and transport	1,103	6.8
Repayments	846	5.2
Administration	820	5.0
Social policy	772	4.7
Agricultural structures, fisheries	646	4.0
Co-operation with developing countries	509	3.1
Research, energy etc	312	1.9
Total	**16,290**	**100.0**

EAGGF is the European Agricultural Guidance and Guarantee Fund. Official accounts now refer to the common agricultural policy.

Where the money comes from
Euros, m

1999

Agricultural levies	1,187
Sugar and isoglucose levies	1,204
Customs duties	13,007
VAT own resources	31,332
GNP resources	37,512
Costs incurred in collection	-1,540
Total	**82,533**

1990

Agricultural levies	1,173
Sugar and isoglucose levies	911
Customs duties	11,428
VAT own resources	28,968
GNP resources	285
Costs incurred in collection	-1,351
Total	**41,413**

1985

Agricultural levies	1,122
Sugar and isoglucose levies	1,057
Customs duties	8,310
VAT own resources	15,592
Total	**26,080**

1980

Agricultural levies	1,535
Sugar and isoglucose levies	467
Customs duties	5,906
VAT own resources	7,520
Total	**15,428**

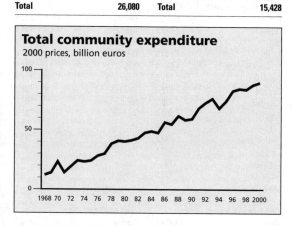

Total community expenditure
2000 prices, billion euros

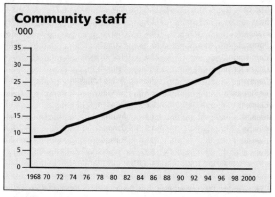

Community staff
'000

Agricultural and regional aid

Agricultural aid by product[a]
Euros, m

	1980	1985	1990	1999
Cereals and oilseeds	1,719	2,360	3,881	17,866
Sugar	575	1,804	1,388	2,113
Fats and protein	748	2,174	5,482	3,495
Fruit and vegetables	687	1,231	1,253	1,454
Wine	300	921	745	615
Tobacco	309	863	1,232	911
Milk products	4,752	5,933	4,895	2,510
Meat, eggs, poultry	1,618	3,477	4,711	6,906
Other	576	963	2,356	3,671
Total	**11,284**	**19,726**	**24,980**	**39,541**

Who got what for what
Euros, m, 1998

Cereals and oilseeds

France	5,678.5
Germany	3,870.5
Italy	1,831.6
Spain	1,699.6
United Kingdom	1,697.9
Denmark	724.6
Greece	472.6
Sweden	450.2
Austria	403.6
Finland	256.4
Netherlands	247.3
Belgium	219.5
Portugal	180.1
Ireland	123.5
Luxembourg	10.0

Sugar

France	607.5
Germany	339.6
Belgium	327.4
United Kingdom	227.4
Italy	201.1
Denmark	111.1
Spain	98.2
Netherlands	67.3
Austria	38.4
Portugal	33.2
Sweden	32.4
Finland	11.3
Ireland	9.5
Greece	8.4

Oils, fats and protein plants

Spain	1,404.6
Greece	1,112.7
Italy	711.4
France	130.9
Portugal	45.7
Germany	22.9
United Kingdom	21.6
Denmark	17.2
Netherlands	15.9
Belgium	8.8
Finland	1.4
Austria	1.3
Sweden	0.5
Ireland	0.3

Fruit and vegetables

Spain	462.1
Italy	378.2
Greece	241.1
France	227.0
Portugal	49.9
Netherlands	42.4
Belgium	21.1
United Kingdom	16.3
Germany	13.3
Sweden	1.2
Austria	0.8
Denmark	0.6
Finland	0.2

a Payments from the European Agricultural Guidance and Guarantee Fund (EAGGF).

Wine		*Tobacco*	
Italy	249.8	Greece	374.9
Spain	192.0	Italy	349.2
France	143.5	Spain	70.6
Portugal	10.3	France	67.6
Greece	9.7	Germany	23.2
Germany	8.2	Portugal	18.3
United Kingdom	0.9	Belgium	3.6
Austria	0.2	Austria	0.7
Sweden	0.1		

Milk products		*Meat, eggs, poultry*	
France	774.2	United Kingdom	1,503.9
Netherlands	662.0	France	1,412.5
Germany	326.9	Ireland	969.5
Ireland	265.7	Spain	938.6
Belgium	213.4	Germany	606.8
United Kingdom	204.5	Italy	364.4
Denmark	177.3	Greece	274.4
Finland	71.4	Portugal	152.3
Spain	39.8	Netherlands	145.7
Sweden	25.2	Belgium	143.8
Luxembourg	-0.4	Denmark	140.5
Portugal	-1.4	Austria	124.8
Greece	-5.7	Sweden	76.7
Austria	-27.9	Finland	45.7
Italy	-214.8	Luxembourg	6.3

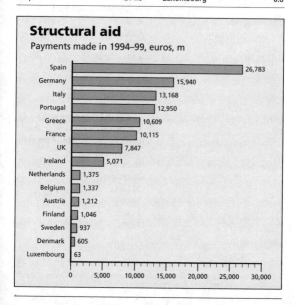

Structural aid

Payments made in 1994–99, euros, m

Spain	26,783
Germany	15,940
Italy	13,168
Portugal	12,950
Greece	10,609
France	10,115
UK	7,847
Ireland	5,071
Netherlands	1,375
Belgium	1,337
Austria	1,212
Finland	1,046
Sweden	937
Denmark	605
Luxembourg	63

The euro

Fixed conversion rates for participants
Dec 31st 1998

1 euro =

Belgian franc	40.3399	Luxembourg franc	40.3399
D-mark	1.95583	Guilder	2.20371
Peseta	166.386	Schilling	13.7603
French franc	6.55957	Escudo	200.482
Punt	0.787564	Markka	5.94573
Italian lira	1936.27	Drachma	340,750

What's to happen when
Notes and coins exchange dates

Supply of notes and coins to financial institutions and retailers	September-December 2001
End-date of national currencies as legal tender	February 28th 2002, except: Germany (Dec 31st 2001[a]), Netherlands (Jan 28th 2002), Ireland (Feb 9th 2002), France (Feb 17th 2002).
Redemption of notes at central banks	Indefinitely except: Greece, France, Italy, Finland (10 years); Netherlands (up to Jan 1st 2032); Portugal (20 years).

Value of euro notes and coins

Notes	There 7 euro notes, in different colours and sizes, but uniform throughout the euro area.
Denominations	€500 €200 €100 €50 €20 €10 €5
Coins	There are 8 euro coins with a common European face. On the obverse, each member state will have their own motif.
Denominations	50 cents 20 cents 10 cents 5 cents 2 cents 1 cent

a In line with the "Joint declaration" the use of DM notes and coins is allowed at least until February 28th 2002.

A bumpy start

1 euro =

	Sterling	Swedish krone	Danish krone	Greek drachma	US dollar
1999					
Jan 1st	0.71	9.52	7.47	329	1.17
Apr 1st	0.67	8.89	7.43	326	1.08
Jul 1st	0.65	8.74	7.44	325	1.02
Oct 1st	0.65	8.74	7.43	329	1.07
2000					
Jan 1st	0.63	8.57	7.44	330	1.02
Apr 1st	0.60	8.30	7.45	335	0.96
Jul 1st	0.63	8.39	7.46	337	0.95
Oct 1st	0.60	8.53	7.45	339	0.88
2001					
Jan 1st	0.63	8.86	7.46	...	0.94
Apr 1st	0.62	9.15	7.46	...	0.88
Jun 1st	0.60	9.17	7.46	...	0.85

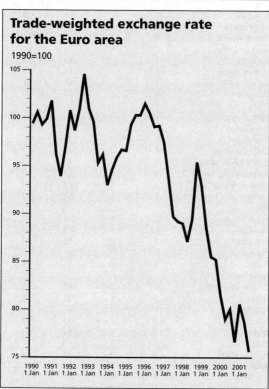

Trade-weighted exchange rate for the Euro area

1990=100

The European Parliament

The 1999 election results

Party	Seats	Gain/loss	% vote 1999	% vote in previous Euro-election
Germany				
Christian Democrats/CSU	53	6	48.7	38.8
Social Democrats	33	-7	30.7	32.2
Greens	7	-5	6.4	10.1
ex-Communists	6	6	5.8	4.7
France				
Socialists/Radicals	22	-6	22	26.5
Anti-EU Gaullists	13	0	13	12.3
Gaullists/Liberal Democrats	12	} -8[a]	12.7	} 25.5[a]
UDF (centrists)	9		9.3	
Greens	9	9	9.7	2.9
Communists	6	0	6.8	6.9
Hunters' party	6	6	6.8	3.9
National Front	5	-5	5.7	10.5
Workers Struggle	5	5	5.2	0
Italy				
Forza Italia	22	-5	25.2	30.6
Left Democrats	15	-1	17.4	19.1
National Alliance	9	-2	10.3	12.5
Emma Bonino List	7	5	8.5	2.1
Democrats	7	7	7.7	0
Northern League	4	-2	4.5	6.6
Communist Refoundation	6	1	4.3	6.1
Centrist parties	11	3	4.3	10
Others	6	-7	15.8	13
United Kingdom				
Conservatives	36	18	35.8	27.8
Labour	29	-33	28	44.2
Liberal Democrats	10	8	12.7	16.7
Scottish/Welsh Nationalists	4	2	4.5	4.5
Northern Ireland parties	3	0	1.8	0.9
UK Independence	3	3	7	0.4
Greens	2	2	6.3	3.2
Spain				
People's Party	27	-1	39.7	40.2
Socialists	26	4	35.3	30.6
Communists	4	-5	5.8	13.4
Regionalists	6	1	15.3	11.1
Greens	1	1	4.5	0
Netherlands				
Christian Democrats	9	-1	26.9	30.8
Labour	6	-2	20.1	22.9
Liberals	6	0	19.7	17.9
Green Left	4	3	11.9	3.7
D-66	2	-2	5.8	11.7
Socialists	1	1	5	1.3
Religious parties	3	1	8.7	7.8
Belgium				
Liberals	6	0	23.5	20.5
Christian Democrats	5	-2	18.9	24.3

Socialists	5	-1	18.8	22.3
Greens	5	3	15.8	11.5
Flemish nationalist parties	4	0	16.4	15.1
Greece				
New Democracy	9	0	36	32.7
Socialists	9	-1	32.9	37.6
Communists	3	1	8.7	6.3
Other left parties	5	3	12	6.2
Portugal				
Socialists	12	2	43.1	34.7
Social Democrats (centre-right)	9	0	31.1	34.3
Communist coalition	2	-1	10.3	11.2
Popular Party/CDS	2	-1	8.2	12.4
Sweden				
Social Democrats	6	-1	26.1	28.1
Moderates	5	0	20.6	23.2
Liberals	3	2	13.8	4.8
Left	3	0	15.8	12.9
Greens	2	-2	9.4	17.2
Others	3	1	13.8	14.2
Austria				
Social Democrats	7	1	31.7	29.1
People's Party	7	0	30.7	29.6
Freedom Party	5	-1	23.5	27.6
Greens	2	1	9.3	6.7
Denmark				
Liberals	5	1	23.3	18.9
Social Demoocrats	3	0	16.5	15.8
Anti-EU parties	4	0	23.4	25.5
Conservatives	1	-2	8.5	17.7
Radicals	1	0	9.1	8.5
Socialists	1	0	7.1	8.6
Far-right	1	1	5.8	2.9
Finland				
Conservatives	4	0	25.3	20.2
Centre	4	0	21.3	24.4
Social Democrats	3	-1	17.8	21.5
Greens	2	1	13.4	7.6
Ex-Communists	1	-1	9.1	10.5
Others	2	1	9.2	8.6
Ireland				
Fianna Fail	6	-1	38.7	35
Fine Gael	4	0	24.6	24.3
Greens	2	0	6.7	3.7
Progressive Democrats	1	0	4.6	6.5
Labour	1	0	8.8	11
Independent	1	1	3.7	NA
Luxembourg				
Christian Democrats	2	0	31.9	31.5
Socialists	2	0	23.2	24.8
Liberals	1	0	20.8	18.8
Greens	1	0	10.7	10.9

a Run as joint list.

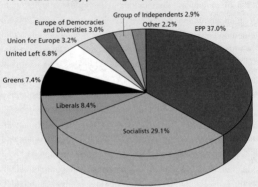

Parliamentary divisions
% of seats held by political groups, June 2001

- Europe of Democracies and Diversities 3.0%
- Group of Independents 2.9%
- Union for Europe 3.2%
- Other 2.2%
- United Left 6.8%
- EPP 37.0%
- Greens 7.4%
- Liberals 8.4%
- Socialists 29.1%

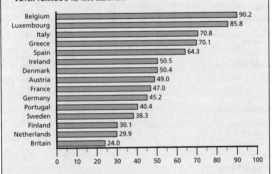

VOTER TURNOUT, %, 1999 ELECTION

Belgium	90.2
Luxembourg	85.8
Italy	70.8
Greece	70.1
Spain	64.3
Ireland	50.5
Denmark	50.4
Austria	49.0
France	47.0
Germany	45.2
Portugal	40.4
Sweden	38.3
Finland	30.1
Netherlands	29.9
Britain	24.0

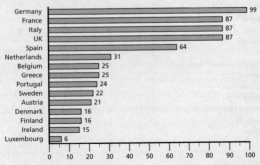

NO. OF SEATS ALLOCATED TO MEMBER STATES

Germany	99
France	87
Italy	87
UK	87
Spain	64
Netherlands	31
Belgium	25
Greece	25
Portugal	24
Sweden	22
Austria	21
Denmark	16
Finland	16
Ireland	15
Luxembourg	6

Sources

Land and the environment
Cassell, *What's what and who's who in Europe*
Europa Publications, *Europa World Yearbook*
Eurostat, *Yearbook*
John Wiley & Sons, *World Facts & Figures*
OECD, *Environmental Data, 1999*
Helicon, *The World Weather Guide* by E.A. Pearce and C.G. Smith
World Bank, *World Development Indicators*
World Resources Institute, *World Resources 2000–01*

Population
Central Intelligence Agency, *World Factbook*
Europa Publications, *Europa World Yearbook*
European Commission
Eurostat, *Social Portrait of Europe*; *Statistics in Focus*
National statistics
Statesman's Yearbook
Summer Institute of Linguistics, *Ethnologue*
United Nations, *World Population Prospects*; *World Urbanization Prospects*
World Bank, *World Development Indicators*

The economy
BP, *Statistical Review of World Energy*
Central Intelligence Agency, *World Factbook*
Economist Intelligence Unit, *Country Reports*; *Country Forecasts*
European Bank for Reconstruction and Development, *Transition Report*
Eurostat, *External and Intra-EU Trade*; *Statistics in Focus*
International Monetary Fund, *International Financial Statistics*; *Direction of Trade Statistics*
OECD, *National Accounts*; *Monthly Statistics of Foreign Trade*
Taiwan Statistical Data Book
Thomson Financial Datastream
United Nations, *Energy Statistics Yearbook*
World Bank, *Monitoring Environmental Progress*; *World Development Indicators*

World Trade Organisation, *International Trade Statistics*

Government finance
International Monetary Fund, *Government Finance Statistics Yearbook*; *International Financial Statistics*
OECD, *Development Assistance Committee Report; Development Co-operation Revenue Statistics*; *Tax/Benefit Position of Production Workers*
World Bank, *World Development Report; Global Development Finance*; *World Development Indicators*

Labour
Economist Intelligence Unit, *Country Reports*
International Labour Organisation, *Yearbook of Labour Statistics*; *World Labour Report*
International Metalworkers' Federation
KPMG, www.tax.kpmg.net
OECD, *Employment Outlook*; *Labour Force Statistics; Revenue Statistics; Tax Database; Tax/Benefit Position of Production Workers; Taxing Wages*
UK National Statistics, *Labour Market Trends*
Union Bank of Switzerland, *Prices and Earnings around the World*
World Bank, *World Development Report*

Business and finance
Euromonitor, *European Marketing Data and Statistics*
European Commission, *European Economy*
Financial Times Business Information, *The Banker*
Food and Agriculture Organisation, www.fao.org
IMD, *World Competitive Yearbook*; *Competitiveness Yearbook*
International Iron and Steel Institute
International Labour Organisation, *Yearbook of Labour Statistics*
Legalease, *The European Legal 500*
Lloyd's Register, *World Shipbuilding Statistics; World Fleet Statistics*
Privatisation International, London
Standard & Poor's *Emerging Stock Markets Factbook*

Swiss Re
Time Inc Magazines, *Fortune*
UNCTAD, *World Investment Report*
United Nations, *Monthly Bulletin of Statistics*
World Tourism Organisation, www.world-tourism.org

Tourism and transport
Airports Council International
International Civil Aviation Organisation (ICAO)
International Road Federation, *Road Transport Statistics*
Lloyd's Register, *World Fleet Statistics*
Rail Europe, *European Rail Fares & Schedule Information*
World Tourist Organisation, www.world-tourism.org

Health and education
ERC, *World Cigarettes: The 1997 Survey*
European Centre for the Epidemiological Monitoring of AIDS, *HIV/AIDS Surveillance in Europe*
UNESCO, *World Education Report; Statistical Yearbook*
Unicef, The State of the World's Children, 2000
United Nations, *World Population Prospects; Demographic Yearbook; Statistical Yearbook*
World Health Organisation, Europe, *Health For All Database*

Society
The Economist
Eurolink Age
Euromonitor, *European Marketing Data and Statistics; World Consumer Markets; The World Market for Petfood*
Eurosecretariat of the national Danish organisation for gays and lesbians (LBL), *Euroletter*

International Metalworkers' Federation, *The Purchasing Power of Working Time*
International Planned Parenthood Federation
International Federation of Phonographic Industry, *The Recording Industry in Numbers*
International Telecommunication Union, website www.itu.int/ri/industryoverview/index.htm
Interpol, *International Crime Statistics*
King's College London, International Centre for Prison Studies
Network Wizards, www.nw.com
OECD, *Employment Outlook*
Screen International
Stonewall
UNESCO, www.unesco.org; *Yearbook*
World Bank, *World Development Report*

Government and defence
Embassies
Europa Publications, *Europa World Yearbook*
International Institute for Strategic Studies, *The Military Balance*

The European Union
DBS, *The European Companion*
The Economist, June 12th, 19th, 1999
European Commission, *Annual Economic Report; The Community Budget; Eurobarometer; Infeuro newsletter; europa.eu.int*
European Parliament, *Session News*
Official Journals of the European Communities, *Court of Auditors Reports*
Thomson Financial Datastream